I0879375

CLASSICS IN CALIFORNIA ANTHROPOLOGY

YUROK-KAROK BASKET WEAVERS

Yurok-Karok Basket Weavers

Lila M. O'Neale

INTRODUCTION

by Margot Blum Schevill

PHOEBE HEARST MUSEUM OF ANTHROPOLOGY
UNIVERSITY OF CALIFORNIA, BERKELEY

Editor: Ira Jacknis
Project Manager: Barbara Takiguchi
Designer: Sarah Levin
Printer: Publishers Press, United States of America
10 9 8 7 6 5 4 3 2 1

The paper used in this publication meets the minimum requirements of American National Standard for Information Sciences—Permanence of Paper for Printed Materials, ANSI Z39.48–1984.

Cover photo: Lila O'Neale and an unidentified Klamath River basket weaver, 1929. Photograph courtesy of The Bancroft Library, University of California, Berkeley.

LIBRARY OF CONGRESS CATALOGING-IN-PUBLICATION DATA:

O'Neale, Lila M. (Lila Morris), 1886-1948.
Yurok-Karok basket weavers / Lila M. O'Neale ; introduction by Margot Blum Schevill.
p. cm. — (Classics in California anthropology)
Originally published: Berkeley : University of California Press, 1932 in series: University of California publications in American archaeology and ethnology ; v. 32, no.1.
Includes bibliographical references.
ISBN 0-936127-06-6 (hardback : alk. paper)
ISBN 0-936127-04-X (paperback : alk. paper)
1. Yurok baskets. 2. Karok baskets. 3. Basket making—California—History. 4. Baskets—California—Design—History. 5. California—Antiquities. I. Title. II. Series.
E99. Y97054 1995
746.41'2'089973—dc20 95-36643
CIP

PHOEBE APPERSON HEARST
MUSEUM OF ANTHROPOLOGY
103 Kroeber Hall
University of California
Berkeley, California 94720

CONTENTS

CLASSICS IN CALIFORNIA ANTHROPOLOGY:

Introduction to the Hearst Museum Reprint Series

The Phoebe Apperson Hearst Museum of Anthropology seeks to preserve its collections and improve their documentation and accessibility, sponsors research on its collections, and presents research relevant to its collections and mission in the form of publications, programs, and exhibitions. The museum recognizes a special responsibility as a repository of perhaps the largest collection in North America of the material culture produced by the Indians of California. With the inauguration of a series of reprints on Native California, the museum seeks to fulfill its commitment to making knowledge about Native California more widely accessible.

The series initiates a new chapter in the long and distinguished history of publications of anthropological research from Berkeley. Prominent among these are the studies produced by researchers from the Anthropology Department and Museum of Anthropology, published in the series University of California Publications in American Archaeology and Ethnology (UCPAAE). Volume one, number one of the UCPAAE, *Life and Culture of the Hupa* by Pliny Goddard, marked the strong focus on California that would characterize the entire series.

The UCPAAE was initiated in 1903 with the financial support of Phoebe Apperson Hearst, and was modeled on the annual reports and bulletins of the Smithsonian Institution's Bureau of American Ethnology. Like BAE publications, the UCPAAE volumes were not for sale to the general public but were exchanged with libraries and scholars. Studies varied in length from long articles to monographs of several hundred pages. In 1937, a second series was added, called Anthropological Records. According to a publisher's note, the UCPAAE was "restricted to papers in which the interpretative element outweighs the factual or which otherwise are of general interest." The new series was "issued in photolithography in a larger size. It consists of monographs which are documentary, of record nature, or devoted to the presentation primarily of new data." In 1964, the series Publications in Anthropology superseded the UCPAAE. By then, fifty volumes subdivided into 237 separate numbers had been published in the UCPAAE. The vast majority of original research from Berkeley about California Indians was published in the three series. Today, almost all of these important works are out of print.

Classics in California Anthropology will present selected volumes from these series and other older sources, enhanced with new introductions by contemporary scholars and, when appropriate, additional illustrations. We intend that Classics in California Anthropology will make available to new audiences landmark works created by a pioneering generation of anthropologists.

Rosemary A. Joyce, Director
May 1995

INTRODUCTION

In 1932 the University of California published one of the classic studies of American Indian art: *Yurok-Karok Basket Weavers* by Lila M. O'Neale.[1] This volume, O'Neale's doctoral dissertation in anthropology, was distributed largely to scholars and academic libraries and has been out of print for years. Although similar studies, like Ruth Bunzel's *The Pueblo Potter* (1929) and Gladys Reichard's *Navajo Shepherd and Weaver* (1936) are well known, the comparable importance of O'Neale's meticulous and imaginative study has been unjustly obscured. A few Xeroxed copies of *Yurok-Karok Basket Weavers* have been consulted by Northern California Indian basket weavers; one weaver, Vivien Hailstone (Karuk-Yurok, member of the Hupa Tribe), referred to it as "*that* anthropology book."

Lila O'Neale based her book on a trip to the Klamath River area of Northwestern California during the summer of 1929. Investigating the entire cultural complex of basketry in the region, she considered materials, basket types and their traditional features, care of baskets, proportion and contour, color combinations, design, and technique. She practiced an innovative field method, now known as ethnoaesthetics, that concentrated on Native aesthetics and criteria for excellence in basket weaving. For example, based on information given to her by the weavers, O'Neale looked at "intolerances" (p.59) or elements that were unacceptable to the aesthetic standards of the weavers. Men's attitudes toward the craft, foreign work and workmanship, design ownership, and the commercial aspect of Yurok-Karok basketry were explored in detail. These interviews and the information elicited contribute to the significance and contemporary value of this book.

O'Neale identified Karok, Yurok, and Hupa style baskets. She focused on the weavers as individual artists with personal tastes and idiosyncrasies. In her publication, the weavers are identified by tribal affiliation and by a number she assigned to each one interviewed;

respecting the anonymity of informants was common practice by social scientists of her time. In O'Neale's field notes in The Bancroft Library at the University of California at Berkeley, the weavers are identified by their husband's names and sometimes their own (see Appendix).

Until recent times, *Yurok-Karok Basket Weavers* was one of the few comprehensive works on California basketry.[2] Publications that had preceded O'Neale's study include those by John W. Hudson (1893), Roland Dixon (1902), Alfred Kroeber (1905), and Samuel Barrett (1908). Kroeber, the first professor of anthropology at the University of California, was the teacher of both Barrett and O'Neale. Reviewing Barrett's volume, the department's first doctoral dissertation, Kroeber concluded that among the Pomo there was a "tremendous predominance of unmotivated custom and habit over conscious utilitarian, artistic, or religious purpose" (1909:249). Lila O'Neale would expand and correct his conclusions because she looked at the *process* of basket weaving and placed it in the context of Yurok-Karok life. By interviewing the weavers themselves, she discovered what Kroeber had missed: that Klamath River weavers did have conscious purpose in the creation of each basket, whether it was made for religious or utilitarian purposes or for sale. O'Neale learned that innovation in design was alive and well and an inexhaustible, exciting topic for discussion. *Yurok-Karok Basket Weavers* is modern in tone and rich in information, and it continues to be utilized and admired by scholars, students, and teachers in the fields of Art History, Anthropology, and Native American Studies, by collectors and dealers, and by contemporary California Indian basket weavers themselves.

THE EARLY YEARS OF LILA M. O'NEALE

Of Irish and English heritage, O'Neale was born on a farm in Buxton, North Dakota in 1886 and grew up in Minneapolis and San Jose, California. She received degrees from Stanford University and the (California) State Normal School in San Jose. Inbetween periods of teaching in the public schools, she also attended Columbia Teachers College in New York City on two occasions: 1912–13 and 1915–16.

Perhaps she encountered cultural anthropology and Franz Boas, who had been teaching the subject at Columbia since 1896. She may have heard about Kroeber—who earned his doctorate under Boas in 1901—and his work on California Indians, but her records do not include any anthropology courses at Columbia University. O'Neale received a Bachelor of Science in Household Arts in 1916 and taught for the next ten years in Wisconsin and at Oregon Agricultural College, Corvallis. From the beginning of her teaching career, O'Neale focused on textiles. Her curriculum included the history and development of textiles, study of fibers, processes for manufacture, and dye analysis. She taught these courses for the next thirty-eight years until her untimely death from pneumonia at the age of sixty-two in 1948.

THE UNIVERSITY OF CALIFORNIA YEARS

Dissatisfied or perhaps frustrated by the limitations of teaching household arts, O'Neale took a leave from her tenured teaching position and enrolled at the University of California in Berkeley. She wanted to complete a master's thesis on lace in the Department of Household Arts. Kroeber had just returned from field work in Peru and required a textile analyst to work on the archaeological cloth he had recovered. O'Neale was recommended because of her prior knowledge and experience with textiles. This was the first of many such collaborations over the next twenty-year period (O'Neale and Kroeber 1930). O'Neale switched her thesis topic from lace to Peruvian archaeological textiles (O'Neale 1927).

After receiving her A.M. in 1927 from the Department of Household Arts, O'Neale decided to enter the doctoral program in Anthropology and went to Kroeber for consultation. In spite of his admiration for her textile skills, Kroeber did not encourage O'Neale to pursue a Ph.D. O'Neale, nevertheless, completed two years of course work, proving to Kroeber and others that she was a fine scholar, as well as an accomplished textile analyst. She was ready for material culture studies among Native peoples of Northwestern California, a far cry from Peruvian archaeological textiles. Kroeber had ongoing field studies with the Yurok, Karok, and Hupa peoples (1905, 1925).

Most of his colleagues and graduate students such as Barrett, Edward Gifford, Pliny E. Goddard, Thomas T. Waterman, and later Harold Driver, Cora Du Bois, Anna Gayton, and Isabel Kelly, were or had been engaged in field work with Native California Indians. Kroeber suggested that O'Neale study the material culture of the Klamath River groups, emphasizing basket weaving, and in the summer of 1929, she journeyed to the region. U. C. Berkeley anthropologist David Mandelbaum recalled that Kroeber had given O'Neale only the "skimpiest instructions," a map, and advice on where to stay (pers. comm. 1983).

THE YUROK-KAROK BASKET WEAVERS

In only six weeks, O'Neale accomplished a marathon of investigation. Frequently traveling by canoe, she went from camp to camp, accompanied by Native interpreters who were also weavers. She interviewed some fifty women, including one family. The tribal representation was twenty-five Karok, sixteen Yurok, and seven Hupa weavers. Forty-three of these interviews appear in her publication. She chose not to use the Hupa interviews, however, although she did include photographs of their baskets. O'Neale concluded that the Hupa "can tell a very few of their own baskets by design, none by workmanship" (1932:9). She also noted that their baskets were very innovative and showed "modern extravagance" (1932:70).[3]

O'Neale derived her research practice from a publication she reviewed for *American Anthropologist* (1930). This Bureau of American Ethnology monograph, *Coiled Basketry in British Columbia and Surrounding Region,* published in 1928, was written by H. K. Haeberlin and Helen H. Roberts and edited by Franz Boas. It included field notes by James A. Teit, who was interviewing weavers as early as 1909 (Jacknis 1992). Of particular interest to O'Neale was Boas's statement in the preface: "The problem I set myself was an investigation into the attitude of the individual artist toward his work. Much has been written on the origin and history of design without any attempt to study the artist himself. It seemed necessary to approach the problem from this angle" (Haeberlin et al. 1928:131). O'Neale acknowledges, in the introduction to her dissertation, to "having freely adapted to a study of the tribes on the Klamath River whatever methods appeared to have been successful among the British Columbia tribes" (1932:5).

O'Neale did not actually make baskets with the Klamath River weavers. She talked with them individually, however, in their homes and in small groups, and was able to observe all aspects of the basket-making process. In order to learn Native aesthetics, she elicited responses by showing them large photographs of northwestern California baskets from the collections of the Museum of Anthropology, the California Academy of Sciences, and private collections. Categories of baskets represented in the photographs included women's dress caps, fancy baskets, made-for-sale baskets, Jump-dance baskets, acorn soup and cooking baskets, openwork baskets, and seed baskets. Klamath River weavers had been producing made-for-sale baskets since contact with the whites in the mid-nineteenth century, stimulated first by the placer mining activities in the area.[4]

O'Neale reported on the reactions of the participants, who were asked first to segregate the images according to tribal affiliation and function and then to comment on them:

> Each informant was shown every print. The method has obvious advantages. Different women reacted in greater or lesser degree to pictured objects of art they had known through two generations at least.... This eagerness [to examine the pictures] may be partly explained by recalling two facts: up to a comparatively recent time a woman's baskets were destroyed at her death, leaving no old ones to become objects of sentimental regard; and also, these same pictures were of the very baskets obtained from their people within their own lifetime, some baskets they might even recognize...The Yurok-Karok basket maker of any age is an enthusiast on the subject of her craft (1932:8).

The women asked O'Neale for copies of the photographs of some of the baskets that interested them. Her gender allowed for an informality that was not possible with male investigators due to restrictions of Yurok and Karok social practices. The women enjoyed talking about basket weaving with someone as knowledgeable as O'Neale, as indicated by the enthusiastic responses she gathered when she presented the photographs. These images generated conversations about design motifs, property marks, acceptable standards for workmanship, sources for materials, care of baskets, proportion and contour, color combinations and techniques. Other topics included male-female involvement in basket making, Yurok and Karok knowledge of each other's work and of the work of outside tribes, influence of white patronage, and Yurok and Karok attitudes toward innovation.

O'Neale's use of multiple reactions, including her own, to the work of a single basket weaver is a contemporary method. This layering of interpretations would prove useful in her other ethnoaesthetic field work on Papago color designations (O'Neale and Dolores 1943) and with Maya weavers of Guatemala and Quechua potters in Peru (O'Neale 1945, 1976).

Kroeber acknowledged *Yurok-Karok Basket Weavers* to be "one of the most important and liveliest [reports] ever to be made in the field" (1948). In 1983, Lawrence E. Dawson, Research Anthropologist at the Lowie [now Hearst] Museum of Anthropology, responded to my query about the influence of O'Neale's work on his own basket research: "O'Neale helped me to distinguish between the many made-for-sale pieces in the collections [Lowie Museum] and the traditional baskets. I was able to obtain a clear picture of white influence through different media" (pers. comm. 1983). Dawson also commented that he learned about the "set of traditional baskets with all their culturally conditioned features," and that these sets, or functional groupings, constituted the proper basis for comparative study.

O'Neale may have been one of the first researchers to isolate "tourist art," a topic that has attracted many scholars in recent years (Graburn 1976, 1984; Jules-Rosette 1984; Baizerman 1987). The Klamath River basket weavers were becoming separated from their subsistence patterns in which baskets played such an important role. It was a time of transition. Money was needed to purchase goods in the non-Native world that surrounded them. Mrs. Rosy Jacks of Requa told O'Neale: "We made baskets every day. Only way to get clothes" (1929). Another weaver sold through the local storekeeper.

The late nineteenth century was a period of intense collecting of California baskets, not only by anthropologists salvaging "traditional" material, but by dealers and collectors. Made-for-sale or tourist art was being produced by the Klamath River weavers for this new market. O'Neale's book documents the reasons for these new forms from the weaver's perspective.

CONCLUSION

Although the legacy of Lila M. O'Neale's innovative field work and publications has passed on to contemporary archaeologists, anthropologists, art historians, and textile specialists, why is she not better known today?[5] Larry Dawson wrote:

> While the work was extraordinarily insightful for the time, it had practically no effect on other investigators, largely, I think, because there was no one in the field at the time who could appreciate the quality of her approach. There were some who certainly *should* have, but didn't, and published much inferior works. Then, too, there was the problem that field ethnology of American Indians was just drawing to a close, and everyone suddenly believed no such studies could be made anymore. So O'Neale's basketry work stands all alone (pers. comm. 1983).

Yet academic trends fluctuate. By the 1970s, anthropologists were again turning their attention to material culture of Native peoples and the treasure troves of objects created by Native artisans, now part of museum collections. Information was needed that could only be gained by questioning the Native artists themselves. O'Neale's elicitations of terminology, process, and other aspects of basket weaving serve as important resources for contemporary basket weavers, especially for those who are still learning (Nancy Richardson, pers. comm. 1992).[6] Graduate students and anthropologists acknowledge the importance of her field work and method (Dides 1992, Niessen 1991). In 1991, Ron Johnson, professor of art history at Humboldt State University, acknowledged O'Neale's contribution (Johnson et al. 1991:17):

Lila O'Neale's field notes offer insights into individual basket makers that were largely eliminated from her published report. Although there is little individual or biographical information in these interviews, there is a sense of each weaver, of their tribal pride, of their standards of basket making, of their concerns for materials, and what they were willing to do in baskets made for sale. Something of the dignity [and] respect for earlier basket makers...[is] revealed...From O'Neal[e]'s field notes we can gain some sense of the art, beauty, and creativity of a past generation, whose creations still live and speak with spirit.

Margot Blum Schevill

NOTES

1. See Schevill 1986, 1988, 1992, 1993. The first two are biographical articles that discuss other aspects of O'Neale's career, in addition to her work with northwestern California Indians. The Native peoples of California now prefer the spelling *Karuk* instead of *Karok,* and it has become common practice. Karok is employed here for historical consistency.

2. Recent contributions include Bates (1982), Bates and Lee (1990), Bernstein (1985), and Cohodas (1979).

3. See Schevill 1992, pp. 166–67 for further discussion of Hupa basket weaving. O'Neale's Hupa field note books discuss some aspects of their social structure that differ from both the Yurok and Karok: the women, outside of their own family units, never worked together, and, therefore, could not identify the caps or other baskets by personal marks or other attributes.

4. Dorothy K. Washburn (1984) has discussed the influence of dealers and collectors on Indian baskets at the turn of the century.

5. Scholars who have benefited from O'Neale's ethnoaesthetic approach to field work include Mari Lyn Salvador (1978), Ann Lane Hedlund (1983, 1992), Christine and Edward M. Franquemont (1988), and Sandra A. Niessen (1991). In the spring of 1993, Professor Nelson Graburn's museum studies class curated an exhibition at the Phoebe Hearst Museum, *Creating Tradition: Expression and Diversity in Canadian Inuit Art.* In an article in *The Daily Californian* (June 9, 1993), Graburn explained that ethnoaesthetics was one of the several perspectives on Inuit art presented by the exhibition.

6. Commenting on the state of basket making today among the Yurok, Karok, and Hupa, Ron Johnson has noted that there are around thirty weavers between the ages of thirty and sixty years. Six can still make the cap, but most of the weavers are making trinket, medicine, and tobacco baskets (pers. comm. 1993).

APPENDIX: THE WEAVERS

The following list of O'Neale's informants is located in the archives of the Anthropology Department (Cu-23.1), The Bancroft Library, University of California, Berkeley. The numbers correspond to those that O'Neale used in her text.

1. Mrs. Annie Williams (Yurok)
2. Mrs. Rosy Jacks (Yurok)
3. Mrs. Nellie Griffin (Yurok)
4. Mrs. Kitty George (Yurok)
5. Mrs. Melissa Meyers (Yurok)
6. Mrs. Frank (Annie) Roberts (Karok)
7. Mrs. Fanny Smoker (Yurok)
8. Mrs. Emily Gordon (Yurok)
9. Mrs. Tommy (Bertha) Peter (Yurok)
10. Mrs. Elsie Young (Yurok)
11. Mrs. Willie (Nellie) Dowd (Eliza Billy) (Yurok)
12. Mrs. Edward (Francis) Wicks (Francie Horopop) (Yurok)
13. Mrs. William (Maggie) Turk (Maggie Weitchpec M.) (Yurok)
14. Mrs. Willie (Amy) Smoker (Amy McCarthy) (Yurok)
15. Mrs. Allie (Lottie) Markussen (Lottie James) (Yurok)
16. Mrs. Sonie Boskey (Yurok)
17. Mrs. Nellie Cooper
18. Mrs. Jim (Carrie) Robert (Carrie Jim) (Yurok)
19. Mrs. Nellie Ruben (Karok)
20. Mrs. Nettie Ruben (Karok)
21. Mrs. Frank Reece (Karok)
22. Mrs. Mary Ike (Karok)

23. Mrs. Emily Donahue (Karok)
24. Mrs. Georgia Orcutt (Georgia Henry) (Karok)
25. Mrs. Daisy Jones (Karok)
26. Mrs. Red Cap Tom (Karok)
27. Mrs. John Allen (Karok)
28. Mrs. Lizzie Hickox (Karok)
29. Miss Lousia [Louise] Hickox (Karok)
30. Mrs. Hazel Harry (Karok)
31. Mrs. Frank Offield (Karok)
32. Mrs. Shaw (Dora) Davis (Karok)
33. Mrs. Elsie Mac Glaufin (McGlaughlin) (Karok)
34. Mrs. Annie Super (Karok)
35. Mrs. Nellie Johnson (Karok)
36. Mrs. Maggie Charley (Karok)
37. Mrs. Susy Pepper (Karok)
38. Mrs. Lucinda Jake (Karok)
39. Mrs. George Jake (Karok)
40. Miss Eliza Elliott (Karok)
41. Mrs. Mary Jacobs with family
    (Daisy, Sara, Fraser, and Frank) (Karok)
42. Mrs. Cora Wells (Karok)
43. Mrs. Madeline Charley (Karok)
44. Mrs. Josephine Smoker Campbell (Hupa)
45. Mrs. Ellen Quimby (Hupa)
46. Mrs. Carrie Steven (Hupa)
47. Mrs. Abraham (Lucinda) Jack (Hupa)
48. Mrs. Emma Dushey Frank (Hupa)
49. Mrs. John (Sarah) Davis (Hupa)
50. Mrs. Redwood Sam (Hupa)

REFERENCES

Baizerman, Suzanne. 1987. Textiles, Traditions, and Tourist Art: Hispanic Weaving in Northern New Mexico. Ph.D. dissertation, Department of Design, Housing, and Apparel, University of Minnesota.

Barrett, Samuel A. 1908. *Pomo Indian Basketry.* University of California Publications in American Archaeology and Ethnology, 7(3):133–306.

Bates, Craig D. 1982. *Coiled Basketry of the Sierra Miwok: A Study of Regional Variation.* San Diego Museum Papers, no. 15. San Diego: San Diego Museum of Man.

Bates, Craig D., and Martha J. Lee. 1990. *Tradition and Innovation: A Basket History of the Indians of the Yosemite-Mono Lake Area.* Yosemite National Park: Yosemite Association.

Bernstein, Bruce. 1985. Panamint-Shoshone Basketry, 1890–1960. *American Indian Basketry and Other Native Arts* 19:5–29.

Bunzel, Ruth L. 1929. *The Pueblo Potter: A Study of Creative Imagination in Primitive Art.* New York: Columbia University Press.

Cohodas, Marvin. *1979. Degikup Washoe Fancy Basketry, 1895–1935.* Vancouver: Fine Arts Gallery, University of British Columbia.

Dides, Judith. [1992]. Speech Acts of Yurok Basketweavers. Paper presented at the Eighth California Indian Conference, University of California, Berkeley.

Dixon, Roland B. 1902. *Basketry Designs of the Indians of Northern California.* Bulletin of the American Museum of Natural History, 17(1).

Franquemont, Christine, and Edward M. Franquemont. 1988. Learning to Weave in Chinchero. *The Textile Museum Journal* 26:55–78.

Graburn, Nelson H. H. 1984. The Evolution of Tourist Arts. *Annals of Tourism Research* 2:393–419.

Graburn, Nelson H. H., ed. 1976. *Ethnic and Tourist Arts: Cultural Expressions from the Fourth World.* Berkeley and Los Angeles: University of California Press.

Haeberlin, Herman, James A. Teit, and Helen H. Roberts, under the direction of Franz Boas. 1928. *Coiled Basketry in British Columbia and*

Surrounding Region. Annual Report of the Bureau of American Ethnology for 1919–1924, no. 41:119–484.

Hedlund, Ann Lane. 1983. Contemporary Navajo Weaving: An Ethnography of a Native Craft. Ph.D. dissertation, Department of Anthropology, University of Colorado, Boulder.

———. 1992. *Reflections of the Weaver's World: The Gloria F. Ross Collection of Contemporary Navajo Weaving.* Denver: Denver Art Museum.

Hudson, John W. 1893. Pomo Basket Makers. *The Overland Monthly* 21(126):561–78.

Jacknis, Ira. 1992. "The Artist Himself": The Salish Basketry Monograph and the Beginnings of a Boasian Paradigm. In *The Early Years of Native American Art History: The Politics of Scholarship and Collecting,* ed. Janet Catherine Berlo, 134–61. Seattle: University of Washington Press.

Johnson, Ron, Julian Lang, and Coleen Kelley. 1991. *Elizabeth Conrad Hickox (1873–1947): Baskets from the Center of the World.* Arcata, Cal.: Reese Bullen Gallery, Humboldt State University.

Jules-Rosette, Bennetta. 1984. *The Messages of Tourist Art: An African Semiotic System in Comparative Perspective.* New York: Plenum Press.

Kroeber, Alfred L. 1905. *Basket Designs of the Indians of Northwestern California.* University of California Publications in American Archaeology and Ethnology, 2(4):105–64.

———. 1909. California Basketry and the Pomo. *American Anthropologist* 11:233–49.

———. 1925. *Handbook of the Indians of California.* Bureau of American Ethnology Bulletin, no. 78. Washington, D. C.: Smithsonian Institution.

———. 1948. Letter to Margaret Harrison, March 4; Correspondence, 1927–48, Alfred L. Kroeber papers, The Bancroft Library, University of California, Berkeley.

Niessen, Sandra A. 1991. More to It than Meets the Eye: Photo-Elicitation Amongst the Batak of Sumatra. *Visual Anthropology* 4:415–30.

O'Neale, Lila M. 1927. Design, Structural and Decorative, with Color Distribution Characteristic of Ancient Peruvian Fabrics. M.A. thesis, Department of Household Arts, University of California, Berkeley.

———. [1929]. Field Notes on the Basketry of Northwestern California, 11 notebooks. Ethnological Manuscripts, Department of Anthropology Archives, The Bancroft Library, University of California, Berkeley.

———. 1930. Review of Franz Boas, H. K. Haeberlin, et al., Coiled Basketry in British Columbia and Surrounding Region. *American Anthropologist,* 36:306–08.

———. 1932. *Yurok-Karok Basket Weavers.* University of California Publications in American Archaeology and Ethnology, 32(1):1–184.

———. 1945. *Textiles of Highland Guatemala.* Washington, D.C.: Carnegie Institution of Washington Publication, no. 567.

———. 1976. Notes on Pottery Making in Highland Peru. *Nawpa Pacha* 14:41–60. Berkeley: Institute of Andean Studies.

O'Neale, Lila M., and Juan Dolores. 1943. Notes on Papago Color Designations. *American Anthropologist* 45:387–97.

O'Neale, Lila M., and A. L. Kroeber. 1930. *Textile Periods in Ancient Peru.* University of California Publications in American Archaeology and Ethnology, 28(2):23–56.

Reichard, Gladys A. 1936. *Navajo Shepherd and Weaver.* New York: J. J. Augustin.

Salvador, Mari Lyn. 1978. Yer Dailege! *Kuna Women's Art.* Albuquerque: The Maxwell Museum of Anthropology, University of New Mexico.

Schevill, Margot Blum. 1986. Lila M. O'Neale. *Kroeber Anthropological Society Papers,* no. 65–66:129–37.

———. 1988. Lila M. O'Neale. In *Women Anthropologists: A Biographical Dictionary,* eds. Ute Gacs, Aisha Khan, Jerrie McIntyre, Ruth Weinberg, 275–81. Westport, Connecticut: Greenwood Press.

———. 1992. Lila Morris O'Neale: Ethnoaesthetics and the Yurok-Karok Basket Weavers of Northwestern California. In *The Early Years of Native American Art History: The Politics of Scholarship and Collecting,* ed. Janet Catherine Berlo, 162–90. Seattle: University of Washington Press.

———. 1993. Lila M. O'Neale and the Yurok-Karok Basket Weavers of Northwestern California. In *Museum Anthropology in California, 1889–1939,* eds. Ira Jacknis and Margot Blum Schevill. *Museum Anthropology* 17(2):67–71.

Washburn, Dorothy K. 1984. Dealers and Collectors of Indian Baskets at the Turn of the Century in California: Their Effect on the Ethnographic Sample. *Empirical Studies of the Arts* 2(1):51–74.

YUROK-KAROK BASKET WEAVERS

by Lila M. O'Neale

University of California Publications in American Archaeology and Ethnology
Volume 32, No. 1, pp. 1–184, plates 1–58, 36 figures in text
Issued February 6, 1932

University of California Press
Berkeley, California

Cambridge University Press
London, England

YUROK–KAROK BASKET WEAVERS

BY

LILA M. O'NEALE

CONTENTS

PLATES

(Following page 184)

FIGURES IN TEXT

INTRODUCTION

The basketry craft of the Indians on the Klamath and Trinity rivers in extreme northwestern California has long been recognized as having attained a high degree of excellence. It is limited with minor exceptions of finish to the twining technique; it is molded by a set of traditional form proportions and stylicized design motives; and it is maintained at present by a group of weavers as jealous of classic conventions as were their teachers and theirs before them. This is not to say that modern ideas and commercialism have failed to penetrate; numbers of these Indians have known whites from the placer-mining days of 1850. It is true, however, that the older women who at present make baskets are conscious of deviations from time-worn attitudes to the extent that they judge today's products by yesterday's criteria. Paradoxically enough, Yurok-Karok contact with white buyers explains at once the maintenance of the craft's oldest aspects and their abandonment for fantastic effects.

A study of the relationship of Yurok and Karok women to their craft was suggested by the paper on coiled basketry in British Columbia prepared under Professor Boas' direction.[1] In contradistinction to the more familiar examination of objective evidence, Professor Boas and his associates set themselves the problem of investigating the subjective attitude of the weaver, of determining individual reactions to craft aspects. My own approach has similar aims and I acknowledge having freely adapted to a study of the tribes on the Klamath river whatever methods appeared to have been successful among the British Columbia tribes.

Analyses of the major and minor differences in the elements of ornamentation have been presented by Kroeber[2] and Goddard.[3] The present investigation made use of the same museum material in addition to accessions since available. What is attempted here from the design standpoint is to relate the weaver to the conventions, or to whatever variations seem to have taken place in form or pattern, and to let her define in terms of the tenets of her craft the relative

[1] F. Boas *et al.*, Coiled Basketry in British Columbia and Surrounding Region, BAE-R 1919–1924: 131–615, 1928. Cited as Coiled Basketry, hereafter.

[2] A. L. Kroeber, Basket Designs of the Indians of Northwestern California, UC–PAAE, 2:105–164, 1905. Cited as Basket Designs, hereafter.

[3] P. E. Goddard, Life and Culture of the Hupa, UC–PAAE, 1:1–88, 1903. Cited as The Hupa, hereafter.

importance of its aspects. I found no woman so inarticulate that she could not indicate conformance to or violation of the traditionally correct expression. The least helpful informant might be able to say a certain basket was not good and to point out exactly where it failed,

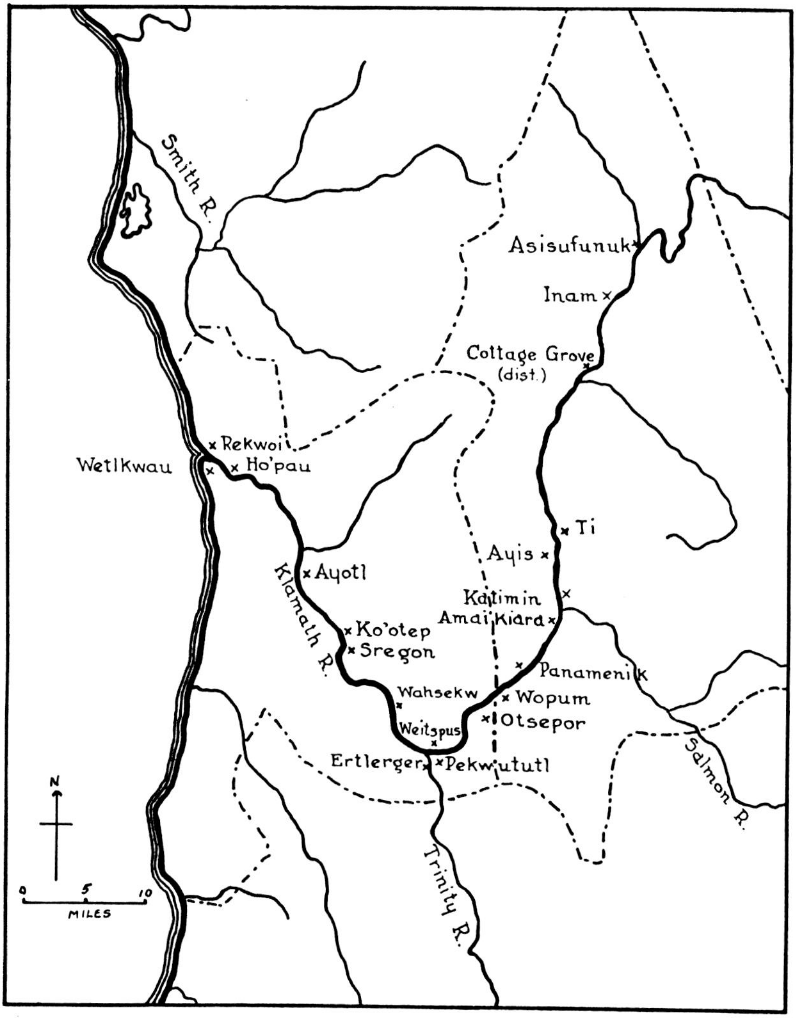

Fig. 1. Localities represented by informants: down-river, Yurok; up-river, Karok.

even if she could not explain why she interpreted it as a failure or what specifically the weaver of that basket should have done. If, then, one informant's view seemed unusual or warped, it was entirely probable that the next woman could make clear in words what a finger had pointed to so readily.

The results as given in this paper are based upon a six-weeks' field trip, financed jointly by the University of California and through a grant from the Bureau of American Ethnology. During this trip weavers representing most of the localities from the mouth of the

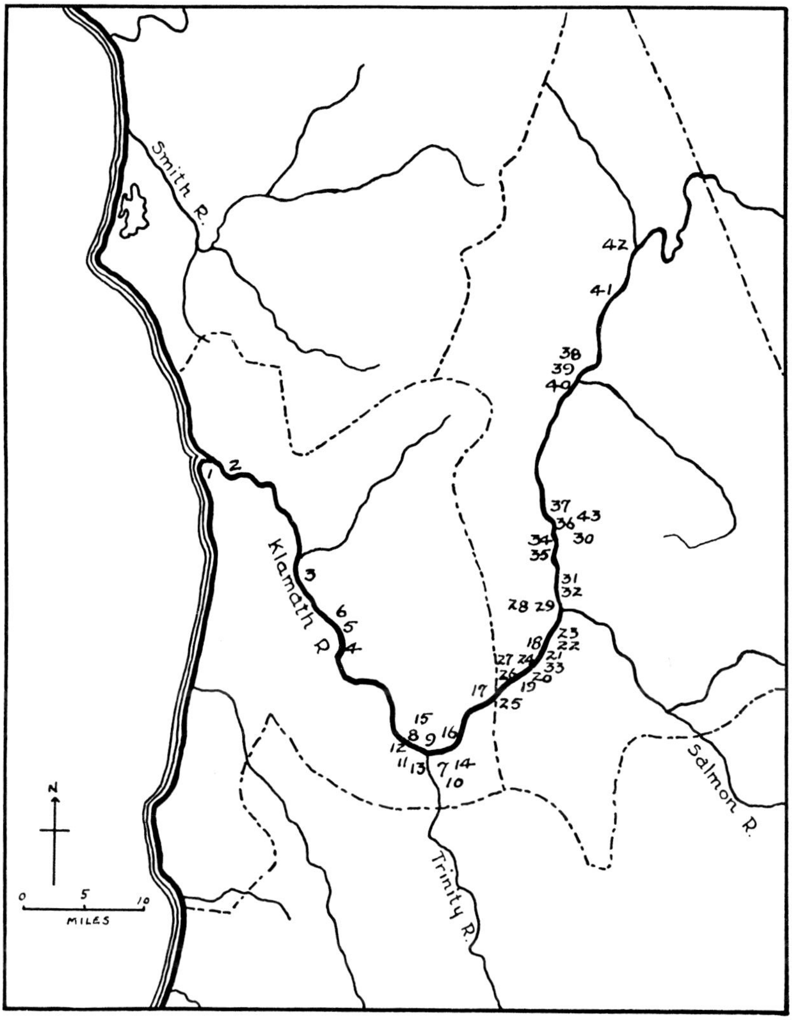

Fig. 2. Localities of informants: 1–18, Yurok; 19–43, Karok.

Klamath to what is the present town of Happy Camp were interviewed (figs. 1, 2). An attempt was made to see every woman who is now making or had made baskets. Certain omissions were unavoidable. Regular fishing days are still adhered to by the Karok and long visits remain in vogue, so that between one day and the next a prospective informant might disappear for a matter of weeks. In all, about forty-seven women were seen, forty-three of whom are referred to by number. Wherever an interpreter was necessary a weaver was selected to act. These cases are the only ones in which composite opinion is known to have been given.[4]

Photographs of the baskets in the University of California Museum of Anthropology, a group from the former collection of the California Academy of Sciences, and a number taken by Pliny E. Goddard during his work among the Hupa were an important element in assembling information upon individual attitudes. Each informant was shown every print. This method has obvious advantages. Different women reacted in greater or less degree to pictured objects of an art they had known through two generations at least. Much detailed information on phases no one but a weaver could have known to exist, came out during the handling of the prints: technical details, special uses, facts about other weavers in connection with this or that design, incidental remarks leading to important distinctions, and casual phrases corroboratory of other opinions. Doubtless, too, some points as self-evident to a worker as the right and wrong side of a leaf of *Xerophyllum* were never mentioned at all. Psychologically, the prints were more productive of results than were questions, whose very simplicity sometimes led an informant to doubt her comprehension of them. With a basket print in her hand, the Indian woman became my superior in knowledge and correspondingly helpful. Several times a coolly appraising demeanor became speedily transformed at the disarming sight of objects familiar and yet fascinating. The Yurok-Karok basket maker of any age is an enthusiast on the subject of her craft. Questions might seem pointless, childish even, but the interest was sustained by the pictures. I found a few informants willing to go back to them again and again to clarify a statement or to add examples illustrating some important detail. This eagerness may be partly explained by recalling two facts: up to a comparatively recent time a woman's baskets were destroyed at her death, leaving no old ones to become objects of sentimental regard; and also, these same pictures were of the very baskets obtained from their people within their own lifetime, some baskets they might even recognize. Informants occasionally showed surprise at baskets of such age as they had never thought to see again.

---

[4] See Appendix for characterizations of informants.

In view of the fact that excellent descriptions of the tribal life along the river are contained in A. L. Kroeber's Handbook[5] and T. T. Waterman's Yurok Geography,[6] it seems unnecessary to go into the environmental and other background material essential for an understanding of any single phase of native life. The down-river, or Yurok, territory extends from the mouth of the Klamath up about thirty-six miles. The Indians set the boundary beyond which is Karok or up-river country at the rocky pass through which Bluff creek rushes to join the main stream a mile below. The pass represents a linguistic as well as a tribal boundary, the former much the more real. Down-river informants married to Karok men spoke very acceptable English because of more frequent use of it as a common tongue.

Investigators of the river tribes agree that their material culture, including that of the Hupa, is identical; that they visited each other, participated in each others' religious ceremonies, and intermarried. The same coincidence is illustrated in their music[7] and in their basketry,[8] as Kroeber has pointed out. For the purposes of this study no segregation of Hupa baskets was attempted. Some of them purchased under conditions rendering certainty of origin impossible are labeled "Hupa or Yurok." Two or three more tribe-conscious informants declared their baskets were like those of the other two tribes in all particulars, and then acknowledged an intuitive feeling for those undoubtedly their own. The results were about even: a triumphant guess on one was often matched by virulent criticism of another basket which could not possibly be theirs, but was so recorded. The fact is that they can tell a very few of their own baskets by design, none by workmanship (table 17). A predominant use of certain locally available materials and minor departures from the typical of a familiar region are clues, not determinatives.

---

[5] A. L. Kroeber, Handbook of the Indians of California, BAE–B 78, 1925 Cited as Handbook, hereafter.

[6] T. T. Waterman, Yurok Geography, UC–PAAE, 16:177–314, 1920.

[7] Kroeber, Handbook, 96.

[8] Kroeber, Basket Designs, 116.

LEARNING AND TEACHING THE CRAFT

A composite account of how almost any Indian woman was taught to make baskets would be somewhat like the following. As a very little girl she watched the older weavers of the family. Usually she and her age mates attempted to duplicate the efforts of their elders with any kind of sticks and green grasses available. This was only playing; it resulted in nothing recognizable as a basket and no one paid any attention to it. But if the child persisted in working she was finally noticed by her elders. She could not be trusted to go on with a basket in process of construction, so her mother would start a root basket on discarded sticks for her. After a round or two of the child's weaving the older woman took it from her to make a course, straightening the sticks where twining turns had been put in with uneven tension. The work alternated between them in this way until its abandonment as a diversion or its completion as a rough little bowl (pl. 4*a*).

Variations from this account are unimportant. A few weavers taught themselves, from the play stage to respectable attainment; fewer, even, give credit for their teaching to older companions. A story often told and hugely enjoyed is concerned with the childish certainty that a good basket required nothing more than good materials. A half-dozen old women confessed that they had pilfered roots and sticks from their mothers' supplies thinking by so doing to solve all future difficulties.

The teacher was generally the mother if living, otherwise an aunt or a grandmother. The child was six or seven years old when the first basket was started for her; it would be five years probably before she could begin her own baskets. In this interim she might make a dipper which is always plain, or possibly an acorn soup basket with simple grass overlay pattern, or a small trinket basket in which twining elements regularly progress over two sticks at a time (diagonal twining according to Mason).[9] The Indians always speak of this technique as "double sticks." Anything might excusably be wrong with these first products. Old weavers still laugh at memories of their first baskets. Some were so sharp at the bottom they could only be hung up, surfaces were fluted from the insertion of too many sticks,

---

[9] O. T. Mason, Aboriginal American Basketry, USNM–R 1902: 234, 1904. Cited as Mason, Basketry, hereafter.

and dippers were so loosely woven that they could not be swollen sufficiently to hold water. Yet between a girl's first efforts and her results which had value for use or exchange, a young weaver learned certain of the established requirements. She gathered and dried materials for the old people of her family who could not get to the patches themselves, and was commended or criticized for quality; she helped "cook" and split tree roots for twining elements; she was taught to set an acorn basket on the ground during its making to watch its shape and proportions—features every beginner must know, and she did considerable ripping out of work in order to make the necessary corrections. Even little girls could help prepare for the crowds that came in the old days to the bar near Panamenik for the new year's dances. As incentive, whatever acorn cups and stick plates the girls finished they might take home with them after the festivities.

A young weaver was also shown when and where to put in new sticks for a cap and how to pull them in to make it fit the head. She learned the right size and the placing of a design in a basket. This was advanced instruction, attempted only after her weaving began to show quality. The age at which a girl's basket might have value other than its use to her family was variously given: No. 27 was selling to white people when ten years old; Nos. 20 and 14 began to sell at twelve, although the latter suspects her baskets were bought only out of pity for her youth; Nos. 18 and 26 were selling root caps to Indian women at about that same age, asking twenty-five and fifty cents for them. Other informants traded their work for clothes but did not make baskets to sell until after their children came.

Grown women will refer to their training with pride. If one's mother or aunt was a "good hand at baskets," presumably she taught the right methods which would never have to be relearned. If those methods produced basketry of traditional type, there is no shadow of reason for modifying them now. A Yurok weaver explained it to me thus: there is only one way to weave a basket; you might change the design, but basketry is not like writing which can be changed to typing; the weave always stays the same. She had of course no knowledge of coiling.

It is a fact regretted by older weavers that young girls of today cannot make baskets. Their elders feel certain the girls would like to weave if only they knew how. But they leave for schools at six years of age, just at the time when their mothers were imitating for them the grown women's work in discarded sticks and grass. Perhaps girls do crocheting or embroidery at school, but never basketry. When they come home they have forgotten all they might have observed and they think it smart not to know the old craft. Some less tolerant elders characterize this ignorance as inability or lack of good sense. A very attractive young girl told me she would like to make baskets but the making included so much preliminary preparation that it discouraged her.

Several informants brought out the first attempts of young daughters or granddaughters whose ages at the time of doing the weaving ranged from six to eleven years. The method of teaching had been identical to that used by craftswomen from thirty to seventy years ago. They were immensely proud of their students' work. One little basket, the size of a cup, had had incorporated within its weaving four materials, simple two-strand and three-strand twining, and patterning of straight and slanting stripes. The six-year-old sat by her grandmother, No. 39, copying everything in her small basket that the old woman put in her own larger one. The work was rough but the shape was fairly good. Everyone in the Ko'otep district makes baskets, even young girls of eleven or twelve. The favorite pattern for first work in that locality is double-stick twilling, with one twining element plain root, the other faced with grass overlay. Twilling is quickly done, simple, and attractive. No. 5 has a daughter of twelve. The girl stayed with her mother and me the entire morning, commented intelligently on patterns, and chose standard shapes with confidence. Her first basket is shown in plate 4*a*. Two girls of the same age hovered around to look at the prints. Evidently a sophisticated attitude is less desired by the girls on the lower than by those on the upper river.

From Rekwoi to towns in the Ko'otep district is about twenty-five miles. My Ayotl informants take the better part of two days for the journey by motor-equipped rowboat. It must have taken several times as long by canoe. All the way the women sit quietly, their hands folded. Surrounded by basketry materials they may have made an especial trip to obtain, they are forbidden to work at any phase of their craft while in a boat. It was not done in the earlier days and it is still against Indian law, "bad luck." Urged to be more specific as to what might happen if one disregarded the rule, a weaver admitted she had never asked the reason behind the prohibition. A second Yurok said a violation might make one sick. Both women had learned of the danger when little girls. Still another Yurok remembered a similar rule that was taught a child: she must stop her basket making at sundown. It was bad luck to go on with it, with the usual implication that illness would follow. But as she grew older a girl might circumvent the menace of misfortune by going to sleep a little while, after which she could work with safety on her basket.

MATERIALS

To sit down to the actual weaving of a basket presupposes hours and days of preparation. A basket maker does not minimize the labor involved, but accepts the difficulties and tedium of the preliminary steps without question. All the processes of gathering, preparing, sorting, and storing of materials the Indian weaver describes by the single word "make." Every woman who can "makes" her own basket stuffs, and it takes direct inquiry to bring out so obvious a fact. Sometimes an informant denies in her answer the suggestion of laziness she feels is implied by the question. Small children in the home, physical disability, or extreme old age are legitimate reasons for not going after available materials. Each weaver regrets such limitations, conscious that her ability to choose for her own work is superior to any other's. Women over sixty are as tenacious of the habit as younger ones.

Several informants admit having secret locations to which they regularly return for various supplies. This one goes for black fern to a certain creek bed; others have special trees from which they have tested samples of the roots or tried out the dye yielded by the bark. All know good materials and all could get good qualities, they tell me, but the one who goes far back into the hills to an unfrequented spot feels an added assurance. And, as a matter of fact, those who confess to these secret patches are the best makers.

Few women will gather a surplus of any supply in order to sell it, and no woman on the Klamath makes a business of selling materials, although she may make baskets for sale to her own people. It would seem that some opportunities are lost because of this reluctance. A Karok woman pays a dollar for three bunches of hazel sticks, about enough for four soup baskets; a "bundle" of willow roots with the bark still on or a handful of white grass about two inches in diameter brings seventy-five cents. These latter supplies are plentiful in Yurok country, but each woman there seems intent only upon her own needs.

On the other hand No. 27, an expert, would almost rather go without than have to buy a quantity of unsorted supplies. A poor worker may be able occasionally to buy the spare or discarded sortings of a good weaver. Other women say of her, "she runs out her grass," meaning that she is improvident. Or, a good worker may gather a surplus to give away. Basket materials are particularly acceptable in localities where certain kinds are scarce. Exchange is fairly common, although the permanent arrangement between a household of weavers at Pekwututl and their relatives at Rekwoi is commented upon often and with some envy. Grass, hazel sticks, and black fern go from the interior annually; redwood and spruce roots come from the coast. Both lots have been made ready for use. The women in the Ko'otep district on the lower Klamath also send grass and fern to the coast in exchange for redwood and spruce roots of better quality than those growing in their own vicinity. Grass goes from the Weitspus region to the Karok country as far as the Asisufunuk district in exchange for porcupine quills. Cottonwood roots, admired for their whiteness, are sent from Hoopa to a Karok weaver near Katimin. She has planted a small tree which she hopes will ultimately furnish her with a dependable supply.

More casual exchange takes place between members of the same group who may go together in the fall to pick the giant ferns. Sharing at that time is part of the spirit which sends the women out together. This seems to be less common among the up-river people than among the down-river people for whom supplies are readier at hand. Giant fern, too, is the most available of the basketry materials. Cooperation may, in the case of some weaver like No. 14, be her sole means of getting supplies. She herself is unable to leave home, but her aunt, mother-in-law, and sister-in-law divide their stores with her annually, besides saving for her use ends of sticks and roots too fine for their own work.

FOUNDATION MATERIALS

All basketry of the Klamath river region is twined, a technique which implies sticks and twining elements. Whatever decoration is made in the basket is by the overlay or facing process. Therefore we may speak of foundation sticks, twining roots, and overlay materials. Comparatively few types of baskets are of one material only; the great majority require at least three different materials in their making.

Hazel Sticks

Hazel sticks are conceded by the women of both tribes to be the best, but the most difficult to procure nowadays. New little shoots from a ground recently burned over are the ideal. This statement is followed, however, by the lament that fires cannot be set as they used to be by the old-time weavers, and by the regret that accidental burnings occur so seldom in places where they do basket makers any good. The lower Klamath people seem to be most fortunate in this matter of fires. Lucy Thompson recounts the burning over of the hazelnut flats as part of the program for their preservation.[10] The nuts were pounded into a gruel flour which was of special value to invalids and the shoots formed the frames of all baskets, hence the flats were worth care. People on the lower Klamath went to burn the brush during a dry summer or in the early fall. The following spring the young shoots sprouted but were left uncut until their second year. They were then from twelve to thirty-six inches high. It is the second-year growth that weavers seek for their work. In the Karok country what new growth does appear is destroyed by cattle—another handicap to the modern weaver.

Hazel is gathered in the spring, April or May at the latest. It is peeled, cured in the sun, graded as to sizes, and often wound around with strips of cloth to keep the lengths uninjured. The most ambitious supply seen during my trip was gathered by informant No. 10. She had gone out with a pack horse, had spent two days cutting the shoots, and brought home a year's stock for four weavers (pl. 3*a*). Preliminary sorting yielded four grades; more careful selection from each grade for the sticks of a particular basket would be made when the weaving was begun.

1. Finest quality: sticks approximately 15 inches long. These are for fancy baskets especially.

2. Medium fine: sticks approximately 18 inches long.

3. Medium coarse: sticks approximately 25 inches long.

4. Coarse: sticks approximately 31 inches long. These are for wood packing baskets.

After the piles of sticks had been subdivided into small bunches about an inch to two inches in diameter and had muslin strips twined between them, the whole sheet was rolled up like a tule mat for storage.

---

[10] L. Thompson, To the American Indian, 29, 1916.

In the old days, before the introduction of cloth, the bark peelings were knotted together to serve for the twining strips.

Quality of stock depends primarily upon the newness of the growth, after that to a large extent upon the curing. Two days is sufficient for hazel sticks; one day, if hot; less time if the wind is up. Careful preparation means watching the process. The sticks must be straightened out while drying. If this is not done the final result will have lost its original value appreciably.

Willow Sticks

Down-river every basket maker uses hazel entirely or to a large degree; up-river, willow predominates. Willow is interchangeable with hazel as a foundation material. Because new growth of the latter is scarce and willow is everywhere abundant, Karok women have to be satisfied with it for most of their baskets. On the upper Klamath, above Katimin, the quality is fine because of continual cutting down of shoots. When gathered at the right time they do not break easily. In actual appearance willow is smoother and straighter, but it is for all that a substitute, a makeshift. It is too flexible, complained a Yurok weaver in describing a cap made on willow foundation sticks. The result is limber, an attribute which no standard cap for work or dress should have. If a cooking basket is to be made, hazel is the choice. It is tough, the best qualities will not break in working them, and the basket is more sturdy to withstand strain.

Near the end of the season when supplies run low, Karok weavers apologize for having to use willow sticks in the same basket with hazel. Down-river women say they would not mix the two. Besides, willow sticks stored for more than two years may be infested with larvae which crumble portions of the sticks to dust. A basket in use stands in no such danger. Hazel sticks are immune to pests. One very good maker continues to go out for her annual supply, although she has remnants from each of the past ten years or so still usable.

Preparation of willow sticks is a tedious rather than difficult process (pl. 1*b*). A woman takes up a bunch of sticks in her right hand; she nips the bark at the butt end of one between her teeth. The left thumb opens the slit and loosens the bark for a short distance whereupon the whole shoot is pulled out of its sheath with one twisting motion of head and right hand together. A woman will strip from five to seven shoots in a minute, depending upon their freshness.

A Yurok informant, who came in with her load late in the afternoon, sat up most of the night to peel her sticks and could not be interested in any conversation which would delay her task. It is hard to strip dry sticks. If willow is cut later than August it is customary to put the shoots into boiling water to soften the bark. That practice, according to a skilled weaver, is an admission of lack of standards.

Myrtle Sticks

Myrtle for foundation sticks is favored by some of the most skillful Karok weavers, Nos. 28, 30, 32, and 38. They say the old people used it for sticks; Yurok informants do not know of it. The bush grows in a few places high in the hills. Because it is difficult to gather an adequate supply from any one spot, only the discriminating weaver uses it. Myrtle is peeled and cured like willow, which it excels in strength. No. 28, who makes very small baskets, prefers it to hazel because it is tough and because the sticks in their various sizes are almost the same from base to tip, allowing a uniformly even appearance of the work the whole depth of the basket.

TWINING ELEMENTS

Tree Roots

Aside from the twining elements in the so-called stick baskets, which are composed entirely of hazel or willow, twining elements are of roots. Near the ocean and as far up the Klamath as Weitspus, redwood and spruce roots are used by women who live on the coast, by those who go there to get a quality superior to that obtainable farther inland or who exchange grass, hazel, and black fern for them. Beyond Weitspus no one has redwood to use and the available yellow pine is considered its equal or better. In the Asisufunuk district "bull" or pitch pine, sugar pine, alder, willow, and wild grape are staples; some cottonwood root comes in from Hoopa.

No root can be used as found. The big tree roots require the most preparation. Along the entire length of the river the basket maker "cooks" her roots. The use of this word is not confined to basketry. Kroeber describes the cooking of money or property to be paid by each side participating in a war dance; and also the dance around a fire to "cook the pains" during a Yurok woman's preparation to become a shaman.[11]

[11] Kroeber, Handbook, 50, 63.

For basketry the term "cook," comparable to our bake, is apt. It in no way implies a drying out. A Yurok woman's method for spruce roots will give a picture of the process for all the big roots. She undoubtedly will have tried out samples of roots from different trees before entering upon a series of steps which require much time and skilled effort. If her results prove satisfactory she goes back to her chosen trees for roots three to four feet in length and about the size of the forearm in diameter. The last measurement is not so important; roots five or six inches in diameter will take proportionately longer to cook. A fire is built on sand. When it has burned to coals the roots are buried in a shallow trench about six inches deep. They stay in the hot sand from twelve to eighteen hours. Those left for the longer time are still a little warm when dug up. Larger roots may have to be taken out the second day, turned over, recovered, and left under a slow fire. My informant tested a root in several ways: she made sure it was pliable, light in weight, and that the bark peeled off as easily as the skin from a cold, baked potato, which the root very much resembled to the touch. The woody part was spongy and moist. Two sisters in different localities cook pine roots in a warm oven, continuing the process until the sap stops running out in quantity. This method is not approved by their neighbors because it is not the old way, but there seemed to be no criticism of the resultant quality of the product. Karok informants said they could shorten the time of cooking by building a second fire over the buried roots, which leaves only part of the cooking to the warmed sand. This method takes two hours for the smaller sizes of roots.

While the roots are still warm they are cut crosswise in the center for ease in handling and split into eighths with a hatchet or butcher knife (formerly with a deer horn) which is inserted wedge-like on the side near one end. The bark and inner pith of each triangular section are peeled off with a case knife and discarded. If the basket maker chooses, she may store these small segments. Soaking them overnight at any subsequent time will restore them to a condition in which they are easily handled, or, the preparation may be continued to the next stage while they are still fresh, and a really good weaver will continue the process if she has time. She splits her triangular eighths into ribbons, starting each with a case knife. Then, with the thin splint held between her teeth, she pulls away the main portion with her right hand, the left always just ahead of the split to prevent a sudden veering to another plane (pl. 1*a*). These ribbons are scraped with a knife, bone spoon, or mussel shell to make the roots smooth and pliable. Whatever tool is chosen is held as one would grasp a stick by the thumb and first finger. The length of knife under the palm does the scraping, first on one side of the ribbon, then on the other, a milky sap dripping from the knife during the process.

Each prepared material has a characteristic form in which it is stored. Split roots are folded over once, tied midway between the loop and the ends, and put in a dry place to prevent mildew. When required for use, a single length is dipped into water and subdivided into eighth-inch strands with the thumb nails. The strands which come from the outer brownish layer just under the bark are the finest to work with. The final product, whether redwood, spruce, pine, or alder root, is a smooth, strong, uniformly wide element which furnishes stability to the basket.

Comparing the values of the larger roots, informants seem to rely as much on personal preferences as on actual quality. The old people on the lower Klamath were accustomed to go into the mountains for pine roots for their cooking baskets; but pine has been superseded by spruce and redwood among the workers of today. These go to the coast for the quality they consider superior. At Weitspus spruce roots are not considered as good as redwood. Possibly the attractive color and the scarceness of the latter bias the opinions of informants. Other Yurok weavers affirm there is no difference in quality between the two roots, that spruce is available and that redwood must be brought in from the coast. As further evidence that redwood is not the most ideal material they tell of down-river people coming up to get the yellow pine because acorn soup takes on the color of the redwood root if left in a basket overnight. However, one of my Karok informants had planted a redwood tree to furnish her with a supply. Sugar pine is never the choice, apparently, and is only taken when other materials are unavailable. It is not so good as any of the other roots according to informants in three different districts along the Klamath: Weitspus, Panamenik, and Katimin. In the Asisufunuk vicinity sugar pine is too scarce to be counted on as a staple.

The Smaller Roots

The small roots requiring no cooking are barked with a case knife or a shell. Willow, alder, and cottonwood are gathered along the edge of the river after high water has washed away the sand, exposing lengths from three to six feet. Willow roots are the most common of the smaller varieties. They are a clear white and not unpleasant to the taste. As all materials may occasionally or habitually be held between the teeth to keep them taut or readily available, taste is important. Alder is red-orange in color, stiff, brittle, bitter to the taste. It is less often used than others for fine work although it frequently appears in the beginning rounds of an all-root basket. It has the disadvantage of getting dark and old looking. Weavers objected to its seeming not clean. Alder root ranges from the size of wild grape roots to that of willow roots. It may be split with the thumb nail into as many as six divisions; willow is more often accounted the right size for the twining just as it grows; at most, it is split but once. Cottonwood root is clean looking but not available in quantity in the down-river localities. It, too, may be split for size.

Wild grape root is used, when at all, for very nice caps. It can be easily subdivided into from two to five even strands, as the women say admiringly, "to the size of a hair." Recognized as possessing qualities of length and toughness, it is often the material chosen for the start of a basket. It is mildly poisonous, an irritant to some workers, hence shunned in spite of its quality. But its greatest disadvantage lies in the difficulty of cleaning a basket woven of grape roots. One informant said the reason for its neglect by weavers of former days was the lack of small cutting tools with which to clip off the ends pushed to the inside of the basket during the weaving. Other materials yield to scraping with the edge of a bone spoon or shell. Nowadays a woman of ability and discrimination will use grape root in her nicest baskets; other less able weavers may begin their finest pieces with it; still others consider it as only a substitute for willow root, whereat an expert smiles. The best maker in the Panamenik district buys her grape root. It comes to her in small rings approximately three inches across. Five of these rings sell for seventy-five cents.

Table 1 summarizes informants' use of the various roots.

TABLE 1

USE OF THE VARIOUS ROOTS BY INFORMANTS*

Informant	Large Roots: Redwood	Spruce	Yellow pine	Sugar pine	Small Roots: Willow	Alder	Cottonwood	Grape
1	x	P						
4	x							
5	x	x	P		x	x	x	x
6	x	x				–	L	L
7	x	x	L	L	x	L	L	P
10	x	x	L	L	x	L	L	P
11		x			x			
15		x			x			
17		x			x	x	x	x
18			x		x			P
19			x					P
20	–	P	x	P	x	x	–	x
21	–	P	x		x	x		P
23			x			x	–	x
27		x	x	x	x	P	–	x
28	–	P	x	P	x	x	L	x
29	–	P	x	P	x	x	L	x
30	–	–	x		x			
31			x		x	P		x
32			x		x			
34			x		x			x
35			x		x	P		x
38			x		x			
39			x			P	P	x

* x = uses; P = present but not used; — = lacking; L = little used.

OVERLAY MATERIALS

White Grass

Xerophyllum tenax, commonly called white grass by the Yurok-Karok, appears either as ground or pattern in a large majority of baskets. Only women who confine themselves to all-stick basketry types would choose to do without it. The main difficulty is in locating spots that produce good qualities. The older weavers of the idyllic days knew just where to set their annual fires and a fine growth of long-strand grass would result. At present, fires are offenses against the law, none can be counted on to occur, and thus any spot which has been accidentally burnt over will be visited by women from miles around.

The accompanying map can be indicative only (fig. 3). No grass grows at Weitspus, Wahsekw, or other spots named. An informant answered my question as to supply source by giving the nearest place name. From there she assumes that one realizes she must go several

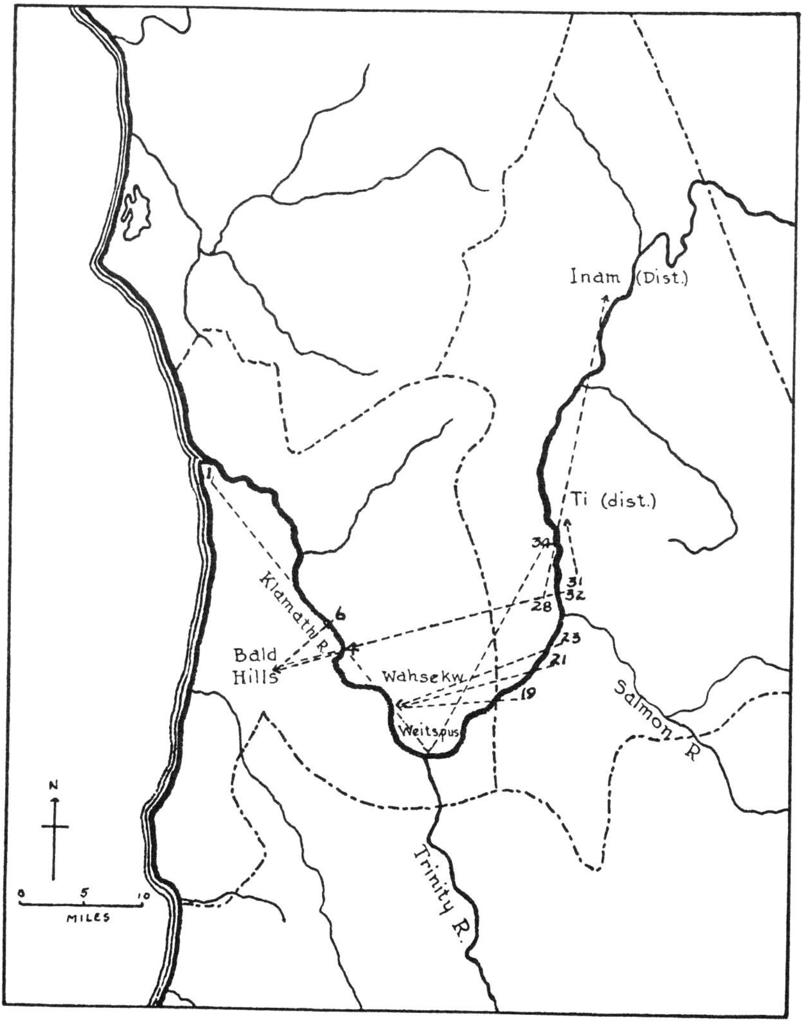

Fig. 3. Map to show locations of white grass patches annually visited by informants.

miles into open country or up on hilltops. The only exchange represented on the map is the previously mentioned one which takes place between No. 1 and her Pekwututl relatives. The other women actually go themselves or pay some one to bring them grass. For example,

Nos. 33 and 20 in the Panamenik district send men, one 18 miles, the other 16 miles out into the country. For a bunch an inch and a half in diameter, the price is fifty cents; larger bunches are relatively higher. The Bald hills shown on the map are in Chilulu territory, about eight miles southwest of Ko'otep and Sregon.

The best quality of white grass is pulled from the center of clumps growing in the shade. In the open, grass is dryer, more brittle. During the curing it is customary to take up a bunch and "work it," which means to grasp the bunch with hands some distance apart and twist it lengthwise between them. This keeps the grass soft while being cured. If left a little green in color it is better, say some weavers, than if dried to the white stage, or worse, to a yellowish tinge which is evidence of burning. Properly done, curing takes two or three days. One informant, No. 14, puts her stock out for three days bringing it in at night. The third night she leaves it out "to soften." It saves time later on when a basket may be in process of construction if grass is sorted into its four or five sizes. A double handful of strands, butt ends even, is tied firmly to braid for storage.

Maidenhair Fern

Black fern patterns against white grounds are characteristic of Yurok baskets. The black is the outer half of the stem of the five-finger type of maidenhair fern. Good stock grows high up in creek beds. To gather it means climbing about in rocky, difficult places miles from home at the risk of encountering bears and panthers. One of my best informants, No. 28, analyzed the Karok name for black fern, yumarekiritapki. Yumare is the tribal word for hell and the milky way is the Karok concept of its location. She suggested, with no intention of being humorous, that the difficulty of getting black fern from high in the creek beds might be the reason for the inclusion of yumare in the plant name. Although plentiful, therefore, maidenhair is hard to get and not equally good from all creeks. June is the best month for quality. Black fern gathered in July must come from spots higher up than those which furnished the June collection. After August, any maidenhair is too brittle for use.

A Karok family of professional basket makers at Inam go a day's journey, camp while gathering and stripping the leaves from their material, and come home with their year's supply all ready for storing. The usual distance is about four or five miles to the head of some near-by creek. No. 5, with her characteristic emphasis on quality, has a secret patch over ten miles from her home at Ko'otep.

Bundles of maidenhair stem may be kept for years. When black fern is needed the amount required for a basket is soaked in water. Most women split the end of a hazel stick, through which they pull each stem separately. At the same time they pinch together the cleft to flatten the stem (fig. 28). To separate the red under-side from the black outer-side they hold one end between the teeth and use both hands to steady the work. The stem splits easily along the side creases, although a narrow irregular strip of red adheres to each edge of the black portion. This remnant must be cut off with the thumb nail and the green lining must be scraped from the inner side of the stem. Prepared strands are coiled and tied in a small ring to keep them in order. Only three informants were found who had ever attempted to make use of the more brittle red side of maidenhair; two of these are Karok women of natural thrift in using basket supplies. One of them combines it with grass in acorn baskets according to an old way to be dealt with later; the other weaver uses it as the only overlay material in root baskets. One Yurok weaver was using the red to wind the edges of baby baskets. The other informants discard it as hard to work with and not worth the trouble for what it adds to the appearance of a basket.

Giant Fern

Indian women call woodwardia "fern" to differentiate it from black fern. It is gathered at any time other than during the spring months and, except where cattle feed on it, most localities furnish enough for the weavers' needs The stems are cut close to the ground and stripped of their leaves. To keep the lengths fresh they are often wrapped in leaves; letting materials dry through neglect means extra labor. When bruised between rocks each stem reveals two long strands which may be taken out intact. These are hung straight until dried, then coiled and stored until needed for some particular basket. Woodwardia is never used in its natural color, but the fern keeps a long time, and its dyeing involves a separate series of processes in no way related to the preparation of the original strands.

Porcupine Quills

The overlay indicative of the greatest degree of skill is that done with quills. Some women never have woven with them: No. 6, who is a good worker, No. 11, average, and Nos. 12 and 19, poor weavers. Not all women are able to manage such short lengths. With great pride a weaver would bring out her store of quills to show me, even though she might not have used any in her baskets for years. The Karok on the upper river told of people in the old days buying caps made by the Indians around what is now Hamburg in the Shasta country. They were soft caps, "like rags," but the Karok bought them in order to take the quills from them. Now they get ample supplies from the Asisufunuk district and the country to the south. One informant had a small box of wavy lengths which she had taken from an old cap of her earlier days. It had been her ambition as a girl to have a new cap for each year's Brush dance. She started work by retrieving the quills from the preceding year's cap. Such economy is rarely practiced now; it is a questionable saving of time and effort, as other women are frank to say.

When a porcupine is killed and skinned at once, the quills are easily pulled out. An ordinary envelope full of unsorted sizes sells for a dollar. Or, the whole skin may be purchased for a dollar since it is useless for any other purpose. The smallest quills are from the sides of the animal. No. 28, near Katimin, uses this size exclusively, trading grass for them. Most baskets have medium to large size quills in their patterns because the widths more closely match the widths of the other overlay materials.

Table 2 is a calendar of Yurok-Karok harvest times for basketry supplies. Each month shows the maturing of some necessity or its continuance at quality level. The later fall and winter months, from October through February, allow the basket weaver to choose her own convenience for gathering root materials and giant fern strands. For hazel, willow, and myrtle sticks, for black fern and grass, the seasons are short and there is a definite superiority in the quality when collected during some one month.

Theoretically, every weaver knows good materials and can get the best. One woman reports that wild grass or fern is ready for picking and they go, singly or in groups, from then on through its season to gather it. Except for secret plots, everybody in a locality goes to much the same places. Expert weavers excuse materials of poor quality in old peoples' baskets. They say that there are too many required kinds of material and too many difficult or dangerous trips to make for supplies for an old woman's basket to be uniformly good. An informant with as high standards as those holding this opinion, but with less tolerance, says few women really know what to use, that they will work with mediocre stuff because that is the kind they carry in from the patches. She does her own grading on the spot by gathering a single quality which requires nothing further than sorting for sizes. Such provision insures a supply to meet orders for baskets of any desired type and of a single grade.

TABLE 2

CALENDAR OF YUROK-KAROK HARVEST SEASONS

	January	February	March	April	May	June	July	August	September	October	November	December
Sticks												
Hazel				x	x							
Myrtle*				x				x				
Willow			x	x				x				
Twining elements†												
Pines	x	x			x	x	x	x	x	x	x	x
Redwood	x	x			x	x	x	x	x	x	x	x
Spruce	x	x			x	x	x	x	x	x	x	x
Alder	x	x	x								x	x
Cottonwood	x	x	x								x	x
Grape	x	x	x								x	x
Willow	x	x	x								x	x
Overlay												
Giant fern	x	x				x	x	x	x	x	x	x
Maidenhair						x	x					
White grass						x	x	x‡				

* The Yurok do not use myrtle sticks because they are brittle, according to No. 10.

† No. 29 says that roots are good at any time except during the spring months when they are growing fastest.

‡ Only good from "high up" in August.

DYES AND DYE-MAKING

The use of color in Yurok-Karok basketry may be summarized by fairly simple generalizations: root twining materials and black fern overlay are always used in their natural state; wild grass is in all but exceptional instances left its pale greenish white; all "red" as the Indians term it, or red-orange as we should describe it, is dyed giant fern; all yellow is dyed porcupine quills, or, infrequently, dyed grass in imitation; all black, other than maidenhair fern, is dyed hazel or willow sticks. Whatever colors fall outside the red-yellow-black category are chemically dyed materials for specific uses. Of these more will be said in connection with the commercial aspect of basketry.

Dyes for Sticks

Dyeing sticks black, often purplish in tone, is a process admittedly old but largely obsolete at the present time. Indian openwork plates, on which fish was dried or served, and wood packing baskets occasionally had groups of colored sticks which formed decorative lines from the center to the rim. The most common dyeing method employed was to bury hazel or willow lengths in mud. Every informant knew of the practice but each said it was of her mother's generation, not done now except possibly by very old people. Even in former times it seems to have been more common among the down-river basket makers than among the Karok. An informant on the lower Klamath remembered seeing her aunt put sticks in a mass of ground rotted acorns, where she left them for about five days. She had never seen sticks buried in mud. Both pine roots and the red side of the black fern stem had been mud-dyed by different Karok informants. This generally discarded half of the stem was rendered less brittle by dyeing it.

Dyes for Giant Fern

All red is dyed fern and all fern is dyed red, according to Indian weavers. This statement requires recognition of variations in color tone from light orange-red to dull red-brown, and of the difference to a basket maker between fern (woodwardia) and black fern (maidenhair). Since the dye is generally from alder bark there must be other explanations to account for the appreciable range of color. Old baskets commonly look duller and darker; those washed often become more faded in appearance. But even among newly made baskets there are visible degrees of brightness.

The method of dyeing woodwardia most often mentioned by writers is that of drawing the strands through the mouth after chewing alder bark. Or, No. 7 said, the juice might be spit out into a basket and water added for the dye solution. No. 16, an older woman in the same general locality, was emphatic in her denial that any such method ever had existed and urged me not to believe so fantastic a statement. Both women were equally sincere, so the difference of opinion is presented for what it may be worth. There are other divergences: two of the most intelligent makers said they knew of the old-time weavers chewing the bark but had never seen it done; No. 7's mother had made the dye just as she has continued to do, by a pounding process to be described. Several informants used to chew the bark but had taken over the modern way, generally giving as a reason that they had no teeth. Only two informants expressed any repulsion at the idea of chewing bark for dye, and this repulsion seemed more an outcome of memories of the very old people who had followed this method than of the method itself. Four women were found who still make dye the old way, among them one very poor worker and one very good one. These women asserted that the old method produced a clearer color than the new method. The dirty red in the baskets of the poor maker, No. 9, may conceivably have been due to the extremely repugnant surroundings.

Practically all basket makers nowadays go through a series of processes similar to that of No. 7 at Pekwututl. She sends her grandson out to the particular tree to which she returns annually; this is the usual custom. Some alder trees give richer, darker colors than others. Bark from too young an alder will make a weak, light dye; a mature tree—it is never too old to be good—will furnish slabs of bark to the women of a locality year after year until it is killed. No. 28 complained that "her" tree was almost dead and that she must test out others to find a new one.

The tree chosen, an area on its trunk about a foot square is cut around with a hatchet and peeled off intact. The bark is about a half inch thick. It turns a brilliant orange in about twenty minutes. The slab is cut into inch-wide strips and divested of any adhering epidermis. Each strip is pounded on a flat rock with a stone mall. The chips are dropped into a pan of tepid water. This completes the first stage of the process. Yurok weavers say it has never been their practice to boil the alder chips; most of them use cold water to draw out the color. No. 7 thought the Karok might boil their dye and that that would account for the darker color in their baskets. On the contrary, No. 20, the most professional Karok weaver in the Panamenik district, uses cold water to make her dye, and No. 21 protested at putting alder bark into hot water. Such a procedure makes a blackish dye, valueless for coloring fern. One Karok made a hot-water dye, then waited for the solution to cool before using it.

For the next step there is general agreement. Coils of fern strands are put into the pan, covered over with the moist bark fragments, and allowed to stand for fifteen to twenty minutes. When taken out the coils are wrapped in a white cloth to develop the right color. This is an important phase. If left too long in the cloth the strands become dark. After a half-hour, not more, they are taken from the cloth, straightened, the butt ends tied together, and hung up in the sun to dry. The only exception to this part of the series of processes was the method of a Karok weaver who leaves her strands in the dye solution until the desired color is reached, then hangs them in the sun all day to set it. Usually the bunches are left out overnight, a method which makes them more pliable for recoiling to store away. Bits of alder bark still cling to the strands. Each strand, when used as an overlay element, will first be moistened in water, drawn between the fingers to clean it, and finally straightened. A reliable Karok informant, No. 22, gave a reason why fern assumed too dark a color. She believed the fern had been allowed to darken too much in the dye bath and that this color was deepened later when the strands were soaked preliminary to their use in weaving. Fern should be left a little too light to begin with. Boiling, she thought, would ruin the color; if the red were to be kept clear the water must be not more than tepid. Whether the bark were chewed or pounded for a water dye could make no difference in the color itself.

Dyes for Porcupine Quills

Porcupine quills are dyed bright greenish yellow with lichen, with Oregon grape, or with mullein, the Karok yivcana. Women from the Weitspus district use moss from pines or scrape it from fences along the road below Wahsekw. The Yurok weavers in the Ko'otep district on the lower river go back into the mountains in their search for yellow pines. They knock off moss with poles from spots high on the tree trunks. They do not use that from fences, but could give no reason for preferring the tree growth. Katimin district weavers, too, climb their highest mountains for their supply.

Dyeing of quills is simple: they are put in water with the lichen and cooked until the color is the desired shade. This takes about an hour; after which the whole mass is turned out on an openwork plate, rinsed, and left in the sun to dry. Each quill is picked out from the moss, rinsed a second time, and dried. The color is permanent. Karok women mentioned a dye made from the bark of the Oregon grape roots, an old-time source of color. Only among these women was the use of mullein observed. They knew no English name for the plant. It grows to a height of from three to four feet along the roads and the river. The dye is made from its roots. One informant in the Wopum district cuts these into small pieces and boils them together with the long moss hanging from pines. When the liquid is cool she puts the quills into it. They remain in the solution for two or three days. She was the only weaver to fear boiling quills might injure the quality of the material. When washed and picked out from the dye-stuff they are placed in the sun to set the color. Other Karok use mullein alone. They scrape the roots, clean, and macerate them; then add water to a cupful of the fragments and boil the quills in the liquid. It is a fairly good dye, but No. 28 had used it only once. It is bitter to the taste, a disadvantage in a craft in which all materials sooner or later may be held between lips or teeth.

As for the comparative color qualities of dyes, all weavers agree that the mountain moss makes the best dye, that Oregon grape lacks depth of color, and that mullein gives a darker yellow than is yielded by moss. The main advantage of mullein is its availability in a country where few materials are plentiful; its disadvantage lies partly in its bitter taste and partly in the fact that its color is not quite the tribally established yellow.

Dyes for White Grass

Porcupine quills dyed bright greenish yellow with mountain moss are the traditionally ideal combination of material, color, and dye-stuff. Up to now there has been no attempt to substitute for the color; substitution for the materials is an old-time device. However, there is no rationalizing by the Yurok-Karok that white grass, the most common alternate, is easier to work with or just as good as quills; it is felt to be a frank imitation of the more elegant effect of quills in a dress cap. Seven of the forty-three informants had never dyed white grass, but only one woman was ignorant of any method of dyeing it.

Oregon grape roots, scraped, macerated like alder bark, boiled to make a solution, and cooled are the dye material and process most commonly described for coloring white grass. Old-time Indian basket makers were remembered to have used grass dyed in this manner before quills were available. A Yurok weaver mixes Oregon grape roots and moss to make her dye. She thought few people knew how to use the combination. Another informant had heard of dyeing

TABLE 3

YUROK-KAROK BASKETRY MATERIALS*

Common	Botanical	Yurok	Karok	Qualities
Sticks				
Hazel	*Corylus californica*	hali L	asis; sarip	Tough, strong; immune to destructive larvae.
Myrtle	*Myrtus communis*†		kisrip	Tough; uniform in size from base to tip, approximately.
Willow	*Salix*	paxkwo	paruk	Smooth, straight, flexible; available; subject to pests.
Roots				
Alder, red	*Alnus oregana*	were'regets	ekvit'ip	Stiff, brittle; red-orange.
Cottonwood	*Populus trichocarpa*			Clean, white; scarce.
Grape	*Vitis californica*		ahip'aha	Fine, strong; easily subdivided.
Pine, yellow	*Pinus ponderosa*		ishividip	Strong; available on upper Klamath.
Pine, sugar	*Pinus lambertiana*	waxpe'u; karamametsaa		Substitute, only.
Redwood	*Sequoia sempervirens*	qiL; hape'		Strong; attractive red-brown color; scarce.
Spruce	*Picea sitchensis*	teiwolite'po		Strong; available on upper Klamath
Willow	*Salix*		koovip	Everywhere available
Overlay				
Fern, giant	*Woodwardia radicans*	paap	tip tip	Long fibers; easily dyed; available.
Fern, maidenhair	*Adiantum pedatum*	rego'o	yumarekiritap; kiritapki	Lustrous black or brownish.
Grass, white	*Zerophyllum tenax*	häämo	panura	Glossy; clear cream color.
Quills, porcupine			kastib	Glossy; takes dye well.
Dyestuffs				
Alder, white	*Alnus rhombifolia*			Rich color; comparatively fast.
Grape, Oregon	*Berberis nervosa*			Less brilliant than moss dye.
Moss, wolf	*Evernia vulpina*	mece'n		Best for brilliant greenish yellow; established color.
Mullein	*Watsica glomerata*‡		yivkana	Not quite the "right" yellow.

* F. V. Colville *in* Mason, Basketry, 199–214.

† L. H. Bailey, Standard Cyclopedia of Horticulture, 1916.

‡ By analysis in Botany Department, University of California.

Spoon Baskets

Holders for the men's horn spoons and for the women's mussel shells were part of the household equipment (fig. 4*f*). They were called spoon baskets although odds and ends were customarily thrown into similarly constructed containers. Curiously, in a region where so much is orthodox, they had no standard shape, although they are all-stick, spaced-twine basketry. Among the examples seen some were high, others medium; some had grass and black fern wrapped upper edges; the sticks of others were cut off close above the last course of twining; some hung by thong straps. I was unable to find any informant to explain what inspired variations in so commonplace an article of daily use. They are not children's products, for to keep spaced twining even taxes the efforts of the average weaver. No. 12, who professed to like to do open twine best of all, turned out indifferent results.

Cradles

Baby baskets are of hazel sticks entirely (fig. 4*i*). Their edges are bound over with willow, hazel, or even the generally discarded red side of black fern. Comparatively few women make cradles now. A weaver is frequently known for her ability to make any kind of a basket with the exception of baby baskets. In former times one woman might make cradles for all the children in a community, no small task, since a fortunate baby will have three or four during his first two years. Mothers brought a measuring string to gauge the required length of the newest cradle. Lucy Thompson says for the Pecwan Yurok that the baby baskets were changed in size as the baby grew, and that the older ones were burned.[13] At Pekwututl it was customary to keep the different sizes. No. 7 had sold her babies' cradles as a group to a collector. A Karok baby is kept in his first basket for ten days, after which it is hung in a corner of the living room to be followed by each new cradle as outgrown. One such room visited has a baby basket from No. 29's infancy in each of three corners. I heard my informant, a grown woman now, order a fourth that the effect might be complete. Their use today is to hold pictures and souvenirs after the manner of our own wall decorations in the early nineteen hundreds.

[13] L. Thompson, To the American Indian, 42, 1916.

CLOSE TWINE BASKETS

Close twining from coarse to extremely fine work characterizes the remaining Yurok-Karok baskets of whatever type. The greater number are similar to bowls. In summarizing the traditional concepts of each recognized variety the classification will be as follows: baskets for preparing and serving food; storage containers; caps; fancy baskets; ceremonially used baskets.

Dippers

Dippers were roughly made of roots, never patterned (pl. 5*e*). They were used especially for serving acorn soup from the cooking basket to the individual containers. For this purpose they were strengthened by three hazel sticks held to the outside by the regular twining strands. Every weaver said the same thing of dippers: no one had ever seen a handle on an old style cup; baskets were not hung up, they were stacked. Whoever ventured to put a root loop on a dipper was simply taking over a feature from the white man's dishes. In the Karok country, they said, there was only one weaver who would think of making a dipper to hang up; No. 20 begins all such digressions from old traditions for her locality.

Cooking and Serving Baskets

Cooking baskets (pls. 11–18) ranged in size from a foot to three feet across, depending upon whether a woman was equipped to make acorn soup for a family or for twenty people at a dance. Both cooking and soup baskets from which one ate were made on hazel or willow sticks with root twining elements and white grass overlay patterns. That these are the only materials proper to use for food types is still axiomatic among Indian women. Old style food baskets had two encircling roots on the outside to strengthen their walls. This strengthening device was especially needed for the cooking basket, and the feature has been retained by the modern weaver who intends to cook with hot rocks. Even now the older women are sure acorn soup tastes different when stone-boiled. At some undetermined time the soup baskets lost their outside roots. Hot rocks might be put into them to keep the contents warm, but the combined weight was too slight to make reinforcement necessary. No. 3, from Ayotl, declared the strengthening roots were there by virtue of an Indian law. Now, with white people buying baskets, the practice of omitting the outside roots has been extended even to those baskets in use among themselves. She noted each violation of the old tradition in looking at the basket prints.

Long ago soup baskets were flatter and larger; now they are rounder and higher, according to women in the Ko'otep district (cf. pls. 6*c* and 8*a*). A Karok informant remembered that soup baskets in the early days were about seven inches across, while now with bread and other white man's foods in the diet, a five-inch basket is a good size. A boy's acorn basket (pl. 5*b*) is like a man's; any design is appropriate. A girl's (pl. 5*a*) is smaller and has an "easy" pattern like points or stripes in it. For each meal there were four different sizes of food baskets: the big basket holding sweetened flour, the "dough" as they call it; the basket in which the cooking is done; the serving or acorn soup baskets for the family, usually six to a "set"; and the dipper for serving. The woman placed before the man his basket of soup, on top of which rested a ten-inch Indian plate with his portion of fish (pl. 5*c, d*). She then served the children, after which she retired to the fire to eat her share of fish from a larger plate upon which she had prepared it, and her share of soup from the cooking basket.

Food baskets in ceremonial.—Goddard speaks of a cooking basket kept exclusively for boiling deer meat.[14] No. 7's grandmother and aunt had told her that those baskets in which deer meat was to be cooked were left undecorated. They also said the weaving was done at night only, but questioning brought out no further information on this point.

Acorn soup baskets have significance on certain occasions. An unused one together with a new plate are used by the doctor at a Brush dance. The herbs are cooked with hot rocks in the new cup. The baby is held in the rising steam. After the dance both the cup and the plate on which the herbs were laid are given to the doctor to be used in any way. When the Karok medicine man in training goes into the sweat-house for his first evening meal after two days and nights of fasting, he is served fish and acorn soup. The basket must be a new one with an old tribal design in it. It could not be sold, it was explained, without bringing down upon the community a torrential rain, even in August. On another occasion a medicine man

[14] P. E. Goddard, The Hupa, 23.

eats from a new plate and acorn cup. During the Pickiawish or new year's making of the Karok, which is held at the dark of the August moon on bars in the Inam district, the medicine man stays alone by his little fire. A queen, as English-speaking Karok call her, is chosen for the dance. She goes to a certain place for wood for the medicine man's fire and cooks for him. The soup basket from which he eats was finished on the bar the first night; he uses it for five days. After the Pickiawish, for one day only, he uses a plain acorn cup made by the double-stick method (pl. 35*a*). It has a special significance at this time. After that day he eats with the others and from any sort of container.

Water Baskets

One other basket type was mentioned by some women as belonging to the household equipment—a bucket for carrying water or for bringing home sweetened acorn meal from the river shore. Usually it was an all-root basket, undecorated. Occasionally grass and even black fern might be used in a design although water is not friendly to fern. The chief respect in which the type differed from cooking baskets was in its proportions: it was higher and smaller at the top than the ordinary cooking basket (fig. 4*g*).

Hoppers, Sifters, and Mealing Trays

Three of the most important baskets in a family's supply were the hopper, the sifter, and the large tray on which to catch the fine acorn meal. These with the stone pestle formed a set (fig. 4*k*, *m*, *r*). Indian women have enviable reputations for their ability to weave strong hoppers; those who do not attempt the work themselves boast that their mothers or aunts were able to make good ones. The hopper bottom is like the center of any basket with spaced twining. It holds the sticks equidistant. Spaced twining changes to close twining with plain root elements, and after a number of courses, overlay patterning begins. One root with grass overlay, together with one plain root, results in the simple striped decoration so often found in the less aesthetically important articles. The groups of sticks bound to the outside and the very heavy stick sprung under the braided top edge are characteristic of the hopper. Upon completion of the weaving the bottom is cut out.[15] Some Indian women were found still using

[15] The hopper picture in this series, vol. 1, plate 24, number 1 is typical.

hoppers in the old way because they like to follow the methods of an earlier time; others use hoppers only in the preparation of meal for acorn soup to be served at the Karok new year's ceremonial.

The sifter is an almost flat plaque of sticks, roots, and white grass reinforced on the under side with heavy sticks. It is said to be the only flat basket made by old-time Indians. It is stiff and will last indefinitely. Women still use their mothers' sifters. It is held lightly between the thumbs and first fingers, tilted sharply, and shaken to allow the larger particles to fall back into the hopper for more pounding with the pestle. The adhering fine meal is emptied with a smart tap on the back from the sifter onto the large tray. Deer bones were formerly the instruments used; women now use their knuckles.

The tray (pl. 52*a*, *b*), which completes the set, is of roots closely twined; its sometimes elaborate pattern is developed in white grass overlay. It is appreciably curved and flexible. The work is done as on any ordinary basket, with the outside held next to the weaver. All ends of strands and added sticks are pushed to the inside. Shaping a flexible object thirty inches in diameter presents problems. For control of shape and temporary stiffening a weaver bends hazel sticks into circles of varying sizes to fasten to the inside by root lashings. When the tray is finished it is dampened thoroughly and turned so that the smooth patterned side is uppermost, the rough plain side with its rubbed-off ends is underneath.

Storage Baskets

Numbers of Indian women recalling memories of older days describe the better-class house with its earth ledge at shoulder height. On it were set all sizes of covered baskets storing food supplies, clothing, and other belongings. Ideally, the sides of the room were lined with fine baskets, all full. The coarsest of the old-time containers were the all-stick, close-twine receptacles for fish and cracked acorns. Yurok women sometimes put in mud-dyed black sticks for longitudinal stripes, but generally they were woven plain. Inverted conical baskets of the same technique served as covers. Dried salmon might be put into an old type of container, similar in form to the high acorn cup shown in plate 35*a*. This is of double-stick work, made by the quickest possible method, in which weaving elements are carried across two instead of a single stick with each twining turn. No. 16 said an old woman would make this type and that circling lines of grass were as much patterning as would be considered worth while.

As many as six closely woven baskets were necessary to store the different seeds for a well provisioned family: the bunch grass seed ground fine to use in a kind of bread, tar weed, clover, and sunflower seeds, together with others the English equivalents of which the Indians had never known. Sizes varied. A basket might be so large that the basket maker would have to stand to work on it (pl. 39). Informants sometimes tried to express their memories of fright when as children they had leaned over too far, to find themselves heels over head in the big cipnuks.

Close-twine storage baskets were also covered with inverted conical baskets (pl. 54*b*), often marked with the same design as the container. The covers are identical with the type used for carrying in fine seeds from the patches. One informant said covers and carrying baskets were interchangeable; two other weavers disagreed with the assertion.[16] The baskets might be the same shape, size, and decoration, but each basket had its own specific use. In this connection No. 17 declared that berries were always eaten from a leaf-lined Indian plate, never from a soup dish. I had no mention of such a distinction for foods from any other informant.

One old Karok woman said poor people did not have storage baskets with covers, that such were only for elkskin dresses; another, very reliable, said only the big fish baskets had inverted cone-shaped covers, others had covers with low knobs or were left open. That this is too sweeping a statement seems to be indicated by those informants who pointed to plate 35*b* as an example of a cipnuk for valuables but protested that it was incomplete without its inverted cover. No 41, about seventy years of age, remembered her great-great-grandfather's baskets of this covered type. Some storage baskets were covered by specially made plaques tied down with buckskin thongs, like the tobacco cipnuks (pl. 48*b*); others might have small trays set over them. Shapes like that in figure 4*o* in open or close twining were old-time covers for little baskets. The four specimens in the University museum are alike in design, an alternating dark and light turn made by overlaying only one of the two twining strands. The cover was described by informants as "coming up to a point to take hold of." The point is not a knob, which they insist is a modern feature adapted

16 Dr. Kroeber considers it probable that covers were the partly worn seed baskets relegated to a use making no demand on strength.

from the earlier form to meet white demands. On the subject of round knobs there was majority agreement.

The only basket print definitely pointed out as picturing a container for clothing shows in reality a small globular form. It serves to bring out an interesting detail. Two Yurok women described it as the sort a mother might have for holding her baby's things. No. 11 had had an all-stick basket of this type, about fifteen to eighteen inches across. She was accustomed to set it in a corner of the room and against it prop the baby in its cradle.

Tobacco cipnuks.—Medium-sized baskets, very round by comparison with other types, and with smaller mouth openings, are for tobacco storage. It is not likely that women of from thirty-five to forty years of age will have made them, since their use went out with the arrival of the white man's tinned product. In earlier days an Indian burned a log to make the ground ready for a room-size planting of tobacco; he gathered and dried it, crumbled it to powder between his palms, filled baskets with it, and hung them from various parts of the house. Tobacco was never stored in big baskets, so one year's crop might be divided among four or five to ten or a dozen cipnuks. Men in the Karok country kept their tobacco in old work caps which had been creased through the center like a scoop and oversewn along the edges (fig. 4*j*). A little hole was left at one end of the semicircular pouch from which to pour the powder into their pipes. Generally old caps were used, but new pouches might be made cap shape. These, provided with loops to hang them up by, were in addition to the regular tobacco cipnuks which they also had. Kroeber gives the value of a capful of tobacco as equal to the second smallest dentalium shell, and a partly filled cap the equivalent of the shortest length shell, a high price.[17]

Typical examples of tobacco cipnuks are baskets of closely twined roots without overlay, or baskets decorated with a simple arrangement of stripes in white grass (pl. 48*b*). There is some difference of opinion as to which basket is for tobacco and which for small valuables. The decision seems to hinge upon elaborateness of pattern rather than upon shape. For instance, five museum specimens are named tobacco cipnuks by a fourth of my informants without dissent. The determining factor, apparently, is the presence or absence of a basket pattern. Although these specimens are striped, that feature in itself does not constitute a decoration according to the implication.

[17] Kroeber, Handbook, 88.

Three specimens, however, similar to that in plate 48*b*, although shaped like tobacco baskets, are cited by eleven women as examples of cipnuks for valuables because they have fancy markings (pl. 34*a*). Five other informants think they might have been for tobacco.

If a small basket was not used for storing tobacco it was a receptacle for shell money, paint, beads, woodpecker crests, carved rocks, obsidian blades, and trinkets. Not everyone had these things; only the chief man of a vicinity possessed such valuables. They were often kept in a trinket basket with a tied-on cover. The small container was placed in a large storage basket together with elkskin garments, also signs of prosperity. The use of a small basket for treasures explains why basket makers are disposed to believe the more elaborate basket is connected with the infrequent need for such an article, and that it is not merely a tobacco cipnuk. Trinket baskets (pl. 34*b*) were marked with ambitious patterns similar to those on the larger baskets. Yet, in spite of its insignificant stripes the round little object mentioned above (pl. 48*b*) was admitted to the trinket basket class by five women who may have been impressed by its perfect shape, workmanship, and general air of quality.

Gift Baskets

Basket makers among the Yurok-Karok are wont to repay gifts with an especially well made basket. There is no conventional type, size, or decoration for this. Caps are less commonly given than acorn soup baskets; in fact, I never heard of or saw a gift cap. Skilled cap makers are also women with knowledge of the worth of their products in time and effort. Occasionally the recipient is informed she is to have a gift and is asked to choose a design for it. A weaver's best work is taken for granted by both donor and recipient. Sentiment is not lacking, however; in a country where few baskets are without a price, a gift basket will not be sold. If two baskets are exchanged by friends neither woman will part with hers, considering the basket a gift. Modern gift baskets are illustrated in plates 44, 45, 46.

Caps or Hats

Caps, or hats, as the Karok speak of them, are of two kinds: work and dress (fig. 4*a*, *d;* pls. 19–33). Work caps were made round on top to fit the head closely, so that pressure of carrying basket straps would be lessened. Dress caps were and still are flat; they fit only at the edge. Men wore the plain root work cap when they packed in deer from the hunt; among the Karok it was often a tobacco storage basket, and it sometimes served as a dipper, which it resembles in shape. One weaver will say that a man's hat was always plain; another that slant or straight stripes of black fern or grass were the only decorations used. Both statements may be looked upon as equivalent, since stripes in themselves are not always considered patterning. Women's work caps, obsolete now, usually had a design in white grass and one or both ferns, all of which turn medium golden brown with age and wear. Some weavers believe black fern is too fancy for a root cap; this is a matter of individual taste worth noting in a region where little is left to the decision of a basket maker.

Widows wore root caps, undecorated. A Karok informant told of widows cutting holes in the centers of their caps through which their cropped hair stuck out. A very old Yurok informant corroborated the statement. The idea, however, was derided as a good story by women from several different localities. The hole was there but it had worn through. It was her oldest clothing that a widow affected to make her remember her husband; she did not have to cut anything. Besides, a Karok informant explained, a widow put on a worn-out hat for the first and fifth days only. It is barely possible that a cap not having an appearance of sufficient age for mourning apparel would be mutilated on occasions too rare to attract general attention.

Caps are named according to the material used in their construction: root caps, fern (alder-dyed woodwardia) caps, grass caps. The full description of a dress cap involves a number of additional points which old weavers murmur to themselves when they look at the picture of a particularly satisfying example. Besides the type name, root, fern, or grass, there is the design name for the little pattern around the bottom, as the cap is held in weaving; the name for the small pattern at the turn to the side; the name for the main design or its parts, if a composite; and still a fourth for the top pattern which in good caps bears a definite relationship to the main motive. This complete description is generally shortened to include only the ground material and the name of the largest design.

Arav is the Karok name, vutsierau Yurok, for the three-strand cords found on all caps at conventionally established points. These will be spoken of again in connection with design zones. The cord effect is stylicized not only as to placing but also as to composition. Nos. 28, 34, and 36, all expert makers, stated the possibilities thus:

for a grass and black fern dress cap the arav is of roots; for a red-dyed fern dress cap the arav is of white grass; for the common root cap an extra encircling root similar to those on old food baskets may be held by grass-overlaid twining elements to the outside. Each type of arav gives texture through slight surface irregularity, as well as color contrast.

A good cap is an achievement. As far back as any woman remembers, cap making was the technical eminence to which a weaver aspired. A cap represents even today a choice possession, and a weaver's ability to make a good one will give her a widespread reputation as an expert. All might weave baskets, only a few could make a wearable cap. These women filled orders for all the others in the vicinity. Caps have always had a sale value among Indians themselves above that of any other type of basket. Into them, as everybody knew, went the most carefully selected materials and the best workmanship. Younger women bought them from older weavers with reputations for fine work, paying the equivalent of a dollar to a dollar and a half in shell money. Today a cap with porcupine quills in its design will bring more than any combination of white grass, red or black fern. It is still customary for a cap maker to take several caps with her to community dances. She lends them to young girls to wear and often makes sales. Few caps are sold in stores; for their size they are too expensive to attract tourists' interest. No. 7, a professional, had not filled an order for a porcupine quill cap in two years.

Fancy Baskets

With the purchase of Indian things by white people there evolved in the Yurok-Karok region what is known as a "fancy" basket similar to their own cipnuks, a basket to put things in (pls. 34–49). Sometimes it is called a work or a sewing basket, but the adjective fancy has the same meaning to every weaver: it classifies shapes for which an Indian woman would have no specific use. She believes that baskets made to sell to white women are largely decorative, that they are on shelves, tables, and against walls.

The fancy basket is a composite affair. Without going into eccentric shapes the commoner forms may be grouped according to the Indians' own concepts of their antecedents. First, the fancy basket is the same to them as the old-time trinket cipnuk, but smaller and more elaborately patterned (pl 45*b*). Designs and color arrangements formerly typical of dress caps are often specified in orders from white buyers. Whereas the older storage basket was plain or with characteristic space divisions, its new relatives display curious vagaries. Informants agree, however, that though a mixture of designs to be woven in the same fancy basket may be ordered, white buyers are dissatisfied with any pattern they suspect of being un-Indian. Second, the fancy basket may be a container patterned after our waste basket shapes (pl. 53*b*), one in which bands of spaced twining alternate with bands of close twining. The only old style type in which this combination occurs is the carrying basket for fish (pl. 53*a*) as described under the section on all-stick types. Older women protest against such combinations of techniques put together without reason, but admit they sell well.

Practically every weaver makes some sort of fancy basket. It is an easy type by contrast with caps as far as shaping is concerned. In a cap new sticks must be added continually to within an inch and a half of the final course; in a fancy basket the adding of sticks is over when the turn is made to the side wall or very shortly after this.

There is one type of basket to which both the Yurok and the Karok give a name implying a narrowing or shaping near the bottom (pl. 54*a*). Most of us would interpret these footed bowls as the efforts of a virtuoso to copy the lamps and fruit dishes of the nineties. In attempting to discover any historical facts about the form some contradictory statements were met. Naturally, the opinion of a conservative who remembered similar baskets as very old is worth something; but there were many women who declared that all old baskets had flat bottoms, that footed bases came in with the whites. Twenty-three informants had definite ideas on the subject, seventeen of them in the older group. Eleven of these and five younger ones were certain that the style was a copy made in response to white influence. They cited members of the preceding generation who were paid five dollars for such baskets. Six older informants and one younger one were just as certain that the footed bowl is an old type, not a modern fancy basket. No. 39 is the most representative weaver in this latter group. According to her the footed bowl is a very old style of basket which might once have been made in different sizes for spoons or other household trifles. It was also made in openwork technique.

Whatever may be the truth concerning its background, the footed basket had a logical successor in a covered chalice shape (pl. 51*j*) which one maker of the type called a fruit dish. Eccentricity was a phase of the recent fantastic era through which the older weavers have passed. The era had its place in the thorough commercialization of the craft, now practically its only aspect. Under new influences such objects as cups and saucers, handled vase shapes, covered bottles, full-size suitcases, and fishermen's catch baskets came in only to go out like other fashions. The new features in basketry which survived the ebb of interest in fads are looked upon today as the white man's tastes. As such they are catered to by weavers, and often admired, it must be confessed. The subject will be more fully dealt with later in this study.

Brush Dance Baskets

Long ago the close-twine packing basket was for seed gathering. The steps from that utilitarian purpose to an esoteric ceremonial use are unknown. Today the old seed basket, identical in appearance with the storage basket cover (pl. 54*b*), is used only for making Brush dance medicine. In no other kind of basket can the herbs be gathered. People might own the baskets to decorate their houses or to lend to friends. A very fine specimen of the type was made by the great-aunt of a Karok informant, No. 25. She used to lend it to a Weitspus medicine woman, but she would not even consider the hypothetical question of its money value; such a basket was not sold, although she would make a duplicate on order. No. 25 said any kind of a design might be used on the upper half of the basket but that there are always stripes on the lower portion. Other Karok agreed with that. No one seems to have made the type in many years.

Jumping Dance Baskets

The Jumping dance basket is totally unlike any other product in Yurok-Karok weaving (pls. 55, 56). Kroeber gives this description of it: "In one hand is a cylindrical basket, slit along one side. This has no utilitarian prototype, nor do the Yurok put anything but grass stuffing into it or attach any symbolic association to it. This basket, ego'or, suggests in its shape an enlarged money box; but the Yurok do not see the resemblance."[18]

The making of a Jumping dance basket is unquestionably the work of the expert weaver; everyone agrees it is hard and that present sales are too uncertain to encourage effort to attain skill. So few dance baskets are made anywhere on the Klamath river that only one Karok

[18] Kroeber, Handbook, 56.

weaver able to accomplish the whole thing alone, and two informants who have husbands skilled in finishing the baskets, are known from Rekwoi to the Asisufunuk district. The finishing is normally considered a man's job. There are two methods of making. To weave first a cylinder and then slit it straight between two sticks is quicker, easier, and more certain to produce a successful basket. The Yurok weaver for the Pecwan dances, No. 4, makes hers this way. Because this is a new-style way it is not approved by older women. The second method is used by No. 18 in the Panamenik district, a Yurok among Karok, and by one of the daughters of No. 41 at Inam. No. 18 and her husband, who finishes her dance baskets, traced the steps involved in the making.

The width to make the right size cylinder is decided upon and hazel sticks put down on a board or the ground as closely together as is possible. To place the first row of twining across the middle of these is difficult, for each stick must be lifted separately and then be put back into its place, parallel with the others. The work progresses from the center each way to the ends. At the proper intervals new sticks are added to give the characteristic flare. A weaver cannot get a good shape by working from end to end; spiraling is always a danger. No. 18 works from left to right on one course, from right to left on the next. Women say this is one of the hardest things to do in twining; reversing the direction in weaving is only required in cradles, dance baskets, and some modern wall pockets. If weavers were to work alternate courses from the under side of the piece, the greater ease would be discounted by the difficulty of keeping the overlay in position behind the root twining element. Some women go so far as to break the roots and overlay at the end of each course so that they may always progress in the same direction.

The rectangular piece with fan-shaped ends complete, the man's work begins. No. 18's husband went on to detail each step in the finishing process. He turns the side edges over hazel sticks as long as from shoulder to wrist, allowing them to extend equally beyond the corners. Sewing is done with deer sinew; the ends of the sticks are wound with buckskin. He bends a stick the length of the basketry ends to make of it a circle, covers it with skin which turns over the sides of the basket, and fastens the edges down with stitches. The other end is a duplicate in appearance. Feathers are hung from the sticks at one end only. All this must be done in a workmanlike manner, but there would seem to be little about the processes to explain why a woman will keep a dance basket unfinished for years because she dares not attempt the skin work herself. Mr. Jim usually made a circular dot in the center of each end. Around the edges he drew a border of isosceles triangles. The dot is in black "paint," charcoal ground fine to mix with sturgeon glue; the triangles are alder-dye red. Both colors are fast.

A most interesting set of reactions was gained from those women who knew both basketry and ceremonial. Although no one had ever made a Jumping dance basket at Weitspus or in the district, comments were not lacking to show familiarity with traditional standards. There was formerly an old Karok dance place, Amaikiara, across from No. 22's home; and No. 41's daughter, at Inam, makes baskets for the Hupa dances, which are still held; consequently the up-river informants were more dogmatic in their criticisms of proportions, suitable designs, and niceties of workmanship. As to styles, the one shown in plate 56*b* is too long; those in plate 55*b*, *e* are too short according to No. 4, the down-river maker for the Pecwan dances. Disagreeing with the Yurok informant, Karok women said the basket in plate 55*b* is the characteristic size used in the last dance made at Amaikiara about thirty-five years ago. Proportions, too, were matters for argument. The basket in plate 55*c* is the only one with a good shape, said the down-river makers of the baskets; that in plate 56*b* is the best, according to No. 12, at Ertlerger, who felt content with every detail; No. 22 said the one in plate 55*e* is nearest right. The first picture of a dance basket that No. 22, Karok, saw was the one shown in plate 56*c*. Its straight upper edge marked it as having been recently made; long ago, there had been an appreciable curve. She picked up a pair of scissors to cut out a correct shape for me, regretting that there was not a really traditional example among the eleven prints shown her. Other women to whom this statement was quoted said No. 22 knew the most about the old-time standards and that she had been an influential figure at the Amaikiara ceremonies.

It is not necessary to have new baskets for Jumping dances. If a man makes a dance, his friends lend him their baskets. He will expect all his friends to bring their ceremonial objects to add to his own display.

CARE OF BASKETS

Cooking and soup baskets are washed with cold water and a brush made from the discarded hazel or willow stick tips. Whatever particles of acorn meal remain in the crevices, dry there. Some meal, never all by the very nature of the basket structure, may be dislodged as from a sifter by tapping against the bottom of the container. The odor of rancid oil always hangs about the food baskets of a poor housekeeper. After a quantity of soup has been prepared for dance guests, each cooking basket and its complement of six individual cups are stored, bottom up, on shelves. From then until the next event no particular attention is required beyond an occasional dusting.

A cooking basket full of meal and the necessary hot stones is an unwieldy object. It cannot be moved without danger to its structure. When a cooking basket wears through, the break usually comes at the turn or at spots where hot stones have partly burned through the walls. Among the Indian women of both tribes only the old people are credited with wanting to save baskets by mending them. If sticks are broken there are varying opinions as to what can be done: repair may be attempted by drawing together the edges with root strands or new sticks may be pushed up and down through the twining turns for a short distance. The protruding ends of the new sticks are held flat against the inside of the basket with root stitches. This latter device, according to a Karok weaver, is a favored method. The test of the efficacy of any repairing is its restoration of the food basket to a waterproof condition. It can be done, say some; it is the height of foolishness to try, say other weavers. These latter grant that the old people mended baskets—the prints show that clearly enough—but a hole in a basket is the beginning of a general disintegration; it would be better to throw the basket away and make a new one. This last is unquestionably the attitude of the younger weavers. By count, six women had patched food baskets for use; ten thought it a waste of time because it could not be well done.

A work cap gives first near the start, leaving a hole on top; the rounds at the edge pull off where it is handled. Whatever mending is done is attempted with no idea of reconstructing texture; the hole might be left, the weakened edge whipped over with roots or Indian string, in widely-spaced, deep stitches. Dress caps are too seldom worn to need mending. They are sometimes washed to restore gloss to grass and fern. Nowadays, they are wrapped in the finest cloth the owner possesses and hung up in a flour sack for safe keeping. Twice upon my request that weavers show me their nicest caps, the women undid several layers of paper and cloth before their treasures were displayed. If they had been old laces or porcelains, the care could not have been more affectionate.

Yurok women sometimes regretted that so many old baskets had been sold. If the Indians had had money, one thought, they would have kept their possessions. This informant has preserved intact all the old baskets of a deceased relative (pl. 4*b*). When a basket attains an age of about fifty years, No. 29 could not be certain of the actual number, it may be buried with a corpse. Old baskets are never burned, she said. The right thing to do with them is to bury them, or to put them in clefts of trees. She knew of clefts so filled, but she could not be induced to look at one intently nor to touch the baskets; it would bring bad luck to her relatives, even if she herself were to escape consequences.

PROPORTION AND CONTOUR

COOKING BASKET PROPORTIONS

It has been stated that very early in the experience of a young weaver she learns to know the shape of the various sizes of soup baskets: for a girl, boy, or man. Her judgment is trained by comparing her basket with the old one serving as her model, or she will be taught to set her work down to see better the relation between height and width. Yurok-Karok weavers do not measure food baskets; it is assumed they know standard proportions. The same holds true for other household containers: the baskets for storing the sweetened meal, the cooking baskets, the deeper water buckets. Each has three essentials: that it be strongly made; that it sit flatly without support; that it conform to a certain "look" tribally recognized as correct for the particular type. For example, the basket in figure 5*a* has nicely curved sides, not too round; that in figure 5*c* has a better bottom than the one in figure 5*b*. Specimens chosen by informants to illustrate standard shapes or deviations from them are listed in table 4, together with the weavers' own estimations of them. Museum measurements and percentages afford comparisons.

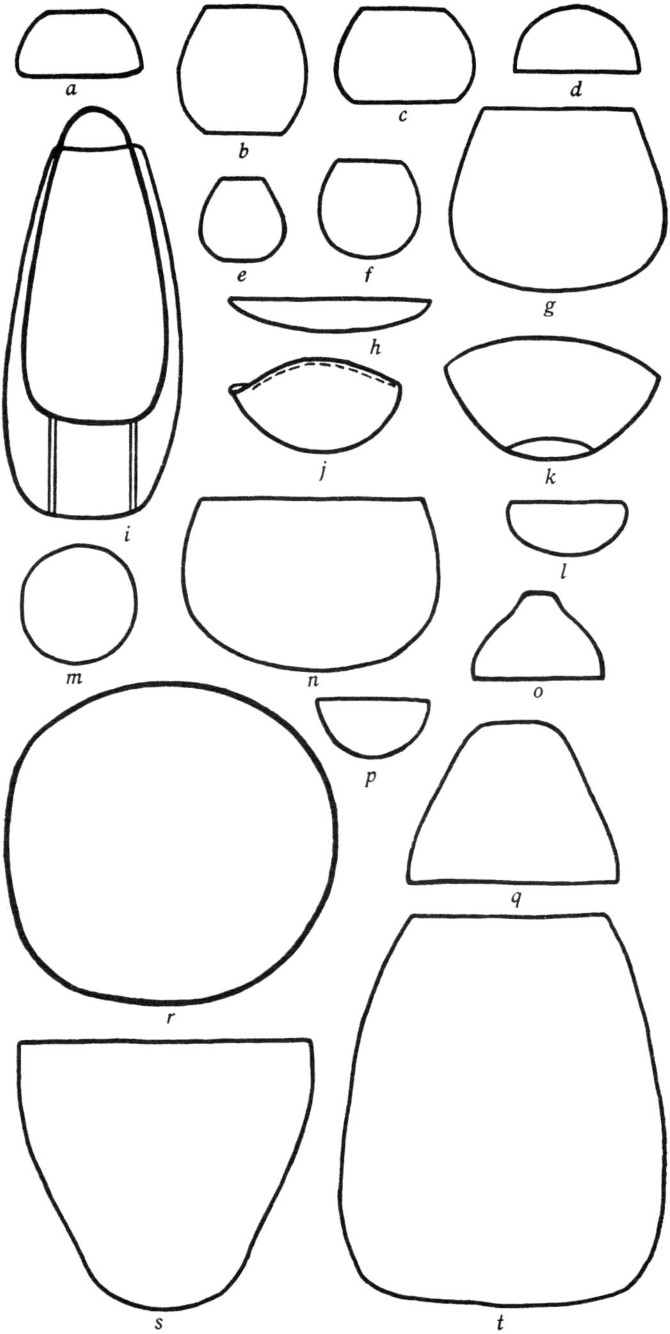

Fig. 4. Traditional shapes and proportions of Yurok-Karok baskets. *a*, dress cap; *b*, fancy basket; *c*, fancy basket; *d*, work cap; *e*, tobacco basket; *f*, spoon basket; *g*, water basket; *h*, Indian plate; *i*, cradle; *j*, cap used by Karok men for tobacco container; *k*, hopper; *l*, soup basket; *m*, sifter; *n*, cooking basket; *o*, cover; *p*, dipper; *q*, cover for large basket or old fashioned seed basket (now used for gathering materials used in Brush dance); *r*, mealing tray; *s*, wood packing basket; *t*, storage basket.

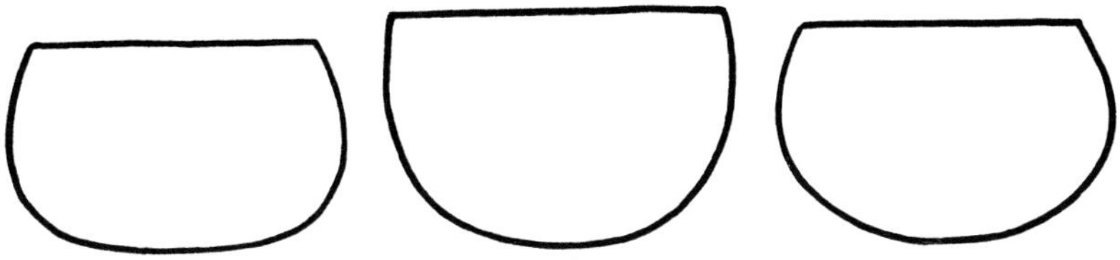

a b c

Fig. 5. Food basket proportions. *a*, nicely rounded sides; *b*, poor bottom for a cooking basket; *c*, good bottom for a cooking basket.

TABLE 4

COOKING BASKET PROPORTIONS

Specimen number	Illustration	Measurements* in inches Height	Mouth	Ratio per cent H : M	Informants' estimates
1-9383	Figure 4*n*	10.75	13.5	79	Good shape, No. 6
1-1764	Plate 16*b*	7.75	10.5	74	Good shape, Nos. 6, 8, 13, 14, 15, 28
1-1579	Plate 14*a*	6.5	8.75	74	Good shape, Nos. 3, 6
CA-411	Figure 5*b*			74	Good shape, Nos. 3, 6, 8, 17 Too small at bottom, No. 15
1-1201	Plate 12*b*	7.	9.5	73	Good shape, No. 6
1-1787		6.75	9.25	73	Just right shape, Nos. 5, 28
1-392		9.25	12.5	70	Good shape, No. 6
G-426	Plate 11*a*			69	Good shape, No. 6
1-1763		7.25	10.5	69	Good shape, Nos. 3, 11, 17, 19
1-1578	Plate 11*c*	5.5	8.	69	Good shape, No. 5
G-438	Plate 18*b*			69	Good shape, Nos. 3, 6, 10, 28 Genuine old shape, No. 41 Just right shape, No. 5
1-936		6.	8.75	69	Good shape, No. 5 Too high, No. 11
1-1761	Figure 5*a*	7.	11	64	Good shape, Nos. 1, 3, 12, 17, 28 Too low, No. 6
1-1202	Plate 12*a*	5.	8.	63	Good shape, No. 5
1-1762	Plate 17*b*	7.5	10.75	61	Good shape, Nos. 12, 14, 17
G-455	Plate 13*a*			59	Good shape, No. 3
1-1880	Plate 13*b*	6.	10.5	57	Too shallow, No. 5

* Where measurements in inches are lacking, the ratio of height to mouth was computed from the photographs.

The range in per cent ratios of height to mouth diameter for those baskets called good is from 59 to 79 per cent; the average or preponderance occurs at 69 per cent. Informants Nos. 3, 5, 6 (Yurok), and No. 28 (Karok) were requested to comment specifically upon proportions of cooking baskets. Table 5 shows the consistency of the reactions. One basket only failed to draw at least one favorable comment from the above four expert weavers. No. 6 approved of baskets representing five ratios; Nos. 3 and 28 included those representing four ratios; No. 5 confined her comments to five baskets, three in the preponderant group. She is the expert cap maker in the Ko'otep district; and cap makers are experienced judges of proportions.

TABLE 5

EXPERTS' ESTIMATES OF GOOD PROPORTIONS

Cases	1	1	2	3	1	2	1	1	2	3	4	5	1	1	1	1	1
Ratio, Height: Mouth	79	74	74	74	73	73	70	69	69	69	69	69	64	63	61	59	57
Experts No. 3			x	x					x		x		x			x	
No. 5						x				x	x	x		x			low
No. 6	x	x	x	x	x		x	x			x		low				
No. 28		x				x					x		x				

SOUP BASKET PROPORTIONS

The range in per cent ratios of height to mouth diameter for soup baskets called good is from 54 to 63 per cent. The average or preponderance is 58 per cent. Eight soup baskets were approved as well proportioned, each of them by at least one informant. Of these, one (pl. 9*a*) was favorably commented upon by four women. Three baskets are not good in the estimation of at least one weaver. The last two baskets (pls. 6*c*, 8*a*) recorded in table 6 were subjects for argument. If they are very old, then they represent the conventional large shallow basket of the days before white men's coming made possible varied foods to supplement the staple acorn soup. As such the two baskets were judged good examples. If, on the contrary, they are of more modern times, their weavers did not carry up the sides far enough. Under the circumstances, they cannot be legitimately placed with either group on the mere basis of proportionate height to width.

Generalizing the reactions of informants to the soup basket type yields one definite result: for so commonplace an article of daily use conventional shape is taken as a matter of course. Whatever attention and interest is aroused by the picture of a soup basket is primarily the result of its design. Technically the form represents no achievement; its possibilities are strictly limited by its size, and everyone has woven several, if not many of them. About half the cooking baskets in the print collection were noticed from the standpoint of their proportions by comparison with a seventh of the soup baskets. Looking at it from another angle, there were forty-five separate comments on cooking basket proportions to balance against twenty-eight for the half again larger number of soup baskets. On the one hand, a weaver has accomplished a rather showy result; on the other, she has provided a necessity.

TABLE 6

SOUP BASKET PROPORTIONS

Specimen number	Illustration	Measurements* in inches: Height	Mouth	Ratio per cent H : M	Informants' estimates
1-1508		3.75	6.	63	Good shape, No. 6
1-1206	Plate 7*a*	4.5	7.25	62	Good shape, No. 28
					Just right, No. 13
					Shallow, No. 12
1-1863	Plate 10*b*	3.75	6.25	60	Good shape, No. 6
1-2232		3.75	6.5	58	Good shape, No. 28
					Not good, No. 17
CA-453				57	Good shape, No. 13
					Not good, No. 6
G-458	Plate 10*c*			57	Good shape, Nos. 13, 39
					Not good, No. 6
1-1517	Plate 9*a*	3.5	6.25	56	Good shape, Nos. 3, 6, 13, 17
G-454	Plate 7*b*			54	Good shape, Nos. 3, 13, 17
CA-15				48	Not good, No. 11
G-448	Plate 10*a*			48	Not good, No. 6
CA-423				46	Not good, No. 3
1-1493	Plate 8*a*	3.25	7.25	45†	Good shape, Nos. 5, 41
					Poor shape, Nos. 6, 11, 12
1-1472	Plate 6*c*	3.75	8.5	44†	Good shape, No. 3

* Where measurements in inches are lacking, the ratio of height to mouth was computed from the photographs.

† Asserted to be the shallower bowls of earlier days.

Informants' attitudes were unmistakable. Only half of the baskets of approved form received more than a single favorable comment. No. 13, upon urging, chose from among sixty-three prints the five baskets that she considered the best. Their percentage ratios of height to mouth are in sequence: 54, 56, 57, 62. No. 28, who has not made bowl forms in many years, forced interest to the selection of one soup basket; No. 6, painstakingly set apart five as good or poor. The shape of a soup basket, to the majority, was too obvious for comment.

FANCY BASKET PROPORTIONS

Fancy baskets also, with their range from traditional to modern shapes and sizes, drew much more comment upon workmanship and admiration for design-to-space adaptation than upon dimensional relations. Those noticed particularly for their shapeliness form a group of eleven out of the sixty-two examples within the print collection. Proportions, in themselves, interested at most three weavers for any single basket. Following the same plan of outline used to classify food baskets shows results as given in table 7.

TABLE 7

FANCY BASKET PROPORTIONS

		Measurements in inches			Ratio per cent			
Specimen number	Illustration	Height	Greatest width	Mouth diameter	Height to greatest width	Height to mouth	Mouth to greatest width	Informants' estimates
1-1661	Plate 34*a*	5.	5.5	2.25	91	222	41	Good shape, No. 13
1-1571	Plate 35*b*	7.	8.	5.	87	140	62	Good, No. 13 Too long, No. 3
1-1507	Plate 35*a*	5.25	6.88	5.5	76	96	80	Good, No. 6
1-11834		3.75	5.	3.75	75	100	75	Good, No. 28
1-26815	Plate 44*b*	5.	6.75	5.	74	100	74	Good, No. 28
1-1888	Plate 48*b*	4.5	6.38	3.	71	150	47	Good, Nos. 10, 11, 13
1-1801	Plate 43*a*	4.5	7.	5.25	64	86	75	Good, No. 11
1-26814	Plate 43*b*	4.75	7.75	5.25	61	90	68	Good, Nos. 11, 28
1-1807	Plate 41*b*	5.75	9.5	7.	60	82	74	Good, No. 3
1-1595	Plate 41*a*	3.75	6.25	5.5	60	68	85	Good, No. 18
CA-444	Plate 40*b*				35	42	88	Good, No. 6
Basket of informant								
No. 34	Plate 45*b*	5.	7.25	6.	69	83	83	
No. 36	Plate 44*a*	4.	6.	4.5	66	88	75	
No. 43		3.	4.75	3.5	63	86	74	
No. 34	Plate 45*a*	4.5	7.25	6.	62	79	75	
No. 14	Plate 46*c*	3.5	5.75	5.	61	70	87	
No. 14	Plate 46*b*	2.5	4.5	4.	55	62	88	

In view of the smallness of the group and the few reactions to proportions specifically, it may be interesting to contrast the findings for the eleven museum specimens with those for a modern group of six fancy baskets made by my informants. It would be natural to suppose that favorable comments upon older baskets are in some degree actuated by sentiment or by similarity to shapes now in vogue; correlatively, today's shapes might be expected to have changed but little from the older ones.

The data, arranged according to the median for the proportion of height to greatest width for both groups, show the ranges of percentage ratios to compare as follows:

Per cent ratio of:	Museum specimens, 11	Informants' specimens, 6
Height to greatest width	35–91	55–69
Height to mouth diameter	42–222	62–88
Mouth diameter to greatest width	41–88	74–88

The range of height to greatest width expressed in per cent covers fifty-six points in the case of the museum specimens as against fourteen points in the case of the informants' specimens. Analysis of the stylistic features shows that today's weavers favor a lower basket than did the weavers of former times. Among the baskets of the old group four approximate the five-tenths to seven-tenths relation between height and width; the remainder, except one (pl. 40*b*), are more nearly of equal dimensions.

The mouth diameter has undergone radical change. The old cipnuk for trinkets was high with a comparatively small opening (pls. 34*a*, *b*, 35*b*, and 48*b*). Range of height to mouth ratios is great for the museum group because it contains baskets acquired during different style periods. Those specimens most nearly approximating the fancy sale baskets of today will be found to have heights from 62 per cent to 88 per cent of their mouth diameters. The ratios at the median differ for the two groups. The basket shown in plate 35*a*, representative of the median for the museum group, has a height almost equal to its mouth diameter. The nearest equivalent within the informants' group of baskets is No. 36's (pl. 44*a*) with a ratio of 88 per cent, the highest ratio within the newer group.

The ratio of mouth to greatest width has changed little for either the old or the newer baskets. The median is 74 per cent for the museum specimens, between 75 per cent and 83 per cent for the informants' baskets. Within the 41 per cent to 85 per cent range of the former are two of the old type trinket cipnuks referred to in the preceding paragraph. Comments in their cases were based on sentiment and appreciation; the style is no longer made.

To sum up: approved proportions for fancy baskets, judging by two small groups, are within the following percentages:

	Per cent
Heights to greatest widths	66 to 75
Heights to mouth diameters	75 to 90
Mouth diameters to greatest widths	75

CAP PROPORTIONS

To make a cap with any degree of success one must have skill, experience, and an eye trained for established proportions. Definite measurements for certain sections of the basket are additional requirements. The so-called exact measurements would not in themselves guarantee correct results from the Indian woman's point of view. Measurements are made with the hand, and a cap weaver must know wherein her hand agrees with, or differs from, that of other cap makers' hands. A majority of my informants told me they did not need to make allowance for the sizes of their hands in measuring; the others said they must add from two rows of weaving to a half inch beyond

noted that a fancy basket had been included among a group of caps; the other informants apparently did not suspect the basket was intended for a cap. Contrasting the contour with that of the majority of caps explains why the example would not excite comment even as a poor cap; it is a typical soup-basket shape.

TABLE 8

CAP PROPORTIONS

Specimen number	Illustration	Measurements in inches: Height	Measurements in inches: Circumference	Ratio per cent height to circumference	Informants' estimates
1-26812	Plate 30*a*	3.75	20.38	18	Good, No. 28
1-371	Plate 26*b*	4.25	23.5	18	Too tall, No. 39
1-27054	Plate 30*b*	3.75	22.	17	Good, No. 28
1-1498		4.	23.	17	Poor, No. 17
1-1593	Plate 21*b*	3.75	22.13	17	Good, Nos. 21, 26, 36 Too high, No. 8
1-1496		4.	23.75	17	Good, Nos. 3, 4, 22, 23, 28, 32, 39
1-11646		3.75	23.	16	Poor, No. 17
1-27055	Plate 31*b*	3.5	21.5	16	Good, No 28
1-20834	Plate 26*a*	3.5	22.	16	Good, Nos. 2, 3, 5, 6, 21, 28, 32, 36, 39
1-27174		3.25	22.38	15	Good, Nos. 28, 32 Not good, No. 3
1-27175	Plate 23*b*	3.5	22.75	15	
1-1692	Plate 24*b*	3.25	22.63	14	Good, Nos. 3, 4, 39
1-4384	Plate 19*a*	3.	21.25	14	
1-1439	Plate 25*a*	3.13	22.25	14	Good, No. 8
1-374		3.25	23.	14	
1-1610	Plate 25*b*	3.25	22.88	14	Good, Nos. 8, 17
1-1804		3.25	23.13	14	Poor, Nos. 8, 39
1-1831		3.25	22.5	14	Good, Nos. 8, 17, 39
1-1609	Plate 24*a*	2.75	20.	14	Good, Nos. 4, 22, 23, 27, 32, 39
1-20824	Plate 19*b*	3.	22.25	13	Good, Nos. 2, 5, 6, 12, 31, 32, 36, 39
1-20822		2.75	22.88	12	Poor, Nos. 20, 36
1-27877		2.5	23.5	11	Poor, Nos. 3, 4, 5, 6, 11, 13, 22, 23, 27, 28, 32, 33

Table 8 indicates the relation between height and circumference of caps. The table cannot avoid being misleading. Caps with the identical proportions and measurements might vary enough in contour to class one as the better. Take, for example, the difference in opinions expressed about the two whose per cent ratio is 18. Both Nos. 28 and 39, Karok, know basketry products from long experience. Again, note the variation between the cap pictured in plate 26*a* and specimen

11646 (not illustrated). The first is commented upon as a good example by nine weavers; the other, of the same proportions, is called poor by an expert. The range of accepted relation between height and circumference is close. With the caps of 18 per cent ratio in doubt, and those of 11 to 12 per cent ratios indubitably too low, the proportions of eighteen caps are condensed within a range of five points.

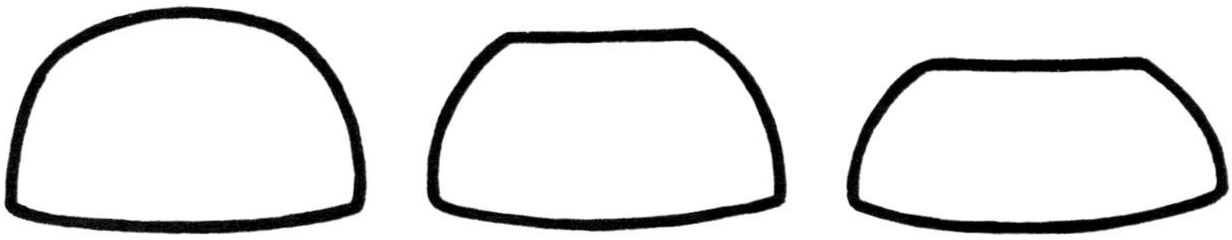

a *b* *c*

Fig. 7. Cap proportions. *a*, too high; *b*, right size; *c*, too low.

COLOR COMBINATIONS AND INTOLERANCES

COMBINATIONS FOR FOOD BASKETS

Color combinations are stylicized for Yurok-Karok baskets. The three baskets shown in plates 7*c*, 8*c*, 9*c*, and others similar to them, came in for a good deal of criticism. The point at issue is the use of black or dyed fern in food baskets. By analysis at the museum fifteen soup or cooking baskets were found in which ferns are either an integral part of the design or used in a manner to suggest an individual property mark. Reference will again be made to this feature of its use. In these baskets black fern, as well as the customarily discarded red half of its stem, and dyed giant fern bar off design zones with horizontal lines or underline portions of motives. There are no solidly woven units, but ferns are unmistakably present. The mystifying element is the almost unanimous disapproval of their use. To my informants baskets like those illustrated represent a radical breaking down of tradition. Food basket shapes with black fern in their makeup were characterized as fancy baskets. With the single exception of a Karok weaver, informants declared that no Indian would eat out of any fern-decorated container, that the baskets within the print collection in which fern appears must have been made to sell. Possibly, it was argued, what showed as black in the picture was the brown outer surface of redwood root. That is used as it comes to hand with no thought of the color contrast presented. The matter of correctness cannot be dismissed simply by feeling that fern stains whatever soup is left standing in the basket, because redwood, also, does that. One informant thought black fern was too hard to put in, but that is an improbable reason since the woodwardia has very long strands and it is equally taboo. The old people, as the former generations are called, would have gone a long time without acorn soup before they would have eaten from such cups; a medicine man would never compromise; they themselves cannot use them. Cups woven with fern are not right, they are against old Indian law, and the usual bad luck is implicated in their use. In former days even the prettiest cooking and eating baskets were not fancy, but nowadays they are more easily sold with the gloss and color of fern to contrast with the dull roots.

The single exception to this concensus of opinion is that of a Karok informant. She remembers an old woman in the vicinity who made food baskets with black fern in the patterning. This old weaver was a good basket maker, as several could tell me, but no one else connected her with any violation of a tradition. That it is a widespread tradition is indicated by the different localities in which it is alive as a memory from a former generation. No. 42 was taught by her mother, a down-river woman, to run in a short series of black fern stitches marking the place to begin each new course. This is a mechanical device, she explained; it does not fall under the description of a basket design; consequently it does not violate the tradition.

All this might be convincing had I not discovered that among the fifteen baskets in the Museum which have fern in their makeup, nine likewise show unmistakable signs of having been used for cooking or serving food. Some specimens were used as far back as twenty-five to thirty years ago. The tradition can neither have grown up since then nor is it reasonable to suppose that all of the seventeen informants who objected to the presence of fern decorations in food baskets should have forgotten in so short a time. I do not know of any statement that gives a hint for the solution of the puzzle.

COMBINATIONS FOR CAPS

Just as white grass is the only traditional contrast for brownish roots in food baskets, so in caps color choice is strictly limited; they may be black and white or red and white. To the black-white combination yellow-dyed quills or their substitute, dyed grass, may be added; to the red-white combination black fern is the one additional possibility. Questions of native tastes are implicated in any other permutation of the four colors. For example, a little black fern gives richness to a red-white cap, but red-dyed fern is never to be put into a black-white cap. The latter is characterized as a "nice" or "dressy" cap. Women of both tribes consider red the more commonplace color, the Karok evaluation largely based on the availability of woodwardia compared with fine white grass and black fern; these must come from a distance. The consequent higher rating accorded to imported materials by the Karok is partly due also to the commercial aspect. They would have difficulty in competing with Yurok basket makers were they to confine themselves to the plentiful giant fern.

As for yellow-dyed quills in a red-white cap, weavers are almost unanimous in saying that the colors do not go well together. Two Yurok women had never seen the combination; a Karok weaver generalized for her tribe by declaring yellow and red were never put in the same basket. Only one informant in the whole number had chosen to work quills and alder-dyed fern into a design. She described to me a flint mark of which the larger area was red, the edging yellow. She said it was pretty. One other woman had seen the two colors in combination; the rest were emphatic that they were never put together. Most of my informants received the question of combining red and yellow in a manner to indicate that it was an unnecessary one.

To basket makers yellow quills are not only evidence of an elegant cap, but the color itself is striking. A down-river cap maker frequently visualized the pictures of baskets as they might be developed in certain colors. In all her descriptions yellow was used in smallest amount. She explained that the larger areas in a motive should be of black fern because the strong color area of quills needs the balance of dark. What she actually said was that no one would ever make a big mark of yellow quills and a little mark of black fern. Either form of expression has the familiar sound of a fundamental principle in color harmony. One other convention is observed by weavers: yellow, wherever it appears, is surrounded by black. A much-discussed cap (pl. 19*a*) which lacks a transition band of white grass on either side of the main decorative zone, was excused for the omission on this basis: if quills were used in the motive then they would need black borders to give contrast; against white they would not show up well and the whole reason for quills in a basket would be lost. The possibility of yellow figures on a white ground with no black elsewhere in the basket was inconceivable to every informant to whom it was offered as an experimental suggestion.

DESIGN

CORRELATIONS BETWEEN BASKET TYPES AND PATTERNS

In theory, any design is suitable for any basket. In practice, the weaver who followed that generalization blindly would find herself running counter to traditional usages. For a big basket one chooses big marks like that in plate 18*b*; for a small basket there are small marks. A plain work cap should have a plain design like a flint mark with no secondary inner motives; elementary patterns of dots and stripes are sufficiently decorative for a tobacco storage basket—these and other conventions indicate a fully developed group of restrictions.

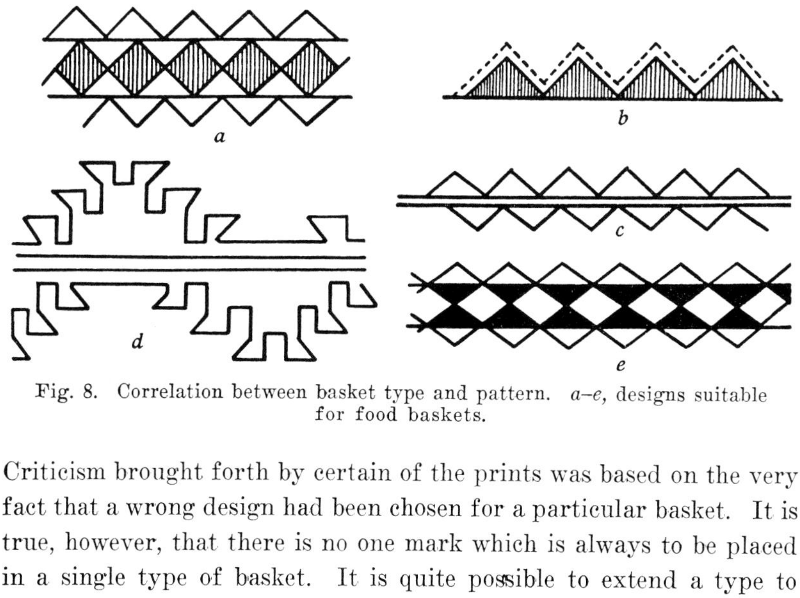

Fig. 8. Correlation between basket type and pattern. *a–e,* designs suitable for food baskets.

Criticism brought forth by certain of the prints was based on the very fact that a wrong design had been chosen for a particular basket. It is true, however, that there is no one mark which is always to be placed in a single type of basket. It is quite possible to extend a type to include several baskets of similar features. Thus, mealing trays, sifters, and the modern table mats use the same designs interchangeably. Modified to suitable proportions these designs are also to be found in the cooking and eating baskets (fig. 8). For caps and fancy baskets the designs must not only be made smaller or modified, but some are eliminated entirely. Informants' reactions on these points are positive.

A good deal of discussion pro and con was provoked by one design (pl. 38*b*). To some informants it was a traditional mark, to others, a new mark. Its place in this connection has to do with expressed opinions as to whether it is or is not a true basket design. Seven women from as many localities along the Klamath declared the motive to be similar to the painted marks on the netted headdresses worn by men in the Jumping dance.[19] Whether the mark is a copy or an old design poorly rendered, as some believe, the most significant feature of the discussion may be stated in a sentence: if it is a dance regalia mark, it is not suitable for a basketry design. Karok weavers say they do not take over the characteristic design forms of one craft to use in another. A woman would not live long who wove a dance painting in a basket. One with a conscience would not weave such a mark in a soup basket for any money, thought No. 38. Through her action bad luck might be passed on to someone who ate from the basket. In the Asisufunuk district on the edge of upper Karok territory, No. 42 knew it was bad luck to mix dance marks with basketry designs although she had never seen any particular design which impressed her as having been taken over from dance forms.

There may have been no connection in the weaver's mind between the painted dance mark and the design under discussion. Basketry design names are applied to decorative figures carved and painted on paddles, purses, skins, and other objects by Yurok men. The figures are without significance; the names solely descriptive.[20] Apparently the prohibition against similarity of designs, if there really is such a prohibition, is directed only toward the women's craft. The Karok position, too, is hard to reconcile with the statement of one of them, No. 26, that the first basket marks were copies of the men's decorations for their arrows.

Food Basket Designs

Plain designs are particularly approved for use in food baskets. Patterns which require frequent breaking of the overlay are less apt to be watertight. A fancy mark therefore is neither correct choice nor good taste for baskets which must hold water. On that score two designs were criticized (fig. 9). That they are more elaborate than some which were admired because they harmonized perfectly with the soup basket type is a matter which cannot be argued very satisfactorily. Just why the design in plate 11*a* should seem easy and therefore suitable by comparison with those in figure 9 was not made clear

---

19 Compare the illustration in this series, vol. 1, pl. 7, fig. 2.

20 Kroeber, Basket Designs, 130.

by any informant, nor did it seem clear to any informant. The motives in figure 8 were accepted as simple, unpretentious designs for baskets in common use.

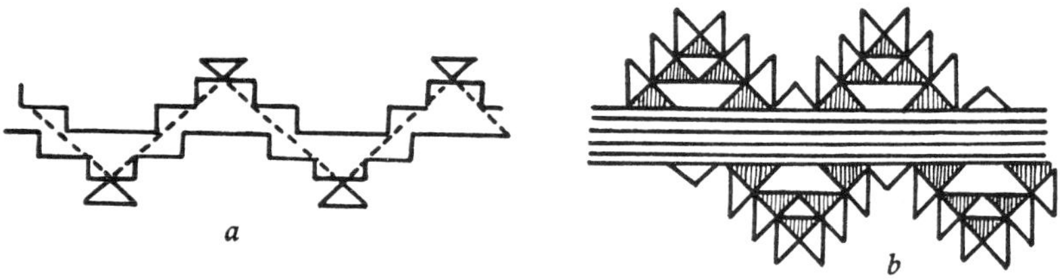

Fig. 9. Correlation between basket type and pattern. *a, b*, designs inappropriate for food baskets.

Storage Basket Designs

Tall baskets like the large containers for fish and seeds were usually marked in longitudinal rather than in horizontal patterns (fig. 10*a, b*). Quite aside from the question of aesthetics, technique is simplified by the choice. Once the "running" mark, as the Karok call a longi-

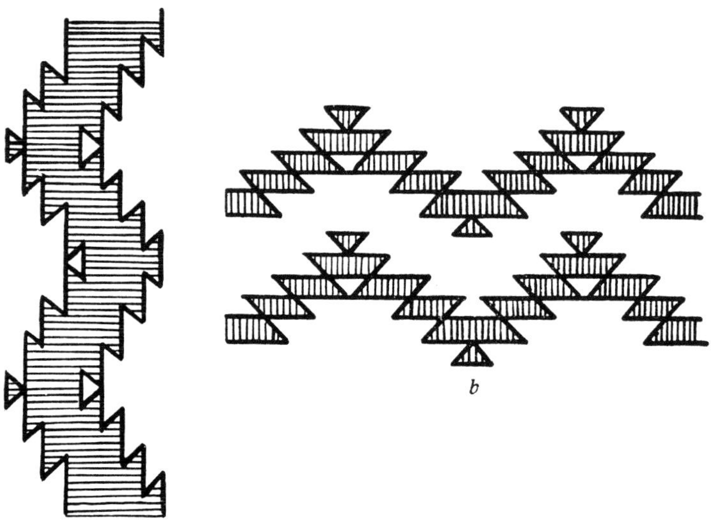

Fig. 10. Storage basket designs. *a*, "running" mark; *b*, the same, called a "double" mark when used in this position.

tudinal mark, is set, the work progresses by regularly twining over more or fewer sticks to right or left of those used for the pattern in the preceding course. Counting the sticks used for the pattern in the first course is all that is necessary in the way of actual computation; after that the design takes care of itself. No single design placed horizontally could pleasingly fill the space on a big basket. Yurok-Karok motives scaled to the size of the large basket would appear heavy and coarse, consequently the need for two or more horizontal bands is recognized. This means counting the sticks used in the design at least twice, occasionally more times (pls. 34*b*, 36*b*). Doubled horizontal designs are hard to do; a running mark is easy after the first pattern course.

Dress Cap Designs

Women tell of going to dances where all was unimportant to them except the appearance of unusual basketry designs or old ones given an individual twist. The finest examples of weaving are displayed during the closing hours of a dance; for these a girl saves her newest or best cap. Formerly it might be embellished by fastening dentalium money and woodpecker crests to the top. Dress caps worn purely

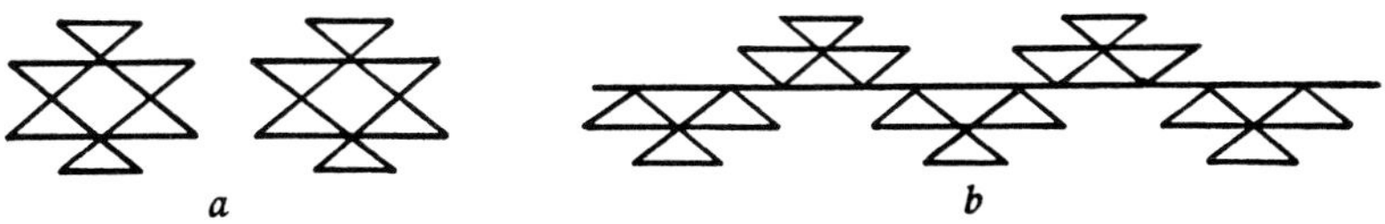

Fig. 11. Relationship between design and use. *a*, suitable for a food basket; *b*, the traditional modification for use on a dress cap.

for display allow the greatest apparent freedom of aesthetic expression. Because they can be indicative of something in the way of real distinction, the failure to make the most of an opportunity is judged severely. To put a design in a cap which would do as well or better in a soup basket is effort wasted to no effect; it merits censure. The designs in figure 8 are not for caps under any circumstances; that in figure 11*a* must be changed to use only half the motive alternately reversing it.

The cap pictured in plate 22*a* was flayed by nineteen out of twenty-seven weavers on the basis of two poor choices: it contains unrelated designs, and worse, the main motive belongs in an acorn cup. Some young weaver who did not know much about baskets might make such patchwork for practice but it is not the design for a cap. In spite of appreciation for the technique the whole thing is wrong. Of that fact six older weavers had no doubts.

The flint mark with all the recently added secondary motives is par excellence the choice for caps. So simple an arrangement as that in plate 24*a* received approbation from the majority of women who commented on it. To them it seemed harmonious and in good taste.

Fancy Basket Designs

Complete freedom in design choice is allowed the maker of a fancy basket. All cap designs are appropriate because they represent the finest Yurok-Karok decorations. Besides these, the range of possible fancy basket sizes permits selection from the large striking designs common in food basket types. In other words, since the white people who buy do not know or care about traditional interrelations and the fancy basket exists to please them, things that every weaver recognizes as heretical may be done in its name. The rejoinder, upon questioning as to harmony of shape, design, and coloring, is that the fancy basket is "just a basket." Informants mean that the type has no standardizing conventions; all that counts is its salability. To take the example shown in plate 41*a*: it is shaped like a soup basket but it is surfaced with white grass overlay; it might have been meant for a cap because of its design areas but it is not cap shape. If, then, by reason of shape or materials, it is neither food basket nor cap, yet it can still be a good sale basket.

The most admired fancy basket in the print collection is that in plate 43*b*. Eight weavers asked for a duplicate print from which to copy. Commendable features are the shape, the simple variation of a traditional design, and the striking space divisions offering possibilities for color contrasts. A group of baskets similar to those in plates 37*b* and 43*a* were also admired. Each shows a lower band of decoration, a recognized detail at the turn of a cap. If the band is decorative on a cap it is equally appropriate for a fancy basket.

PRESCRIBED DESIGN ARRANGEMENTS FOR BASKET TYPES

To have a basket accounted a perfect example of its type is a phenomenal occurrence. Under the scrutiny of working experts irregularities and mistakes rarely escape detection. Appreciation of all the selective phases involved, materials, designs, and proportions, leads a weaver to put her finger unerringly on the weak spot. Basketry is little different from the historical crafts dependent upon eye and hand; as with them it has prescribed conventions. Behind them are the weight of tribal tradition and also the Indian woman's feeling for space division—a feeling similar to our own. Her evaluations will be made more familiar by analysis of examples from the several basket types; these most nearly conform to Yurok-Karok ideas of design excellence.

Prescribed Design Arrangements for Caps

Basket makers commend first of all a time-honored design. If a picture showed one, then its proper disposition within the allotted space was quickly verified. For example, there are three established decorative zones on a cap (fig. 12). The first is from the center to the three-strand twine at the turn of the base to the side wall. Any sort of little pattern may be used around the center but good taste dictates that it shall be a suitable complement to the cap's main design.

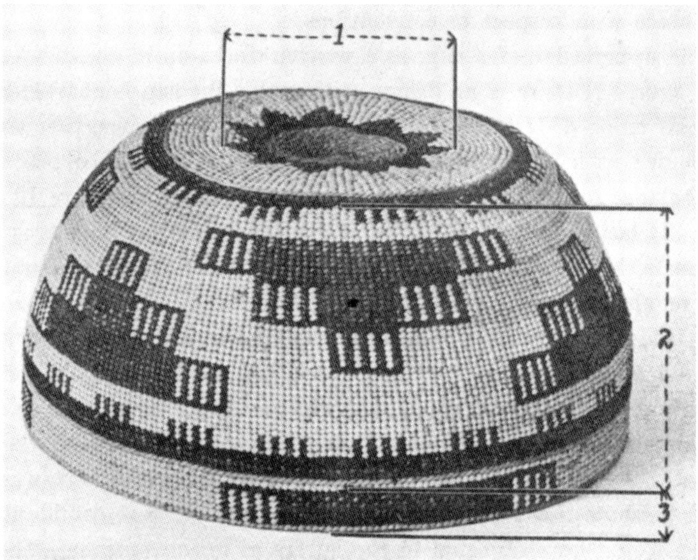

Fig. 12. Traditional number and proportionate size of decorative zones for a cap.

Plates 22*a* and 33*b* show a plain circular band, inadequate no matter what pattern is planned for the side; a band does not do justice to a dress cap. The second, the main zone, extends from the three-strand twine at the turn on the side to the same cord-like effect near the top edge. Long ago, the oldest Yurok informant said, a weaver did not start the main mark right at the turn; there was always a shallow border of straight or slanting stripes which extended over the edge; after the stripes there were several rows of plain white grass overlay and then the big mark. The cap in figure 12 is good, but the one in plate 19*a* lacks the plain white courses to set off the main motive. To those weavers intent upon design arrangement the cap looks unfinished; to older women, with memories of earlier ways, it is not a conventional cap treatment. An old woman, according to one of them, would not wear a cap like the latter example although a young woman might not know it was wrong. On a good cap there are always three or four units within the main decorative area. This is a pleasing space division not crowded. The cap in plate 26*a* is a good example. Whatever number of courses of plain grass-overlay border the lower side of the main zone, that same number should be woven for the upper side. After this the border used at the turn of the cap is duplicated. One example was proved to be imperfect because it had seven courses on the lower side, only six on the upper; the cap in figure 12 still holds first place with respect to conventions.

The upper edge of a cap, as a weaver works on it, constitutes the third zone. If there is no design within this the cap is characterized as "half finished" (pl. 23*b*).[21] Whatever motive is woven here should harmonize with the main one in particular; it should be placed to give balance to the whole effect. Here the specimen in figure 12 loses rank. It lacks the required rows of overlay, according to Karok professionals, Nos. 36 and 41. Seven rows are too few; there should be nine or eleven rows. As judgments were finally checked, two caps (pls. 19*b*, 26*a*) were able to measure up in all particulars; they were admired for their shape, design choices, and workmanship without a dissenting voice. It was often said whoever made them knew exactly how caps should look. However, the original photograph of the cap in plate 19*a*, upon which my informants gave their opinions, was not tilted to show the T-forms as this view does. I feel confident the women would have objected to the letters as unconventional, "new."

There was equal unanimity of opinion regarding the two poorest caps in the print collection. Every informant commented upon either one or the other. They are too shallow to fit the head; the shapes are weak; the main design in the one illustrated (pl. 27*b*) is lost in the surrounding space. Any of these points we ourselves would second without question.

Prescribed Design Arrangements for Food Types

Ordinarily, the crosswise axis of designs in food baskets is placed well above the side center of the basket. Sometimes the two strengthening encircling roots are made a part of the pattern; occasionally,

[21] "No California language is known to have any expression for fractions. There is always a word for half, but it seems to mean 'part' or 'division' rather than the exact mathematical ratio." Kroeber, Handbook, 879.

they confine a smaller subsidiary band above the main design unit. Where they are lacking, the alternately reversed motive, so favored by Yurok-Karok weavers, gives the impression of a center axis. Two food baskets (pls. 7*a*, 12*b*) are similar in design. Both are good but the latter is the better; the difference rests upon the few courses of unfaced twining root which edge the basket. A young weaver eager to finish her work rationalizes that a design extending to the top is prettier, newer; the old weaver says someone was in too much of a hurry; that a good basket has the rounds of plain root at the top, always.

The specimen shown in plate 12*a*, and the basket just analyzed (pl. 12*b*), were pointed out as good examples. They have the approved shapes, the simple old flint marks, the well proportioned design units to which every weaver responds. Moreover, the relationship between the size of the container and the design is harmonious. By contrast with such standards, the designs in plates 7*b* and 8*b* are out of scale with the basket sizes, the design in plate 11*c* is too crowded, and those in plates 15*b* and 16*b* are placed too low. The small rectangular motives below the main mark in the last basket were interpreted as a confessed error. Obviously they are not part of the big wax'poo mark; they indicated to my informants that the weaver did not rip out her work, but abandoned the false start to begin a different design higher up where a pattern band is conventionally set.

Prescribed Design Arrangements for Fancy Baskets

For the so-called fancy basket there are no conventional zones of decoration because there are no traditions governing it. Designs therefore must be judged independent of established arrangement, solely from the standpoint of whether they do or do not fill the space well. One basket design (pl. 43*b*) has been referred to as a favorite. It represents an extension of the two or three superimposed flint marks familiar in work and dress caps. The spiral is not particularly common in the old storage baskets; in them the decoration is more often longitudinal or horizontal. Designs spiralling from the lower turn of the basket flourished during the era of covered bottles (pl. 51*c*) and cylindrical flower containers. The advantage of a running mark over a series of horizontal bands has been mentioned in a preceding section. Spiral designs still hold favor in fancy baskets as evidenced by plates 38*a* and 45*a*.

One of the most familiar arrangements is the inversion of alternate design units. There is no attempt to give a true reciprocal effect to the ground and pattern. Informants expressed a feeling that the smaller motives should be organized by attachment to a center line. The design in plate 29*a* was judged better proportioned and better unified than the one in plate 29*b*, which is practically the same mark. The latter is not wrong, according to some informants, but the elements look scattered. Conventional treatment involving a center line holds less often for the larger than for the smaller baskets. The design in plate 38*b* depends upon a line for unity; the one in plate 37*b* represents the same placing of the motive without the line and the arrangement was very generally admired.

Prescribed Design Arrangements for Jumping Dance Baskets

Only six of the forty-three informants have made Jumping dance baskets. It is somewhat surprising, in view of the small number, that there should be such unanimity of opinion upon the subject of the correct decorative treatment. No. 22 described the old dance baskets as patterned at each end of the woven piece and left plain through the center.[22] The nearest correct among the prints shown here are those illustrated in plates 55*e* and 56*d*. No. 11 said the old baskets had a little design but that the new kind have a pretty design. This seems to state the difference fairly well. The older women agree that there should not be too much decoration on a dance basket and that the design should be unified; that it should consist of a single composite mark or its elements. Plate 56*a* has too many little marks along its length for good taste. The print which aroused almost universal condemnation pictures a basket (pl. 56*c*) with three motives: triangles, stripes, and the wax'poo mark. The last element spoils the entire effect. Informants interpreted the mixture as due to a liking for display of technical ability. Or, the basket might be the work of a Hupa weaver, synonymous, from the Yurok-Karok standpoint, to saying that the work is touched by modern extravagance. Eleven informants held similar views to these. One dissenter, a young woman, felt sure that a dance basket ought to be floridly decorated.

---

[22] Compare Goddard's description: "Four bands of small designs encircle the basket." The Hupa, 86.

PRESCRIBED TREATMENT OF DESIGN MOTIVES

One cannot say with certainty what disposition of motives is due to tradition and what to crystallization of technically simple methods into habits. Of some details weavers speak in terms of "should" and

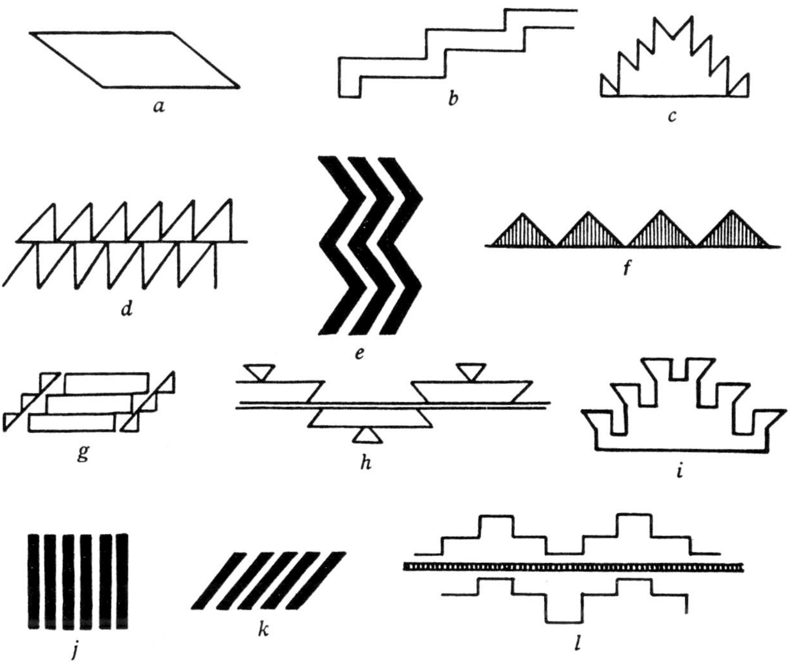

Fig. 13. Design elements in frequent use. *a*, flint (Y), flint-like (K); *b*, snake (Y), long worm (K); *c*, spread finger or spread hand (Y), frog hand (K); *d*, sharp tooth (Y), points (K); *e*, zigzag; *f*, sitting (Y), snake nose (K); *g*, ladder (Y), cut wood (K); *h*, wax'poo (Y), apxanko'ikoi (K); *i*, foot; *j*, straight stripes; *k*, slant stripes; *l*, elk (Y), cut wood (K).

"should not." Where no technique is implicated, even remotely, these are conventions. For instance, the direction in which a series of superimposed flint marks progresses. It was emphasized many times that the Yurok-Karok series always go from lower left to upper right in a basket and that the slant of the flint mark ends is in the opposite direction. Exceptions to this rule are considered errors. The three examples varying from the standard were discovered by several weavers.

happen in a majority of cases. Two Yurok women even went so far as to say that the quadrilaterals must equal in width the height of the triangle used with them. Most triangles have a base line of eleven or thirteen twining turns; the apex is reached in six or seven courses. Under the limitation imposed by the Yurok informants the whole motive would be very thin. Usually this point, if it is a real one, is ignored.

"OLD" AND "NEW" MARKS

Basket designs among both Yurok and Karok weavers are spoken of as marks. The word appears as noun and verb: a woman marks her basket, or she makes a mark *in* her basket, an unconsciously correct statement concerning any form of structural decoration. Incidentally, I never heard a woman say she put a design "on" her basket.

Whatever the subsequent characterization, a weaver's first reaction to a design motive is to place it within the category of old or new marks. The validity of the classification depends to some degree upon locality, the informant's age, and her real knowledge of designs. There is a universal assumption that everyone knows every old mark. It would be more nearly correct to say that everyone is supposed to know them. A design has certain identifying stylistic features, but far more important is the fact that each old design has its name or names; the number in itself does not raise or lower standing. Design names are essentially identification tags. They call to the weaver's mind specific forms. Women make no effort to interpret basketry motives subjectively; I met with no attempt to render any of their phases mysterious. In fact, one or two informants became self-conscious, ill at ease, when asked for a design's symbolic meaning. It was as if a meaning were something they ought to know but were unaware of. Karok women told the story of the snake who watched the old-time weavers use many isosceles triangles in their baskets. When he saw the design was a favorite he said, "Here is my nose for a basket mark." On the upper Klamath weavers tell the same about the deer and his excrement; at Rekwoi there is the story of the elk and his hand. In this version the elk places his mark in a basket. The stories are amusing to the tellers. No. 28 explained that the triangular mark need not really look like or represent a snake nose; it is just called that.[23]

---

[23] Cf. Kroeber's discussion of symbolism in California basketry in Basket Designs, 159–162.

In most instances the name given to a design by Yurok and by Karok women, although it might be stated in different ways, was virtually the same. Thus, the same motive (pl. 27*a*) is interpreted as a flint element diagonally bisected by a band of stripes, and also as two isosceles triangles separated by stripes. Another well-known design (pl. 28*a*) is called "points going up" with the snake mark through the center; or, it is described equally well by its three elements: flint, points, and snake. In the first case the native names imply division of a complete unit; in the second, the units are reduced to their component elements each of which is recognized by name. However, the simplicity of the criterion by which a design is accorded rank as a tribal mark is only apparent. To be able to resolve a design into elements bearing traditional names is not unquestioned proof to a weaver that the mark is an old one unless, also, the grouping of those elements is conventional. The necessity of this latter recognition may be read from informants' reactions toward the design in plate 6*b*. The same basket has been mentioned in another connection; it drew comments from thirty-two women, an unusually large percentage. Ten of the number analyzed the motive as a legitimate rearrangement of the widely known foot mark plus an extra element, the bar. For the bar, a stripe element in horizontal position, there is no name. The remaining twenty-two informants failed to see familiarity in the elements, or repudiated the whole motive by dubbing it "copied from a patchwork quilt." A second similar example (pl. 24*b*) shows two countered isosceles triangles, apices touching the opposite ends of a horizontal bar. Eleven of the fourteen informants saw in this arrangement something clearly unconventional. The device of counterchange, to one aspect of which Yurok-Karok weavers are addicted, and the mere addition of a rectangular element, an indispensable portion of several well-known marks, threw both designs out of the class of old designs and into the new, nameless class. Even without an extra element, triangles in different relations to each other may be disapproved of. No. 18, Yurok, and No. 21, Karok, compared the designs in plates 6*c* and 8*a*; they called the latter an innovation, an old mark put together the wrong way (fig. 14).

Since most weavers assume that every basket maker knows the complete catalogue of tribally recognized designs, their names, and their correct arrangement, an informant's declaration that she has never seen a mark is usually equivalent to her statement that the mark lacks tribal standing. In that case it has no name, and, according to any Yurok-Karok weaver, it can never hope to have one no matter how old in years and familiar through usage it may become. No. 5 was the only woman to remember having seen the motive in plate 28*b*. She had been taught the design when a child because it was easy. It had no name then and my explanation of an X mark as a countering of two portions of the time-worn zigzag did not really bear on the matter. A mark *has* recognition, it can in no way achieve it. Any new design is handicapped. Some basket maker, they say, will always be left to know that the mark is outside the pale. The old people of earliest days named the patterns; since then whatever new marks have come into use are called "made-up," to be described in terms of their resemblance to tribal marks or as copies of foreign inspiration.

a *b* *c*

Fig. 14. Arrangement of elements. *a*, familiar combination of sitting (Y) or snake nose (K); *b*, bases joined through center, called "right"; *c*, apices joined through center, called "wrong."

The swastika is known by a few informants as an Indian design. Half of it is pictured by Kroeber among standard basketry design elements; it is also to be found carved on acorn soup paddles. It is supposed, according to his informants, to represent the tail of a swallow; it has a name.[24] Nos. 28 and 29 had never seen the swallow mark; they call it part of an Indian good-luck symbol, of no rank among Yurok-Karok weavers. Farther up the river at Inam, when the family's collection of baskets had been arranged for photographing, No. 41 hurried forward to snatch from the group a small soup basket marked with five swastika elements. She had copied the design while it was having a period of popularity in the locality, but the design was not on a par with the older ones and it should not appear in the picture.

Karok women were given to comparing the decorations in the print collection with their memories of old storage basket designs. If the two tallied, it was by way of accrediting the later designs as worthy successors of traditional forms.

[24] Kroeber, Basket Designs, 127.

A curious irregularity to the rule that every old pattern has a name is illustrated by a type of design whose origin may have been accidental. A Karok informant admired the ideal planning of the basket design in plate 9*a*: background and pattern are duplicates. When the two are truly complemental as in plate 11*c*, either is conceivably the objective the weaver had in mind; that is, she may have been working toward a positive or a negative color effect. The first old basket makers, said No. 29, had experimented with possible divisions of a pattern zone to the stage where right placing of some motives automatically created for weavers a second design, complemental to but not identical with the first design. A basket mark of this latter type, one which owes its origin to the negative ground become positive pattern, has no name. Yet, it cannot be relegated, consistently, to the status of a new mark since it is so often a resultant of calculated or accidental placing of the most orthodox designs. The motive in plate 11*b* is the ground complement of the foot mark. In spite of the exact duplication of each detail its position in the Yurok-Karok scheme is anomalous. Similarly, the basket design in plate 11*c* was described by four informants as being "like the foot mark." They could offer no reason for denying the two designs rank along with the old, but they and their kind can never attain it.

I found no one who had made a point of developing the potentialities of the ground-as-pattern idea; the woman with limited repertory does not undertake experimentation, and the best weavers care little about playing with technique.

Lost Designs

An old design with a long history may be lost to a community. Informants often recognized an element or basket mark which was once familiar but has dropped out of the local repertory. A few of the prints requested of me were to renew a memory of patterns which weavers had known but remembered too faintly to produce. Possibly their oldest baskets had been burned or sold off. In that case a hard mark, which presents difficulties in setting its first pattern row, disappeared from sight the more speedily since models to copy from were lacking. In the course of time these designs are forgotten by the older women; the younger generation of weavers have never known them and so they descend to the status of copied or invented marks. Some of those almost scornfully condemned as new, must have had a former history. One or two such cases were recalled by my informants. No. 26, very old, and her sister, No. 24, in another locality, looked through the basket prints unsuccessfully to find the crane foot mark which they had known. It was a hard design to set but had been a favorite among the women of their mother's time.

A mark which used to be common is the "crab, his hand," to be seen around the bottom of the cap in plate 33*a*. Another cap in the collection shows the motive in three countered pairs of widely separated units (pl. 22*b*). The reactions to this pattern were definite: twenty-nine women had never seen the design or else characterized it as an invented mark; two women thought it might be a copy from linoleum or a patched quilt; one weaver thought it a little like Yurok points (fig. 13*g*); No. 18 gave it a name. The same mark appears on several baskets made by No. 16, a very old informant, who copied it from her mother's work (pl. 2*b*). The last three weavers are Yurok. I found a variation of the pattern on one of the basket fragments which No. 27, a Karok, keeps for guides (pl. 4*c*). My suggestion that the design clearly is a portion of a foot mark failed to draw the slightest acquiescence from the women who denied it tribal standing. Nevertheless it was the crab hand mark to those with long memories in spite of the majority opinion against its being a named design. A comparison of the motives in plates 6*b* and 22*b*, both adaptations of the element countered on a horizontal bar, brings up a question: by what reasoning is a design (pl. 22*b*) in one instance to receive a traditional name because it started out with elements recognizable as belonging to a standard mark, and why on apparently just as good grounds is another design (pl. 6*b*) denied the badge with its attendant rank? No Yurok-Karok weaver to whom I put the question could see the similarity in the two marks, to begin with; and the designs as examples of principles were not visioned.

Designs with Histories

Baskets and their designs traveled up and down the Klamath river as did the people. Gifts of baskets are still made, and sometimes, if a mark is a tricky one, a basket will be bought from a distant weaver solely for its pattern. Or, at a dance new caps appear and an individual turn to an old mark or an entirely new design is noted by a weaver to be memorized. Obviously, for most patterns there is a complete blank as to origin. There was never the mildest attempt to attribute an age to an old mark: it always has existed.

A story purporting to give the origin of a new design (pl. 21*b*) was told me by an expert maker from the Ko'otep district. A number of years ago a woman of the vicinity wove into her basket the shape of the metal slide on her son's suspenders. The circumstances were well known to my informant whose sister married the son. Offering further proof that the very cap in the picture was the work of the down-river weaver, No. 5 pointed to the border of sharp triangles on either side of the main design zone, a mannerism the older woman affected for all her nice work. The inventor often visited in Weitspus. She took caps to the dances to sell. Other weavers admired and copied the new mark. No. 14, a young Weitspus weaver, declared she had always made the design. The statement is doubtless true since it was at her mother's house that the visitor stayed. Now the pattern has been seen, at least, by my informants as far up the river as the Asisfunuk district. A Karok at Ti had also noticed the mark at the Weitspus dances; she remembered the down-river caps offered for sale. In disagreement with its so-called history, two women spoke of the design as a variation of the wax'poo idea (fig. 13*h*), countered alternates on a center line. The motive does resemble the wax'poo mark. Kroeber says of the motive that the name "sitting" was given to it, but that the design is probably modern.[25]

An interesting tale of traveling designs is suggested by several disconnected incidents concerning one very striking adaptation of the foot mark. No. 13, at Ertlerger, told me one part of the history. She had brought out her crocheting to show me that instead of taking over crochet patterns to weave into baskets, she was preserving an old basket mark in her bedspread (fig. 15). She had not seen anyone make the design for a long time. There was nothing definite to be got from her about the people involved, nor the place, nor the year at which the incidents took place. It happened "long ago." A friend of hers had taken her little girl to an Indian doctor. An old storage basket, the bottom removed, the side slashed from upper to lower edge to spread out flat, fan-shaped, served for rug on the floor of the doctor's house. "Alice" spit on her hand to clean off a little part of the design, counted the sticks in each basic element and memorized the number. Later, both she and No. 13 made baskets using the mark. Now the crocheting was being done to keep the pattern in memory. The next incident, which may or may not have been before the Ertlerger one, is dated by the last Jumping dance held at the Karok

[25] Kroeber, Basket Designs, 120.

Amaikiara, about thirty-five years ago. Among the soup baskets taken home after the festivities by the Inam family of weavers was a stray whose pattern made instant appeal. Since that time it has been copied by them in their large cooking baskets (pl. 2*a*; basket in front of No. 41). These baskets make an annual appearance at the August new year's ceremony. The copied design is still considered very choice and the baskets in which it is woven are never left around to become models for other weavers. It is, however, identical with the pattern design in the crocheted spread.

Fig. 15. Crocheted bedspread made to preserve the memory of an old basket pattern.

In Yurok territory, striped interpenetrating triangles set horizontally are called sharp tooth marks, sometimes sturgeon backs (fig. 16*a*, *b*). For those set longitudinally none of the eighteen Yurok informants gave a name. No. 17, characteristically analytical, named the elements of the design in one basket print showing the mark (fig. 16*c*). To do it she had to imagine the ground a zigzag pattern band; no other weaver interpreted it as such. In Karok territory interpenetrating triangles are called skunk or snail back when placed horizontally and uswufumas mark when spaced or connected longitudinally (fig. 16*c*, *d*). Two Karok informants gave this last name to the horizontal arrangements. Nine Karok women knew uswufumas as a name, each with an accompanying explanation more or less identical: there is a rock in the river below Wahsekw, near the present Martin's Ferry, which has a marking similar to the basket design. The design gets its name from the rock. No. 36 had heard the story from her grandmother but neither she nor any of the others had ever seen the rock. Nos. 23 and 41 had Yurok mothers who, when they married Karok men, brought with them their own baskets and some down-river variations in designs. Both informants knew of the rock name but no more than that. Up-river informants were sure the down-river weavers would be able to furnish the complete story. Curiously

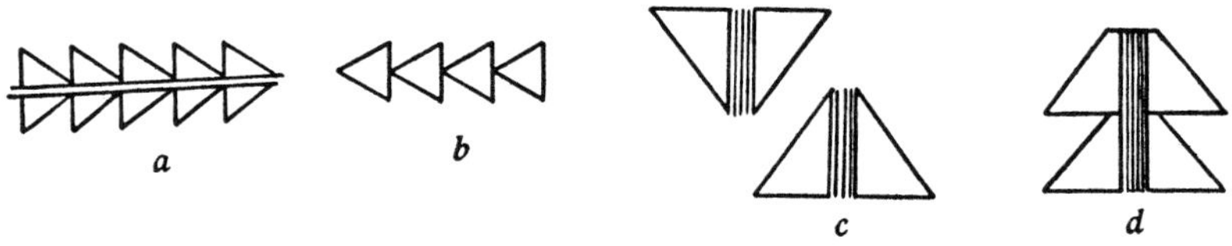

Fig. 16. The Karok uswufumas.

TABLE 9

INFORMANTS' NAMES FOR INTERPENETRATING TRIANGLES

Yurok design names:	Plate 8*c* Figure 16*a*	Plate 35*b* Figure 16*b*	Plate 49*a* Figure 16*c*	Plate 37*a* Figure 16*d*
Chiton mollusk, kwerermetsaa	No. 4	No. 6		
Sharp tooth, veniirpelaa	Nos. 13, 17	No. 17		
Sturgeon back, qaxkwilee	No. 10			
Zigzag and stripes, okrekruyaa and vetseq!seq!oaa			No. 17	
Karok design names:				
Skunk back, cochinimvaci	No. 32	No. 20		No. 21
Snail back, esivaci	Nos. 22, 23, 41	Nos. 22, 23		No. 42
Uswufumas mark	No. 19	No. 37	Nos. 22, 23, 25	Nos. 21, 22, 23, 32, 33, 36, 39, 41, 42
Wild geese mark		No. 36		

enough, not a single woman among the six who live below Wahsekw could recall any rock which might have given a name to a basket design. The nearest clue was the mention of a fishing place Seq'aa, by coincidence a part of the Yurok name for stripes. No. 5 disclaimed that any rock near Seq'aa bore a resemblance to the design. Others were plainly uninterested; the river is full of rocks and perhaps one was like a basket mark. This seems to be an example of a traveling design. One woman who knows the name from her mother is about seventy-five years old; No. 36 who learned it from her grandmother carries back sixty years the possible time of its having been more generally known. If the design came into Karok country as a recognized down-river design, it may have been preserved because it was an importation, while it was being forgotten in its former locality. Or the longitudinally placed motive might have lost its identity through inclusion under a name equally appropriate to both positions of the triangles. It is evidently the remnant of a Yurok story kept alive by Karok weavers. The youngest of my informants, and the least helpful, knew of this one design, its name, and its significance (table 9).

NEW DESIGNS

Designs from White Sources

Basketry motives designated as ''new'' by Yurok-Karok weavers may be from any one of several sources. Because the basic design elements are so uniformly triangular and quadrilateral in form, similarly patterned fabrics of white manufacture invite attention to their easily adapted units. Foremost among these are crocheted fabrics. The majority of my informants crochet; it is taught to young girls at the schools. The patterns, especially those for square-mesh filet laces, are play to copy. I did not see a basket which seemed to me to have within it a characteristic lace pattern, and no one was working with any to my knowledge. The women around Ko'otep make lace but only one converts its patterns into basketry; others make trimming for garments and bedspreads like those in use among white women fifteen years ago. In this type of work the Indian women often use basketry motives (fig. 15). It is my impression that a demand for crochet patterns in basketry could be met at once by weavers. As a lace, however, crochet is completely out of favor among us, so that the occurrence of its common motives in a basket would render the product doubly unattractive. At any rate, Panamenik weavers say isolated motives from crochet will not sell a basket and that the simplest of its continuous patterns, the Greek fret, is a troublesome design to join neatly.

Little embroidery is done: the poorest materials are expensive; and demand for Indian work is wholly lacking. Some women know cross-stitch from pictures, that it is quite similar to a basket pattern made to show each twining element turn, and that it could be easily transferred to weaving. As a result cross-stitch embroidery is classed with crocheting. The two words are pronounced rather contemptuously by old weavers against a suspected intruder into the tribal body of designs.

Oilcloth, a patchwork quilt, a piece of linoleum, a carpet, or a machine-woven "Indian" blanket are unusual in Yurok-Karok houses. Mail order magazines, found all through the country, profusely illustrate these objects and the patterns prove tempting suggestions. I had five informants who had copied geometric designs from white sources. No. 20 took it as a matter of course that she should make use of adaptable motives wherever found; two weavers, relatives, had made caps with patterns taken over from pictured dress materials. They spoke of their results with pride. No. 4, from Sregon on the lower river, brought out a small basket in answer to my question as to the sources of her designs. In the basket was a mark copied directly from linoleum. It had been a feat, rather clever to do, but deserving of no respect as far as design motive went. In the course of a visit to No. 21, she took me outdoors to see an old ingrain rug spread on the ground. She had lived on that rug for a long time before the possibilities of its varied patterns became evident to her. She traced out a half-dozen suitable basketry motives, regretting the circumstances which kept her from weaving. No. 28 once copied a pattern which in itself had looked attractive, but when completed was recognized to be inappropriate, not a real basket mark. Here I suspect the cultivated taste of the gift shop proprietor who contracts for all baskets made by this weaver. The appreciations involved are less the Indian's, perhaps, than the white woman's. Of course this statement does not pretend that a design with no traditional sentiment behind it would not be at a permanent disadvantage.

Invented Designs

In addition to self-evident copies of printed letters, borders, and textile motives, the term "new" includes a number of invented designs of composite character. I could not discover that my informants estimate any more highly an arrangement of selected elements to form an original composition than they do a motive copied directly from modern white sources, but the makers of the two are ranked unequally. If, for example, informants look at the swastika mark, admiration is modified by their knowledge that its source is the ubiquitous cracker box. Likewise a crochet pattern completely planned out by squares, as it is commonly printed, testifies to no real skill. But weavers did not always recognize models like patched quilts or floor coverings because they are unfamiliar. In these cases, copying the designs does not raise the valuation put upon the results, but the adaptation awards more distinction to the weaver. Correspondingly, esteem for a woman who can invent by a process of rearrangement of the local design elements rises several degrees higher.

There are comparatively few weavers along the Klamath with a flair for experimentation. Ingenuity, as it concerns basketry, is at a low ebb. Ask the older weavers one after the other if they ever made up a design which no one about them had seen before, and a majority of answers will be in the negative. Ask them if they ever took a triangle from this mark and a zigzag from that, by way of illustration, to put together in a new way, and the answers will be again largely negative. Or, the last question may be sensed by informants to mean using two or more unrelated designs in the same basket, a combination one occasionally finds in the bottom and sides of a cap (pl. 22*a*). Granted that any basketry mark requiring two identification names to describe it is a composite, repetition of the same arrangement has generally unified the elements to a degree where their original separateness has long since passed from memory. It is so with our own concept of the egg and dart motive. As mentioned in the section on correlations between basket types and patterns, a combination motive often impresses women as lacking harmony. A cautious worker avoids possible incongruities, and she may extend her caution to an avoidance of single design motives which bring together unrelated elements. Just how my informants would have estimated the design conglomerate in a northwestern California basket of unknown provenience (fig. 17*a, b*) would be interesting to know. The weaver in this instance seems to have started out with an idea of rearranging flint marks and right isosceles triangles. The slanting rectangular form is without similarity in the motives of the region. Technical difficulties in setting the mark together with the necessity for a filler explain the arrow, also not found among Yurok-Karok designs. Above the center line the deliberate attempt to do something different has resulted in a compromise in one of the four units, namely, a return to the familiar flint mark diagonally transversed by the eye element. If the design is an invented one, it is farther away from recognizable sources than any except one of those originating among my informants.

The fact that the unstandardized result counts for little by comparison with old named designs does not lessen an amount of half-envious admiration for the woman whose inclination and ability lead her to invent an acceptable basketry motive. The native phrase is "to make up" a design, for which the phrase to copy a design from other than basketry sources is an equivalent. None of my informants acknowledged she had tried unsuccessfully to make up a mark, but to judge by the pride with which the few displayed their original

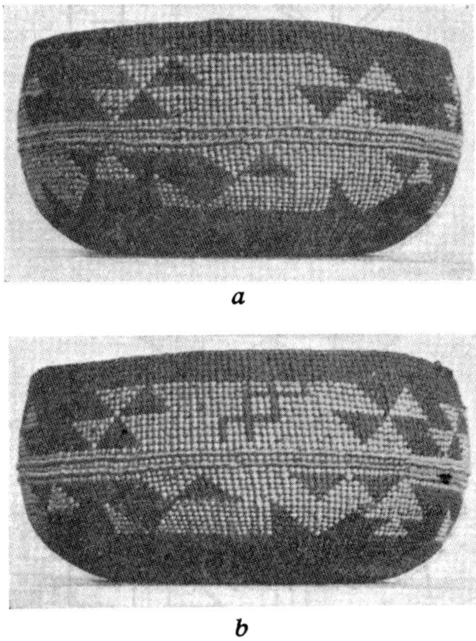

Fig. 17. An attempt at invention? Contains two elements foreign to the region: the rectangular slanting detail and the arrow head.

designs, those who can achieve are thoroughly conscious of the distinction it brings. Even No. 9, a sloven of low average ability, was known to have made up a mark. Yet when the so-called invented designs are analyzed there is little freshness of treatment and less newness in component elements. Tradition, custom, habit, with the strong probability that there never has been much incentive toward innovation, seemingly contrive to sever active connection between basketry and the imaginative faculty. As skillful a craftswoman as No. 18, a weaver who has copied covered chalice shapes and handled vases (pl. 51*h*, *j*), confessed she was not smart enough to make up new designs to go with her modern forms. She loses nothing in prestige although she would gain a good deal were she talented along the inventive line also.

Speaking first of those claimed by my informants to be original with them, I find the patterns to be of two types: invented designs which are undoubted adaptations of motives from white sources to the basketry technique, and other patterns which bear some likeness to the conventional tribal designs.

The Weitspus weaver, No. 9, allowed me to sketch off her own pattern (fig. 18*h*). Two informants, asked for opinions on it, smiled

Fig. 18. Informants' invented designs. *a*, by No. 20; *b*, by No. 8; *c*, by No. 21; *d*, by No. 42; *e*, by No. 21; *f*, by No. 20; *g*, by No. 4; *h*, by No. 9; *i*, by No. 43.

at its claim to originality; they said it came from a patchwork quilt. Two others, one a conservative Karok expert, appreciated a quality of newness and admired a weaver's capacity to evolve something unusual. They made no effort to connect the pattern with an origin; they accepted the motive at its maker's evaluation. Other original designs are seen to be in close relationship to some form familiar to another craft. The incomplete flower motive (fig. 18*a*) made by No. 20 is a commonplace among our own stencil patterns for painted wood and in embroidery. No. 20 considers any adaptable catalogue picture a legitimate source for a basketry mark. No. 4's original pattern (fig.

18*g*) was taken, according to her own boast, from a piece of linoleum. She also uses crochet patterns in her baskets. No. 8 had adapted the Red Cross poster symbol (fig. 18*b*) to a fancy basket modifying the cross with the secondary center design. No. 20 was immensely proud of an original motive (fig. 18*f*) which she uses in basketry napkin rings. The motive combines very old elements: snake nose and the foot mark. No. 42 had encircled her basket with five repeats (fig. 18*d*), combinations of square-end flints with zigzag lines. Both elements are familiar among storage container designs; the arrangement on No. 42's basket is also identical with the usual one for the large baskets. No. 21 brought out two wall plaques (fig. 18*c*, *e*), black designs on white grounds. It is possible to match either pattern with a tribal design so similar in appearance as to confuse the "original" with the authentic at first glance. The informant asserted she had never seen any designs like hers.

By far the most ambitious effort among the original patterns is the design (fig. 18*i*) by No. 43, the youngest of the Karok informants. By her own confession she is weary of the old things and consciously tries to produce novelties. The main design in her basket is a series of four isolated repeats, each a combination of snake marks and a stepped arrangement of right triangles, but not the isosceles triangular forms so common in the region. More unusual is the cover of the basket with its five repeated groups of character-like motives. The asymmetry is marked but the effect as a whole is not unattractive. The conventional flower-petal center is called points and is often found on cap bottoms; it seems a jarring note when used with the geometric elements.

Those who have invented designs do not give any reason for their activity other than desire to vary the mechanical monotony of the work. The practice, as I found it, is fairly limited now by a uniform demand for striking, well spaced tribal marks. Tourists feel these are genuinely Indian in feeling. Older weavers through conservatism, caution, or inability are wont to criticize the desire to change old patterns or to substitute inferior copies, even while they acknowledge the superior capacity of the woman who can do either. Older weavers accuse the dissatisfied younger women of perpetrating the unconventional in form and design. Apparently there was always such a contingency. No. 27's mother told her it was not right to make up marks; that the old marks always had been from earliest times. Men had put the designs on their arrows first and the basket makers had copied them. Changing designs was against Indian law. The older weavers, too, are content to make modifications of some minor detail or to rearrange the color areas to adapt them to different requirements. No. 28 could not remember that there were any new patterns when she was a girl. Although this sounds like the proverbially sentimental attitude toward earlier days, it may be that with the former demand coming only from Indian buyers there was even less than the present impetus to invention.

Ordinarily, older informants explain an invented or copied design in one of three ways: that some young woman wants to show off; that she has become tired of the old marks; or, that the weaver, old or young, has sold all her baskets, leaving no old models from which to copy or by which to check the amount of variation she is giving to

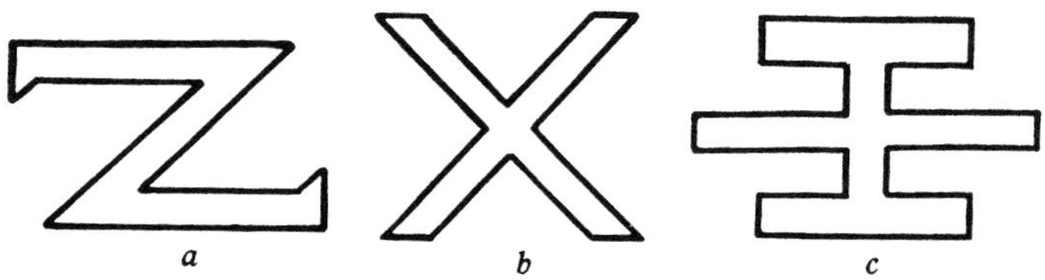

Fig. 19. "New" design elements, by unanimous opinion of informants.

her work. To the first accusation little is added; it is always voiced with tolerance or with wonder that anyone should care to make the effort. The second, weariness with the old marks, is heresy to the basket maker thoroughly content with the traditional. She hastens to add that she herself never tires of the old designs or that a basket would not seem a real basket without an old mark in it. To the third possibility is conceded some excuse. A weaver without models or good memory might be obliged to make up a mark. No. 24, who offered this plausible reason, was sure that if she had had to work independent of old helps that she might have copied from modern white sources. She felt confident of her ability to achieve under these conditions results equal to those in the baskets in plates 25*a*, *b*, and 28*b*. These designs are three of a very small number characterized as invented marks by all who commented upon them. The weight of opinion against them is representative of both tribes, contrasting markedly with opinions on other designs to be discussed in the section to follow. Further development of the subject will show, too, that today's younger women know basket conventions as well as their elders, so that the modern frequency of striking variants from recognized tribal marks is doubtless overestimated by older weavers. If we may judge from my own informants, almost no one picks up basketry by herself; she is consciously taught. Again, as with the weavers much older than herself, the easiest road to a successful result is by way of an old design for which some one knows and will share the necessary pattern counts. Few women will risk failure for the achievement of novelty. It should not be thought from this discussion that the aesthetic quality of the nameless, new design is unappreciated. The attention has been focused so far only on each design's right to a place within the Yurok-Karok system.

MODIFIED DESIGNS

Disputed Modifications of Old Designs

It has been emphasized that an Indian weaver makes no distinction in her characterization between a motive adapted from white sources and an invented design: they are both "new." How she distinguishes between a legitimate variation of an old pattern and an invented one is even more hazy to an investigator. A study of informants' reactions toward designs termed modifications and those definitely carried by opinion out of the old design class into the new, still leaves several questions unanswered. Nineteen of the thirty designs whose recognition as old tribal marks is controversial were put by the majority of informants into the new class. The results must be noted with certain reservations: first, because it is simple for a woman to say a design is new to her without making it clear to her questioner that it is the idea of a legitimate variation of the old mark that is new; and second, because she may not really be aware that the rearrangement of elements *is* a legitimate variation.

The table of reactions (table 10) is presented with the possibility of its errors in mind; even with allowances, the summary tabulations of counts based on it reveal a number of additional facts concerning the attitudes of weavers toward their craft. Table 11 has been made on the basis of informants' ages. Group 1 includes seventeen women from sixty years upward; group 2 includes nineteen women from forty to sixty years of age; group 3 includes seven women from twenty to forty years. It might be predicted that group 1, with thirteen of its seventeen members actively making baskets for sale, would most often conform to majority opinion in recognizing a design as old or new. But some older informants have undoubtedly reached

TABLE 10

Basic Table of Reactions to Designs as Old or New

					Group 1 (Ages 60–)																	Group 2 (Ages 40–60)																			Group 3 (Ages 20–40)						
					Yurok						Karok											Yurok									Karok										Yurok			Karok			
Informants					1	2	7	13	16	17	19	21	22	26	28	33	34	35	39	41	42	3	4	5	6	9	10	11	12	18	20	23	24	25	27	31	32	36	37	40	8	14	15	29	30	38	43
	New designs, undisputed																																														
Specimen number	Illustration	Total	Old	New																																											
1-1439	Plate 25*a*	36		36	x	x	x	x	x	x	x	x	x	x	x	x	x	x	x	x	x	x	x	x			x	x	x	x		x	x	x	x	x		x	x	x		x	x	x	x		
1-1610	Plate 25*b*	21		21	x	x						x	x	x	x	x	x	x	x	x	x	x		x				x		x		x			x	x				x				x			
1-20819	Plate 28*b*	31		31	x	x	x	x	x	x	x	x	x	x		x	x	x			x	x	x	x	x		x	x		x		x	x	x	x		x	x			x		x	x	x		
	Old designs, disputed																																														
Specimen number	Illustration	Total	Old	New																																											
1-373	Figure 20*l*	28	8	20	N			O	O	N	N	N	N			O	N	N	O				N	O				N	N	O	N	N	N	O			N	N	N	O	N	N	N	N			
1-1426		15	7	8				O	O	O	N	N				N		O						O				N	N	O			N		N			O				N					
1-1437	Plate 8*b*	15	2	13			N						O		N								N		N		N	N	N			O	N			N	N							N	N	N	
1-1438		5	2	3			N								O												N						N									O					
1-1441	Figure 20*i*	29	2	27			N	N		O	N	N	N		O	N		N	N	N		N	N	N	N		N	N	N			N	N	N	N	N	N	N		N	N	N	N				
1-1442	Figure 20*n*	14	4	10							O		N	N	N					O			N									N	N	N	O		N	O						N	N		
1-1472	Plate 6*c*	13	9	4	O					O		O	O		O		N	N		N	N									O		O									O			O			
1-1476		7	5	2											N			O		O	O	N	O													O											
1-1495	Plate 9*b*	8	2	6						O					N							N		N					N												O	N		N			
1-1577	Plate 22*b*	34	3	31	N	N	N	N	O	O		N	N	N	N	N	N	N	N	N	N	N		N			N	N	N	O		N	N	N	N	N		N	N	N		N	N	N	N		
1-1593	Plate 21*b*	9	3	6		N										N		N	O					N					N				N					O		O							
1-1598	Plate 38*b*	26	7	19	N			N		N	N	N	O		N		N		N		N		N					N	N	O	N	O	O	O	N		O	N	O	N	N		N			N	
1-1674	Plate 37*a*	10	9	1								O	O			O			O		O											O						O		O	O				N		
1-1692	Plate 24*b*	14	3	11		N				O		N				N	N	O				N			N				N		N		N	N				N									
1-1698	Plate 6*b*	32	10	22	O		O		O	O	N	N	N		N	O	N	N	N	O		O	N	N	O			N	N	N	N	N	N	N	N	O	N	N			O			N	N	N	
1-1762	Plate 17*b*	10	7	3	N										O	O	O			O		O			N						O												N			O	
1-1796		7	3	4						O		N	O									N			N						N	O															
1-1801	Plate 43*a*	9	2	7				N			N	N	O	N															N			O	N												N		
1-1802	Figure 20*g*	8	3	5						O			N		N				O													N	N							O				N			
1-1829	Figure 20*j*	24	3	21				N		O	N	N	N		N		N		N			N	N		N				N	O	N	N	N	O	N	N				N	N	N		N	N		
1-2232	Figure 21*e*	5	4	1						O										O									O								O						N				
1-20807	Figure 20*h*	17	3	14									N				N	O			O		N		N			N	O			N	N		N		N	N				N	N	N	N		
1-27057		7	6	1							O		O																		O	O		N			O				O						
G-2	Plate 31*a*	9	5	4						O			O					O							N						N	O	N	N										O			
CA-14	Figure 6	19	15	4				O	O	O		O	O	O	O					O		O		N						O	O	O	N	O							N	O	N		O		
CA-87	Plate 22*a*	15	5	10		O	N			O				O	N						N				N		N		N				N	O							N		N	N	O		
G-94	Plate 28*a*	15	13	2	O		O	O		O		O			O		O		O						O		O						N			O				O					O		N
G-423		6	5	1	O	O	O																				O	N							O												
G-425	Figure 20*o*	7	2	5									N									N			N						O	N		O	N												
G-455	Plate 13*a*	8	7	1			O			O					O		N								O		O										O							O			

the limit of their design repertory; they have fewer opportunities to compare work with other women and their judgment is at best a reliance upon memory. Again, dim eyes easily may have missed the key details in pictures.

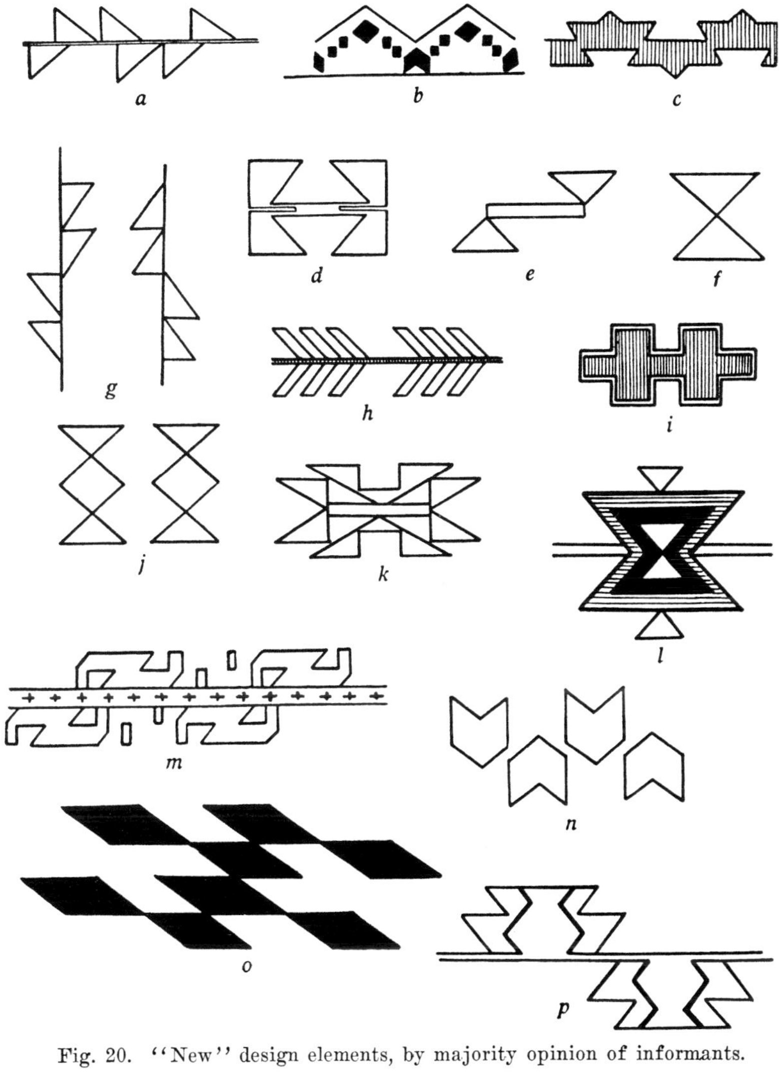

Fig. 20. "New" design elements, by majority opinion of informants.

Group 2 represents the active basket makers of the present, alertly interested in their craft, eager for new ideas. These women have a tendency to dogmatic interpretation. It is significant that within this group, regardless of the locality in which informants live, there is agreement to a marked extent: the group constitutes a majority nucleus which gives or withholds tribal standing to twelve out of the thirty disputed designs. Group 1 controls the decisions for eight other designs, and the remainder are "old" or "new" by virtue of combined efforts.

TABLE 11

CLASSIFICATION OF DESIGNS BASED ON INFORMANTS' AGE GROUPS*

Specimen number	Illustration	Group 1 60–80 yrs.	Group 2 40–60 yrs.	Group 3 20–40 yrs.	Total "old":"new"	Decided by group:
1-373	Figure 20*l*	4 : 7	4 : 9x†	0 : 4x	8 : 20	2
1-1426		4 : 3	3 : 4	0 : 1	7 : 8	
1-1437	Plate 8*b*	1 : 2	1 : 8x	0 : 3x	2 : 13	2
1-1438		1 : 1	0 : 2	1 : 0	2 : 3	
1-1441	Figure 20*i*	2 : 9x	0 : 15x	0 : 3x	2 : 27	2
1-1442	Figure 20*n*	2 : 3	2 : 5	0 : 2	4 : 10	2
1-1472	Plate 6*c*	5 : 4	2 : 0	2 : 0	9 : 4	1
1-1476		3 : 1	2 : 1		5 : 2	
1-1495	Plate 9*b*	1 : 1	0 : 3x	1 : 2	2 : 6	2
1-1577	Plate 22*b*	2 : 14x	1 : 13x	0 : 4x	3 : 31	
1-1593	Plate 21*b*	1 : 3	2 : 3		3 : 6	
1-1598	Plate 38*b*	1 : 9x	6 : 7	0 : 3x	7 : 19	1
1-1674	Plate 37*a*	5 : 0x	3 : 0x	1 : 1	9 : 1	1
1-1692	Plate 24*b*	2 : 4	1 : 7x		3 : 11	2
1-1698	Plate 6*b*	6 : 7	3 :12x	1 : 3	10 : 22	2
1-1762	Plate 17*b*	4 : 1	2 : 1	1 : 1	7 : 3	1
1-1796		2 : 1	1 : 3		3 : 4	
1-1801	Plate 43*a*	1 : 4	1 : 2	0 : 1	2 : 7	1
1-1802	Figure 20*g*	2 : 2	1 : 2	0 : 1	3 : 5	
1-1829	Figure 20*j*	1 : 7x	2 : 10x	0 : 4x	3 : 21	2
1-2232	Figure 21*e*	2 : 0	2 : 0	0 : 1	4 : 1	
1-20807	Figure 20*h*	2 : 2	1 : 8x	0 : 4x	3 : 14	2
1-27057		2 : 0	3 : 1	1 : 0	6 : 1	
G-2	Plate 31*a*	3 : 0	1 : 4	1 : 0	5 : 4	2
CA-14	Figure 6	8 : 0x	5 : 2	2 : 2	15 : 4	1
CA-87	Plate 22*a*	3 : 3	1 : 4	1 : 3	5 : 10	
G-94	Plate 28*a*	8 : 0x	4 : 1	1 : 1	13 : 2	1
G-423		3 : 0	2 : 1		5 : 1	1
G-425	Figure 20*o*	0 : 1	2 : 4		2 : 5	2
G-455	Plate 13*a*	3 : 1	3 : 0x	1 : 0	7 : 1	2

* Group 1, 17 informants; group 2, 19 informants; group 3, 7 informants.

† x=conspicuous agreement.

The youngest age group, 3, has in all but two cases aided the majority whichever way it turned. Where its members' verdicts or failures to comment do not checkmate each other, the group has thrown the weight of its opinion fourteen times to classify a design as new, as against four times to keep it in the old class. Reviewing the personnel of the group makes the result explicable: within it are five daughters and two nieces of expert basket makers. If one woman of a household knows or learns something about the craft, that knowledge is correspondingly available to all around her.

On count, the majority of the classifications within each group are too equally divided to make them settle decisively any argument on a design's tribal "age." For the thirty designs in the table, reactions within groups 1, 2, and 3 may be listed as follows:

Opinions checkmate (includes failures to comment) in..........	5: 0:10 cases
Agreement conspicuous in	7:11: 7 cases
Results too close to be definitive in	18:19:13 cases

TABLE 12

CLASSIFICATIONS OF DESIGNS BASED ON TRIBAL AFFILIATION

Specimen number	Illustration	Yurok "old"	Karok "old"	Yurok "new"	Karok "new"	Total Old : New	Decided by:
1-373	Figure 20*l*	4	4	8	12	8 : 20	Karok
1-1426		5	2	3	5	7 : 8	
1-1437	Plate 8*b*	0	2	6	7	2 : 13	
1-1438		1	1	2	1	2 : 3	
1-1441	Figure 20*i*	1	1	12	15	2 : 27	
1-1442	Figure 20*n*	0	4	1	9	4 : 10	Karok
1-1472	Plate 6*c*	4	5	0	4	9 : 4	
1-1476		1	4	1	1	5 : 2	Karok
1-1495	Plate 9*b*	2	0	4	2	2 : 6	Yurok
1-1577	Plate 22*b*	3	0	11	20	3 : 31	Karok
1-1593	Plate 21*b*	0	3	3	3	3 : 6	
1-1598	Plate 38*b*	1	6	8	11	7 : 19	Karok
1-1674	Plate 37*a*	1	8	0	1	9 : 1	Karok
1-1692	Plate 24*b*	2	1	4	7	3 : 11	Karok
1-1698	Plate 6*b*	7	3	5	17	10 : 22	Karok
1-1762	Plate 17*b*	1	6	3	0	7 : 3	Karok
1-1796		1	2	2	2	3 : 4	
1-1801	Plate 43*a*	0	2	2	5	2 : 7	Karok
1-1802	Figure 20*g*	1	2	0	5	3 : 5	Karok
1-1829	Figure 20*j*	2	1	7	14	3 : 21	Karok
1-2232	Figure 21*e*	2	2	1	0	4 : 1	
1-20807	Figure 20*h*	1	2	5	9	3 : 14	Karok
1-27057		1	5	0	1	6 : 1	Karok
G-2	Plate 31*a*	1	4	1	3	5 : 4	Karok
CA-14	Figure 6	6	9	3	1	15 : 4	Karok
CA-87	Plate 22*a*	2	3	6	4	5 : 10	Yurok.
G-94	Plate 28*a*	6	7	0	2	13 : 2	
G-423		4	1	1	0	5 : 1	Yurok
G-425	Figure 20*o*	0	2	2	3	2 : 5	
G-455	Plate 13*a*	4	3	0	1	7 : 1	

Table 12 divides informants on a tribal basis irrespective of ages. There are eighteen Yurok informants and twenty-five Karok. Some concession in evaluating the totals too strictly must be made to the

Yurok to counterbalance the Karok majority. Informants' reactions when looking at the basket pictures were largely volunteered; a range of topics was covered. Consequently, during my several days' work with her, a woman might talk on many subjects but touch on the age classification of fewer than a dozen specific designs. There are only two cases where an informant's and an interpreter's opinions were duplicated. Mathematical corrections seem impractical under the circumstances.

It should not be inferred from table 12 that Karok women know more about basketry design than Yurok women, but results do show the Karok to be more consistently in agreement, more uncompromising in their definitions of what is and what is not the traditional aspect of a design. Kroeber cites the comparative freedom of the Karok from contact with permanent white settlers and their being left to their own devices. He says that "they yielded their old customs and their numbers much more slowly than the majority of old California natives."[26] Karok pride in their conservatism is self-evident. They are satisfied with "our ways." They tolerate the ways of others' without desire to follow them. These are essential elements in the Karok tribe-consciousness; their attitudes are partly indicated by the tabulations.

Of the thirty disputed designs, eleven are by combined majority of the two tribes to be considered legitimate modifications of old basket marks, to be characterized as "changed wax'poo," or "changed snake nose mark"; nineteen are new, possibly containing elements of tribally recognized patterns but too far removed in appearance from the prototype to be entitled to the old name. Some of the verdicts are almost equally divided; in sixteen cases they were undoubtedly swayed by Karok conservatism, or at least agreement. The results show, too, that a design is classified as old through Karok opinions six times to the Yurok's once; as new, ten times to the Yurok's twice. Allowing for the Karok majority of seven informants the results are definitive.

Table 13 illustrates the agreement between each informant's design classification and the majority's. It shows, too, the consistent quality of Karok opinion within each age group. The greater number of designs are as well known to women of one tribe as to the other. The few exceptions seem to be designs more common to Karok basketry traditions. These are illustrated in figure 6 and plates 17*b* and 37*a*.

---

[26] Kroeber, Handbook, 98.

An outstanding instance is furnished by an analysis of the reactions toward the design in plate 17*b*. One Yurok weaver said it was not a down-river design; a second admired it, knew it was an old motive, but did not know the name of it; a third woman said it was a hard mark to set; two others had never seen it; and the last three contented themselves with commenting upon the shape of the basket in which it appears. Undoubtedly, the design is unfamiliar to most

Fig. 21. "Old" design elements, by majority opinion of informants.

Yurok women, to judge by the eight informants listed. Five Karok women knew the design as a good old mark. They called it by three names: points, the frog hand or foot, and the mountainside mark. The basket was identified by No. 38 as the work of No. 41's mother. Sometime later No. 41, an old lady herself, said it might be her mother's basket, that the pattern had never been a common one because it was so hard to make the join come right, but that once that problem was solved her mother had woven the pattern in basket after basket.

TABLE 13

AGREEMENT BETWEEN INFORMANTS' CLASSIFICATIONS AND MAJORITY OPINION

Place	Informant	With majority	With minority	Per cent agreement	Place	Informant	With majority	With minority	Per cent agreement
Yurok, group 1					*Karok, group 1*				
1	7	8	1	88	1	19	8	1	88
					2	21	13	1	83
						28	14	3	83
					3	34	9	2	82
4	2	4	1	80	4	26	4	1	80
	13	7	2	80		33	7	2	80
					5	22	14	4	77
6	1	6	2	75					
					7	39	6	3	66
						42	4	2	66
						41	6	3	66
					8	35	7	4	63
9	17	8	10	44					
10	16	1	4	20					
Yurok, group 2					*Karok, group 2*				
1	10	8	0	100					
	4	9	0	100					
2	12	14	1	93					
					3	27	9	1	90
						32	9	1	90
4	11	8	1	88					
					5	31	6	1	85
6	3	9	2	82	6	20	9	2	82
					7	24	15	4	79
8	6	10	3	77	8	23	14	4	77
					9	36	8	3	72
					10	37	2	1	66
						40	6	3	66
11	5	5	3	62					
					12	25	6	7	46
13	18	3	6	33					
Yurok, group 3					*Karok, group 3*				
1	14	8	0	100	1	38	4	0	100
					2	29	12	1	92
					3	30	9	2	81
4	8	8	4	66					
	15	6	3	66					
					5	43	0	1	0

If a design is "old" or "new" by the nice selection of determinate design elements and their place relations in a motive, then the exact boundary between the two categories becomes, in the main, a matter of subjective interpretation. Otherwise, there would be no disputed designs. Evidently, too, the weaver who pays greatest heed to the letter of the conventions or falls heir to a crystallized formula is most often in agreement with the majority. Tabulated counts and percentages for individual informant's reactions prove that some of the most reliable women, who know designs, who have long worked with them, and who appreciate the possibilities resultant from rearrangement of elements, often stand with the minority in calling a design old. Generally this is because these informants break up a motive into its component parts and give a name to each. The most helpful informants in group 1 are Nos. 7, 13, 17, 22, and 28. No. 17 lost her chance to vote with the majority ten times out of eighteen because what appeared unconventional to other weavers was at base an old mark. Most of the motives she had woven and she gave no impression of considering them unusual or invented forms. Much the same applies to Nos. 5, 6, 10, 18, and 40 in the second group. Evidence of Karok conservatism is apparent in table 13: their percentage conformance to majority opinion entitles them to positions in blocks from 1–5, 5–10, 1–3 in the three age groups by comparison with Yurok weavers whose percentages leave gaps. The best Yurok informants occupy places at intervals from first to thirteenth. Curiously enough, No. 12, a gossipy little woman who never has been able to make a good basket, stands in second place with only one minority judgment to her fifteen agreements with the majority. Whether or not No. 2 and others who commented upon only five or six designs could have maintained or improved their percentage standings had they been asked to decide on the rank of a dozen designs is speculative. For the most part the oldest women in group 1 were more valuable for information making fewer demands upon eyesight.

Legitimate Modifications of Old Designs

Apart from six designs new to every informant who noticed them at all, and the thirty designs whose position as old or new is controversial, there is a small group of presumably legitimate modifications of tribal marks. It is necessary to assume in these few cases that if the designs were not commented upon as new, and were noted as examples of recognized variations by one or two reliable informants, the opinions are to be considered as representative of group opinion. Each design, in general, has been modified by a change falling under one of four types: an adaptation in size to make possible a series of perfect repeats in scale with the basket; a change in position affecting the appearance of the whole motive; an addition of inconsequential details; and, an omission of appreciable portions of the conventional unit. The variations will be dealt with in turn.

Any weaver will change the count of the sticks to make her design repeat correctly within the pattern circumference or to scale it to the size of her basket. These obviously are legitimate modifications since no one number of overlay twining stitches within a pattern can be considered absolute. So, too, a design usually found within a horizontal zone is permissibly shifted by a quarter-turn to a vertical position if thereby it will fill the space more satisfactorily. Compare plates 34*b* and 36*b* for this. The other advantages of what the Karok call the running mark from the bottom to the top of a basket have been mentioned in connection with appropriate designs for storage baskets. Nos. 29 and 32 thought several examples of quarter-turning the mark might be due to efforts to vary the familiar aspects of an old motive. In each case they described the results thus: the mark in plate 14*b* is an old mark turned; it should be like the one in plate 10*b*. But neither woman suggested that the treatment was unconventional nor was there any question about the design's retention of its old name. Another feature that takes from the familiar appearance of several designs similar to the first mentioned is the use of the designs as evenly spaced motives in a pattern zone. Yurok-Karok designs, except for the flint marks in particular, form continuous horizontal bands. When a single unit is segregated for use, the innovation is noticed. No. 17 gave the term zigzag to the quarter-turned section of an old running mark seen in plate 41*b*; she knew and had used only an older form (pl. 44*a*). No. 27 recognized the different effect of the design in plate 7*a* in contrast with its usual unbroken progression to the right.

The inclusion of an elaborating detail which does not in any way disturb the form of characteristic elements is appreciated for its novel effect. The variation is considered an evidence of ability. One must know the designs well to be conscious of such minor additions as an inner line paralleling the hypotenuse of a triangular form (pl. 23*a*); the small open rectangles, variously explained (pl. 16*b*); the double stripe giving variation to the wax'poo mark (pl. 6*a*).

Finally, omission of considerable portions of a design motive seems to be tolerated. Under the circumstances the design does not lose rank as an old mark. The spaced motives in plate 29*b* lack a center horizontal line to unify the rather scattered effect. Goddard mentions for the Hupa this reliance upon a dividing line through the center of the main pattern zone. He speaks of it as "usually imaginary, but occasionally expressed."[27] I found my informants considered that the smaller motives required the steadying influence of a band,

[27] P. E. Goddard, The Hupa, 44.

although with larger units the integration was successful without one. The line or band, however, is not regarded an essential. More noticeable omissions are overlooked in plates 13*a* and 40*b* in which

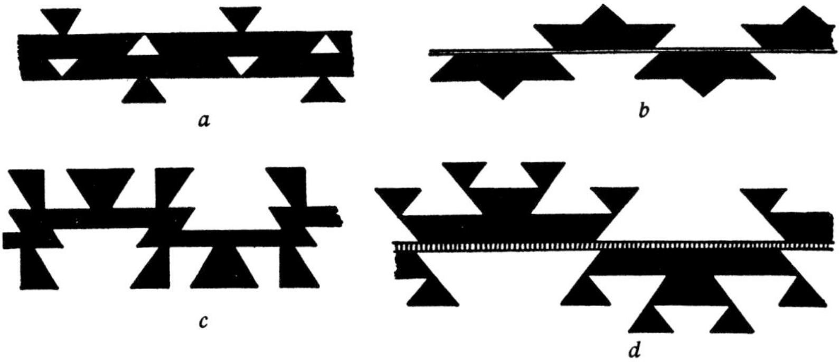

Fig. 22. Disputed modification of the wax'poo mark. *a*, traditional form; *b*, "old mark changed," according to two informants; "new" according to five others; *c*, not recognized as a basket mark by No. 18; *d*, crab hand element substituted for single customary triangle, according to No. 18; not recognized by weavers of the Katimin district.

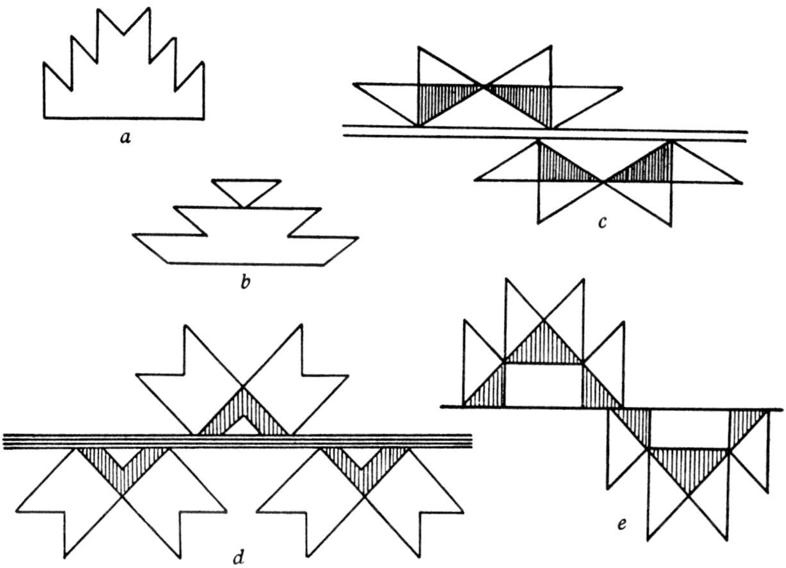

Fig. 23. Disputed modification of the spread-hand mark. *a*, traditional form; *b*, a recognized change, according to No. 10; *c*, copied from linoleum, according to Nos. 4 and 18; legitimate variation, according to No. 14; *d*, from linoleum, according to No. 18; *e*, a legitimate rearrangement of elements, according to No. 18.

the designs represent just half of each motive. The second is an abbreviated edition of the design in plate 41*b*, the first is one side of a unit more often bilaterally symmetrical. The motives were recognized as fractional motives by nine women in the case of one design (pl. 40*b*) but casually, and with no intimation that as old marks the designs had lost standing. This is one of the unsolved questions which appears to depend upon a feeling as intangible as ours for the essentials of good taste. Yurok-Karok women undoubtedly have awareness for the non-existent boundary between what does and what does not constitute a licensed modification; but with the data available for presentation their criteria are obscure. Three Yurok and two Karok weavers considered the basket in plate 6*a* in the light of an aesthetic achievement. Why a bar in one basket design (pl. 6*b*) should, by two-thirds vote, render it an invented mark without a name, while two bars in another should bear witness to some weaver's inspired variation of a most commonplace tribal mark is perplexing.

From the viewpoint of size and shape, no one would declare the old marks to be necessarily better than the new. No. 27 had noticed that the old designs were larger and correspondingly clearer than the new designs and more striking in effect when woven. The newer designs have a tendency to grow smaller and more complicated because of their primary use on fancy sale baskets. There must be, however, a familiar quality in the proportions of an old pattern which is indispensable for an aesthetic appeal, for a regrouping of the same elements will draw forth comments from a number of informants that they can always tell a new design: "There is no sense to it."

TRIBAL TASTE IN DESIGNS

The great majority of Yurok-Karok basket designs are so simple upon analysis, so free from complex rhythms, that an over-elaboration is reacted to in one of two ways: either it was hard to do, or the effort has resulted in mere confusion. The women have no basis for appreciation of minute details except where technical fineness automatically reduces the size of a familiar motive; then admiration is transferred from the design effect to the skill of the weaver. Outspoken praise is accorded the unassuming patterns. That these are in tribal good taste is proved by specific comments on about fifty baskets. Frequently the whole basket was admired: its form, proportion, design, and workmanship. Or, informants had in mind one or two features, ignoring at times, criticizing at others those which did not measure up to standard. Disapproval touched on workmanship, choice of materials, or pattern placing—all technical phases; most often it had to do with the design itself. The older weavers harked back to the days of plainer flint marks; they spoke of the secondary inner motives as an outcome of recent tourist trade. That statement, as has been noted, is open to doubts.

Flint marks bisected by simple diagonal bands are impeccable. The bands may be solid, or striped, or modified to the snake mark. Or, there may be a triangular inset solid or striped. For more than these minor changes there is no enthusiasm; to take over a swastika or a letter from our alphabet for the inner element of a flint is self-evidently tawdry to the Yurok-Karok. It is the same with the wax'poo mark (fig. 13*h*) in its different forms, and with the other old recognized patterns. Whatever variation is made should be the plainest. An illustration of a single informant's reaction to a composite

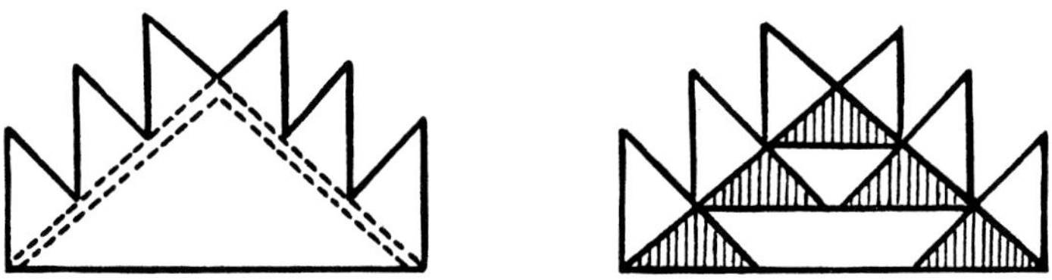

a *b*

Fig. 24. Good taste in designs. *a*, admired for its large unbroken areas; *b*, too ornate.

admired by some women as a striking mark resulted from contrasting figure 24*a* and *b*. The former is the spread-finger design with an inner stripe. Stripes in themselves are not always unimportant; weavers objected to them in one soup basket as making it too elaborate. Here, in a cap, they are fitting. But the design in figure 24*b* represents a superimposition of a second complete motive on the first, and No. 6 criticized the ornateness. All-over patterns, from one standpoint the earliest possible method of filling space, are not popular. The basket in plate 42*a* was hard to weave; the result is unattractive, and crowded looking.

Weavers ask that a design show up well, that it be in definite contrast with the ground, that it have comparatively large unbroken areas of color in most instances, and that it be well spaced. No. 32 criticized the lack of adequate space between the doubled mark in plate 40*a*. It is never good taste, I gathered, to have a basket look as if it had been labored over, as if the design had been an effort as in plate 9*b*. One of my informants regretted that any one should spend time on a mark like that in plate 8*b* when it could not possibly be satisfactory to the beholder. Nor should a basket give an impression of conscious display of skill as the sampler effect in plate 42*b* was interpreted to be. Above all, marks to be used together should bear a noticeable relationship to each other, especially in a cap. Here it is easy to err through wrong choice of smaller marks to combine with the main side motive. The marks most frequently given as illustrations of tribal good taste are listed below; the numbers stand for the times each was mentioned in this connection.

	Times
Wax'poo and variations (pls. 19*b*, 20*b*, 36*b*)	11
Flint mark (pls. 12*a*, 43*b*)	8
Foot mark (pls. 11*a*, 37*b*)	6
Cut wood (fig. 6, pl. 14*b*)	4
Points (pls. 5*a*, 28*a*)	4
Sitting (pls. 8*a*, 10*c*)	4
Spread-finger mark (pls. 7*c*, 41*a*)	3

No. 35, in the Ayis district, brought out a basket to illustrate her concept of a plain, striking mark in good taste. The design in plate 9*a* is nearest the design in her basket. Her flint marks are squares of yellow porcupine quills, the triangles of black fern. Of course it is the elemental square-end flint and sitting mark combination of the Yurok, the Karok flint and snake nose mark. There happened to be no basket with that particular arrangement within the print collection, but it is a very old combination of elements woven by the women of both tribes the length of the river.

There is no abstract admiration for a hard mark, as such. The easiest of designs, the snake nose triangle was noticed in its various forms many times to the foot mark's once. Display is not a part of basketry. It is well and desirable to be known for ability to do the hard things in the craft, but, after all, the prettiest baskets, according to the women in all localities, have the plainest, most easily followed design rhythms.

As an additional means to focusing personal tastes each informant was offered duplicate prints of one or more baskets she might care to make. To about half of those who took advantage of the opportunity some one basket made an especial appeal and a woman limited her request to a single print. Whatever reasons for choices were expressed fell, in the main, under three heads: the pattern had been forgotten, or at best was dimly remembered; the design elements satisfied a sense of proportion and orderly arrangement; or, some feature challenged by its novelty. Doubtless the latter two were interwoven motives. Any picture, too, is a technical aid although that explanation was given but twice. A number of informants expressed no reason for their requests beyond saying they would like to make the pattern illustrated. As expected, choices fell most often upon the showier caps and fancy baskets. Older weavers looked through the prints as eagerly as younger women, but occasionally an old woman would say her memory held all the patterns she could make during her lifetime and she waived the opportunity to ask for a picture. In the following summary it may be noticed that some designs were more in favor among Yurok informants (Nos. 1–18), and others among Karok (Nos. 19–43). The baskets are listed in the order of their popularity.

Cap (fig. 6).—No. 4 selected it because she had forgotten the old patterns; she seldom sees old baskets. No. 10 asked for a sketch instead of waiting for a print that she might begin work without delay. Nos. 22 and 23 knew the design for an old, pretty pattern. No. 23 counted out the sticks to memorize the grouping. Nos. 8, 24, 27, and 41 had never seen this variation of the cut wood mark. Customarily, a line of contrast color follows the stepped portions. No. 41 planned to use yellow quills for the stripes. No. 8 began her basket the very day she saw the print, working from memory. Nos. 32, 38, and 40 gave no reason for their choice.

Fancy basket (pl. 43b).—No 6 knew the motive for an old flint mark variation, but had not seen it for a long time. Nos. 1 and 10 chose it for the design; No. 28 liked the shape of the basket. No. 27 thought the position of the stripes a new variation; Nos. 15, 24, 36, and 38 gave no reason for their choice.

Cap (pl. 28a).—Nos. 28 and 30 thought the mark typical of Karok good taste. Nos. 26 and 39, both within the oldest group of informants, admired above all the workmanship. The former weaver still makes caps; the latter cannot maintain her earlier standards; she has abandoned efforts at any but the coarsest containers. No. 33 gave no reason for her choice.

Cap (pl. 19a).—Nos. 3, 4, 33, and 36 thought it a very pretty cap.

Soup basket (pl. 7c).—No. 35 used to make the mark long ago. No. 32 recognized that black fern in a food basket was not an old-time feature, but she believed the basket would sell with the gloss and color contrast.

Fancy basket (pl. 48a).—Nos. 1 and 3 admired the type and workmanship; they recognized the new-fashioned shape and cover.

Cap (pl. 20b).—Nos. 41 and 42 liked the varying widths which give a new look to one of the oldest marks. No. 41 objected to the design having three white grass courses on one side, four on the other. She would place the motive exactly in the center of the middle zone. What is novelty in one feature, the unequal widths of quadrilaterals, is violation in another, the unequal widths of the borders.

Soup basket (pl. 6b).—Nos. 5 and 40 both admired it. No. 40 liked the "bunched up" arrangement of an old mark. There are comparatively few design repeats in Yurok-Karok basketry which stand free. Usually, motives are dependent upon an encircling line or spiral from bottom to top of the basket.

Cap (pl. 30b).—Nos. 28 and 29 admired the design.

Fancy basket (pl. 37b).—No. 41 admired the design.

Fancy basket (pl. 41b).—No. 25 characterized this as a hard mark to plan for. She said if the weaver made a mistake the design would never come out correctly. She could manage it with a picture from which to copy.

Fancy basket (pl. 40b).—No. 6 chose this because it is an easy way to make an old design (cf. pl. 41*b*). She recognized it as an abbreviated form.

Fancy basket (pl. 58a).—No. 17 had never made a foot mark in this manner. It is a Wintun basket.

Dance basket (pl. 56d).—No. 43 had never made a dance basket but would be able to copy a picture. (See her characterization in the Appendix.)

Cooking basket (UC-PAAE, 2: pl. 20, 4).—No. 20 liked both shape and pattern.

Cooking basket (UC-PAAE, 2: pl. 16, 2).—No. 42 gave no reason for choice.

Soup basket (pl. 8a).—No. 32 gave no reason for choice.

Soup basket (pl. 6c).—No. 6 liked this shape and the separated design units although she described them as "half done." (See footnote 31.)

TECHNIQUE

THE BASKET START

Karok weavers begin their baskets on eight sticks; Yurok weavers begin theirs on eight or ten sticks. The only reason an informant can give for her particular number is that she was so taught. No point is made of choosing sticks all the same length to begin with; any of them may snap off, necessitating replacement. Selection of uniform sizes and quality is a matter of importance. A weaver takes up each stick, places the butt end between her teeth and tears of half its thickness in a sliver about an inch and a half long. If her teeth are poor she whittles down one side with a case knife. Two of my informants had been driven to use knives in their work. They were the only tools I ever saw used during actual weaving and, because they are not essentials for the Yurok-Karok type of basketry, both women apologized for practicing methods foreign to the craft. When the end of the stick is reduced in size its roughened surface is scraped with the thumb nail to complete the preparation. Every stick added from first to last for whatever purpose is treated like the first ones. By doing so the ends are softened and rendered pliable, a condition which aids in the final cleaning of the basket.

The technical details involved in the start of a basket and the introduction of three of the subsequent groups of sticks were analyzed by dissecting a cap disc woven by No. 5. No weaver works slowly enough at this stage, or with her basket start in one position long enough, to make observation very reliable. Also, the more automatic the action the less marked it is apt to be.

The method of placing the sticks and the binding of them into a firm center is told best by diagrams. The process is essentially the same whether eight or ten sticks are used. The first step is placing. The basket maker picks up the first prepared stick, *A*, holding it butt-end toward her. The second, F, is placed parallel to *A* at its right, butt-end away from her. About three inches is allowed for the lap. The third stick, *B*, is placed to the right of the second, corresponding in position to the first; the fourth, *E*, duplicates *F*, the second. Then the weaver crosses the first four with four other sticks in like manner, starting the first of the second group with butt-end away from her. Finally, as may be seen from figure 25, diagonal corners are either all ends or all tips. The end lengths are twined over from the start as if they were independent sticks.

The second step is binding. For this and for the twining which is to follow, split tree root is used by most weavers. Some choose the finer willow root but even in those cases a tree root binder forms an additional layer on top of the willow. To overlay the binding root elements with grass or black fern so that the button-like center of the

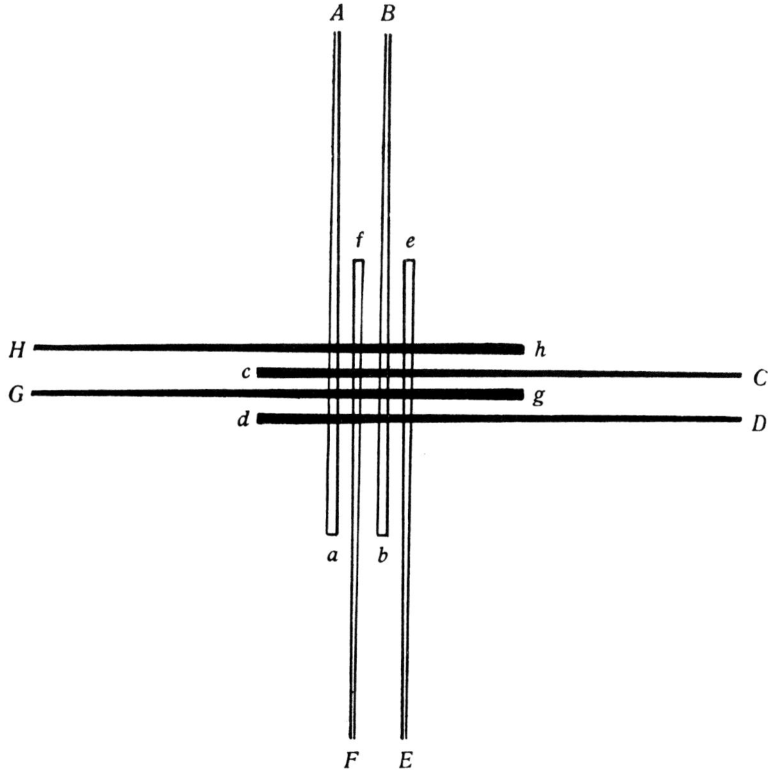

Fig. 25. The method of placing the sticks at the beginning of a basket.

basket may have luster is a technical refinement (pl. 32*b*). Holding the eight sticks close together under her left thumb, a weaver crosses them once diagonally with the binding root, from upper left to lower right. Then she carries the binder diagonally on the under side to bring it out obliquely across the two sticks and two ends at the extreme left, entering it between *F* and *b*. It is crossed diagonally again on the under side to come out at the upper right corner. From here the binder makes a straight line across the two sticks and two ends at the extreme right.

The third step welds each stick to the center. The binding root crosses diagonally on the under side from lower right, where the second step left it, to come out between *A* and *f*; it crosses over to enter between *a* and *F*; up again between *f* and *B*, crosses to between *F* and *b*; finally up again between *B* and *e* to enter between *b* and *E*. This makes a series of straight flat bands on the outer, working side. Bringing the root element up to the right of *e* it crosses *hCgD* and the sticks are held fast, ready for the twining.

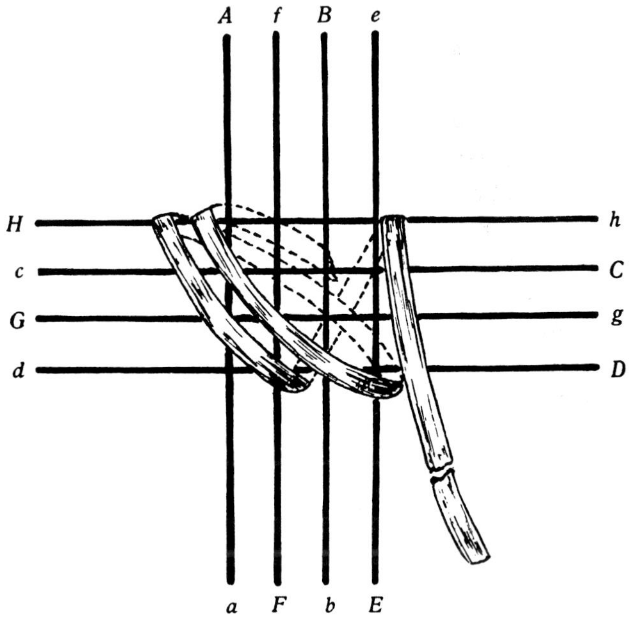

Fig. 26. Binding the sticks at the center with a root element.

All Yurok weavers do not begin their baskets with the identical movements described, nor do the Karok follow a given set of sequences exactly. No. 20, Karok, uses two pine root binders and crosses her basket center with each; No. 7, Yurok, uses two binders, one of willow root, a second of redwood. I was assured that everyone did exactly the same thing in the same way, which declaration probably weights digressions as immaterial. Some baskets have a noticeably bulky center due to width of binding root elements or the number of times they are carried around the start. Flatness combined with strength is the ideal.

At the point of beginning the twining a second root element is introduced. Sticks and ends are crossed in fours by the two root strands for a single round. Upon its completion a third twining element is introduced. This element may be of root, or it and the second may be of split willow, in which case the original root binder will be replaced by a willow graft to make it conform in size to the others. The center of a cap or close-twine fancy basket is its heaviest, most sturdily woven portion. It is a disc of three-strand twining from one and a fourth to one and a half inches in diameter. When the center disc is completed, one root twining element is discontinued. From here to the top the basket is woven in plain two-strand twining, overlaid with white grass, black fern, dyed fern, or porcupine quills as demanded by the pattern.

The outside of the basket is held next to the weaver. Work progresses from left to right. In plain twining the root element behind stick no. 1 comes forward between no. 1 and no. 2; the second root element at the front crosses stick no. 1 and is carried over the first root element, then it passes behind stick no. 2 to come out between no. 2 and no. 3. Each twining strand in front position consistently passes over one stick and over the root strand which came from behind that stick. Overlay material, when used, and its foundation root are in effect one element with the overlay always toward the outside of the basket. Exception to this is described under the section on Devices.

Most of my informants pulled apart the sticks with left thumb and first finger so that the twining elements might pass more easily between them. At the same time each new turn as it was being formed was forced down close to the previous course. No. 32 was working on a large all-stick drying pan in spaced twining technique. To handle the awkward size and manipulate sticks and twining elements at the same time was difficult. She took each twining strand between her teeth, as it was brought to the front, in order to hold it at tension. What seemed necessary in this case was less obviously so with Nos. 28 and 30, both working on very small baskets. The former gave as her reason that there was no chance for the overlay to slacken against its root foundation nor for it to shift its position behind the stick if held taut by the teeth. Her standards are the highest; a vestige of overlay showing on the inside of her baskets is accounted carelessness.

Addition of Sticks

During the weaving of the center disc sticks are regularly introduced to increase the original sixteen (counting the ends of the eight sticks) to sixty-eight (fig. 27). Here, again, the number given refers only to those in the dissected basket start. There may be variations but the principle holds. The large schematic diagram shows courses

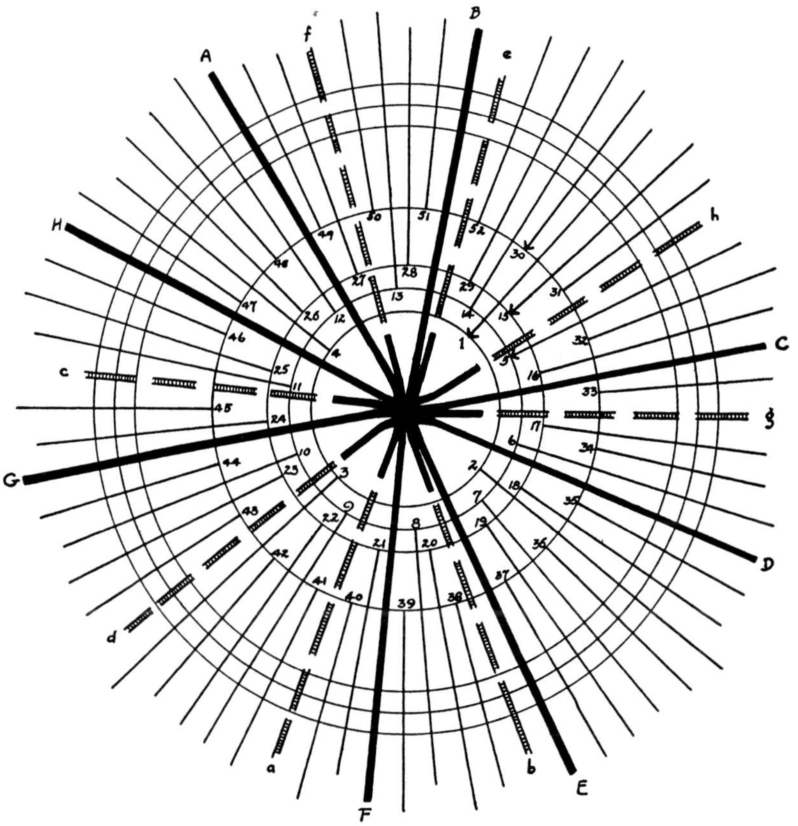

Fig. 27. Addition of sticks to the original eight on twining courses 2, 3, 4, and 7. A basket bottom at this point is about one and one-half inches across.

2, 3, 4, and 7, the only ones within which additions were made. It also shows the number of sticks found to have been introduced during each course and the order of their insertion. For the first entered sticks the problem is less difficult. Every girl is taught to spread out the eight original sticks and eight ends equidistant from each other in readiness for the introduction of the third twining element and new sticks. Regularity is not absolute but most weavers have a rhythmic sequence of additions: one stick skipped, the second to brace an inserted stick, and repeat. If represented by letters with o indicating old, N the added sticks, the sequence would show: O–ON–O–ON–O–ON, etc. When a weaver crowds in new sticks too closely, she makes a rough surface; this error shows in the basket in plate 15*a*; introducing too few for the size of the container results in a lopsided, wobbly basket. A basket maker follows with her left hand the twining elements as they are moved and tightened by her right; frequently she stops to prepare and insert a new stick. Her motions seem automatic. But for all the apparent simplicity, a well shaped basket demands judgment along with skill. Some weavers, informants say, never do learn how many sticks to put in and the places to enter them. No. 13 declared a good weaver could feel when a stick was needed. One like herself did not have the gift, or as she expressed it, it was not "in her." When it is observed that a little fancy basket 16⅝ inches in circumference has the number of its sticks increased from the original sixteen (counting the ends of the eight) to two hundred fifty-two in weaving about three inches, and that a cap twenty-three inches in circumference may have three hundred forty-five at the completion of its less than four-inch height, the achievement loses its casual aspect.

Addition of sticks in caps.—A sixth of my informants do not make caps. Such a statement is not to be interpreted as inability to make medium-fine or fine baskets, or that these women cannot reduce patterns to correct proportions, or weave to a specified height and circumference. The assertion admits a weaver's lack of ability to control contour. The contour of a basket is dependent entirely upon the placement of new sticks. Consequently almost every weaver makes fancy baskets because, in the majority of them, all additions are complete shortly after the turn from the base to the side wall. The newer sale products differ only in materials from cooking and soup baskets, which represent a young girl's first efforts. In these three types it is customary to add sticks on four different courses spacing the additions with concern for the size of the basket. For cap makers the problem of adding sticks is not solved until within an inch and a fourth of the final row of weaving.

To verify this, the cap made by No. 34 (pl. 32*b*) was analyzed. There are ninety-nine courses of twining from the outer edge of the three-strand twine disc to the rim. The following numbers indicate the courses—counting as the weaver holds her basket—within which sticks have been inserted; the capitals *O* and *N* will indicate the changes in rhythm developed to allow greater space between new sticks as fewer additions become necessary.

Course 1, at the edge of twined disc: O–O–ON–O–O–ON, etc.
Course 4, at the edge of first color band: O–ON–O–ON–O–ON, etc.
Course 14, at the base of triangles: O–ON–O–ON–O–ON, etc.
Course 20, two courses before the cord effect: O–O–ON–O–O–ON, etc.
Course 32 at the turn, midway between first and second dark stripes of the main pattern zone: O–O–ON–O–O–ON, etc.
Course 49, only in red ground flint marks: O–O–ON–O–O–ON, etc.
Course 50, only in white triangle bases: O–O–ON–O–O–ON, etc.

Beyond the third stripe, which comes two and three-fourths inches from the edge of the cap, the weaver can observe no regular sequence. At this point, No. 34 lacked thirty-two sticks to accomplish the correct shape. By count, she distributed them as follows:

On rows 51–60	10 sticks
On rows 61–70	19 sticks
On rows 71–76	3 sticks

How she knows where to put this last fraction of the total number of three hundred forty-five sticks is something no cap maker is able to explain. That there is nothing stereotyped in their disposition is proved by the varying spaces between sticks within the same course: they may be inserted three-eighths of an inch from each other or two inches apart. In one area five sticks were entered within two and a fourth inches on the same course. Evidently special attention was needed there. Moreover, sticks were added on rows 56 through 60, 63, 64, 66, 67, 71, 74, and 76. From that angle there is no visible system. One thing is noticeable, however: design motives are disrupted as little as possible by the last scattered entries. To insert a single stick in a small triangle is disastrous. Unless the contingency is foreseen the resultant even number ruins all chances of an apex formed of one twining turn.

From rows seventy-seven through ninety-nine, No. 34 could weave with no thought for size or shape. Within this distance, however, a cap maker must duplicate the top border and arrange an entirely new design motive for the narrow third zone.

Addition of sticks in storage baskets.—From the technical aspect caps rank first in difficulty among Yurok-Karok weavers, and always have. For impressiveness, according to present-day informants, the big storage cipnuks of the old-time Indians have no equal. Cipnuks varied in size from fifteen inches in height up. The largest one in the University museum (pl. 39), stands thirty-four inches high and is about thirty-seven inches in diameter at its greatest width. It has seven sticks, and nine twining courses to the inch. A basket is turned during the progress of weaving by pulling on its sticks. As a result, the sticks of any basket, no matter how small, will show a tendency to spiral to the left. A weaver stops her work frequently, grasps a handful of the sticks and pulls them vigorously to the right in an effort to counteract the swirl. The sticks in the big storage basket at the museum are four and a half inches off the vertical and its craftsmanship is clearly of high standard. The start of that basket is similar to the start for all-stick trays, plates, and wood baskets. In this case two sets of four sticks are crossed by two other sets at right angles. To the original thirty-two ends there must be added enough more to count approximately eight hundred twelve at the basket's greatest circumference. By the time all-stick twining reaches the boundary between

Fig. 28. Cleft hazel stick for flattening maidenhair fern stems before splitting off the black side.

base and side wall, the ratio is about one original stick to seven new ones. This counts up to some two hundred twenty-four, a number still a long way from enough. Just at the turn new sticks are added by two's and four's bringing the total much nearer to the required number. The remainder, when we recall what can be developed from an original sixteen in a cap, does not seem so formidable. No exact analysis has been attempted, but wherever the drawing in the transparent plate cover of plate 39 shows a Y, there a stick has been inserted. At midpoint the top begins to be drawn in definitely. This is the single legitimate occasion for cutting out a foundation stick to combine its stub with an adjacent stick. Although this technical device is condemned in attempts to remedy pattern miscounts, it is regularly resorted to when the top of a basket must be made appreciably smaller than its greatest circumference. The inverted Y's show numerous examples found within a defined area. Here too, as in the cap, rhythm is lacking; similarly, also, fewer increases and decreases come within the patterned areas.

DESIGN SETTING

The hardest single feature of a basket is the beginning or setting of a design. Difficulties of gathering and preparing materials are physical; technical proficiency is a matter of experience plus conformance to tried methods. But the placing of a pattern in a basket presents to each weaver a specific problem which makes unusual demands upon her mental ability. There is no rule-of-thumb method, the knowledge of which will automatically solve the problem. If two baskets have patterns started the same distance up on their sides, they will presumably have had added the same number of sticks to the original eight or ten at the center start. That being the case, the divisions for marks and spaces in each will be identical and a woman saves time by setting the first pattern row on the second basket soon after making her computations for the first. Naturally this binds her to duplicating her designs, but some weavers think repetition is less to be dreaded than planning for a different pattern. If only mediocre or poor basket makers complained of the difficulty of setting a mark, the matter would be comparable to any task requiring effort. Poor weavers bungle the possibilities for perfection through inaccurate calculations; good weavers send the children out of the house while they wrestle with the problem. To talk at this stage is out of the question even for the woman who ordinarily works as well in a sociable group as alone.

There are in practice three methods of apportioning sticks for the pattern and those for the spaces between motives: to measure for both with part of the hand, with a twig, or root; to count for both; or, to combine measuring for spaces with counting of sticks to be used in the pattern motive. Measuring is a gamble, entirely. So many triangular forms are used in Yurok-Karok designs that the first prerequisite is to set off an odd number of sticks for a base so that the apex may come to a single stick. Measuring is not precise enough to take into account one stick. The combination method is the lazy weaver's favorite. Measuring is certain to be inaccurate, informants told me, but an error of from one to three sticks will be tolerated even by weavers of high standards if the basket is intended for household use. The best makers and the more painstaking of the average ones use the second method, counting for both pattern motives and spaces. The usual procedure is to tie sticks together in groups. For a triangular unit this may mean groups of thirteen or fifteen sticks alternating with one stick left free to make the space between bases, or the grouping may be the reverse if the triangle apex is on the first pattern course as in a zigzag design. No. 14, the daughter of an expert weaver, illustrated her way of setting patterns as taught her by her mother. She counts fifteen sticks for the triangle, for example, then thirty-five for the space, fifteen, thirty-five, and so on around, tying each group with a root. If her last space totals thirty-eight sticks instead of thirty-five, she loosens all ties to begin over, this time counting out a thirteen-stick triangle base. Nine, eleven, thirteen, and fifteen are customary numbers to work with; spaces, too, in some designs may be varied in length, a fact which suggests numerous permutations. For really fine work a good basket maker does not begrudge the time nor patience required to perfectly adjust motives and spaces. There are informants who will make recounts for a surplus of one or two sticks. The reason is simple: that same one or two sticks at the beginning of a pattern motive easily pass unnoticed. As weaving progresses, with gradual additions of sticks to increase the size of the basket, the error may grow to make special demands on ingenuity. Since, according to the standard technique of this region, surplus sticks are removed from baskets only in constricting the tops of fancy or storage baskets, and since sticks are regularly worked in two's only at the point of inserting an extra, or in diagonal twining, Yurok-Karok weavers have a paradoxical rule: add more sticks when there are too few or too many for a motive. The necessary increase in number must be foreseen, moreover, at the time of tying up the groups for the first pattern course. If, for instance, it were to be discovered that the last motive or space count lacks a half-dozen sticks to make it right, those cannot be introduced at one spot or the basket will lose shapeliness. They must be inserted at different places on the same or immediately following courses (pl. 17*a*). A weaver considers all these interrelated difficulties a part of the setting of the mark.

Fillers.—Given that an inaccurate division of sticks is made, that a weaver does not rip back her work to start over again, or that she does not provide the necessary number of additional sticks, she must prepare to resort to an expedient. Either she will increase the size of the last motive, or she will fill the space with a pattern unit much reduced in size (pl. 13*b*), or perhaps she will fill the space with an unrelated design element (pl. 33*b*). Fillers are not necessities suggested by a vacancy for which technique is responsible, as in imbricated basketry of rectangular forms.[28] In the circular twined Yurok-Karok baskets there is no need for makeshifts, my informants agree, if correct division of the sticks is made before starting the design. On the whole, the best basket makers are tolerantly inclined toward the implicated carelessness. Even good weavers make such mistakes and it is hard to have to rip work. Besides, the space looks so small at first. As it grows larger it must be decorated and the filler is the solution. These were some of the reactions to obvious fillers seen in plates 13*a* and 40*b*.

"Hard" and "Easy" Designs

An informant's characterization of a basket pattern as "hard" (figs. 31, 32) or "easy" (fig. 29) is synonymous with her estimation of the difficulty involved in planning its first course. Comparison between the flint mark in the cap shown in plate 24*a*, previously analyzed from another standpoint, and the foot mark in plate 11*a* will illustrate this. The flint mark in its simplest variation is divided into two right isosceles triangles. The lowest course of a single motive given in letters to indicate color changes runs thus:

B B/W W W W W/B B B B B B B B B B B B B B B B B B B B B B B B B B (33)

Most caps with isolated design units are encircled by three motives with three intervening spaces. To set this particular type of mark the weaver experimentally ties up three pattern groups of thirty-three sticks, leaving approximately equal spaces between them; from then on she shifts, recounts, and reties groups until trial and error result in a satisfactory adjustment. This may necessitate a slight variation in motive sizes. It will for all but the most exact workers. My analysis of the design in plate 24*a*, as indicated in the draft above shows a flint-motive base on thirty-three sticks. Choice was made of the three motives most nearly mathematically correct. The unit centering the plate has a base on thirty-seven sticks. So small a discrepancy to start with shows up with the increasing size of the basket, as might be noticed with the actual cap in one's hand. No. 3 criticized the corner triangles in this cap; they differ in size. For our purpose, suppose the adjustment to have been made perfectly, since most informants subscribe to calling the flint mark an easy one to set. It has been noted that there is something to argue in this description.

---

[28] F. Boas *et al.*, Coiled Basketry, 281.

Fig. 29. Easy designs from the point of view of starting the first pattern row of twining.

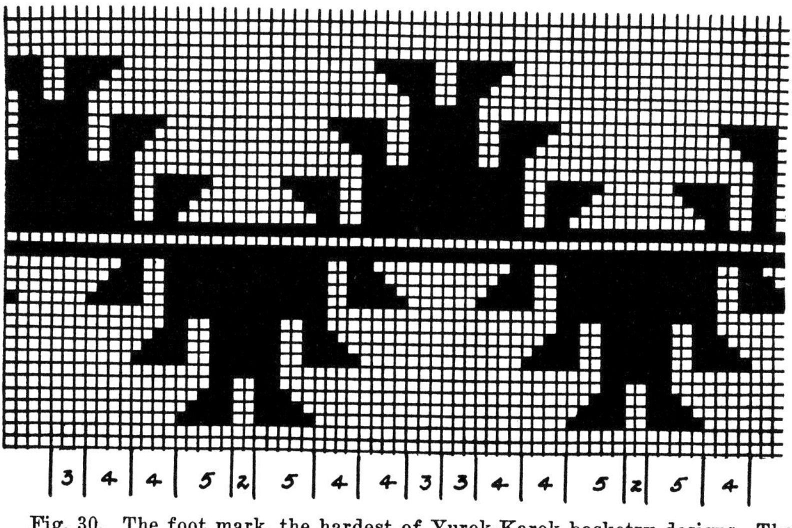

Fig. 30. The foot mark, the hardest of Yurok-Karok basketry designs. The counting for the first pattern row must allow for the subsequent development of the design.

The foot mark is termed hard with reason. In its continuous form it often appears as inverted alternate motives diverging from a center band. From its numerous variations the simplest has been chosen for analysis (fig. 30). The first course is composed of a recurrent series of short unequal element lengths and spaces. This is a much more elusive set of potentialities with which to cope than the group in the flint mark. Upon the correct calculation for the first pattern course depends provision for the subsequent development of duplicate motives inverted above the center band. For the reason that any insertion of new sticks would disrupt the allocation of sticks for design elements and spaces, the foot mark is confined, so far as I know it in baskets made by weavers on the Klamath river, to food types and fancy baskets. In these the final introduction of extra sticks is well below the decoration. Caps on this score are barred out. There are about a hundred caps in the University collection. The foot mark is found in a single cap; the design appears in the form of four separate units around the center root disc. Unfortunately the print shown my informants was small and the design escaped everyone's notice (pl. 30*b*). If it had been seen, the cap would undoubtedly have been criticized as displaying the wrong choice of mark to harmonize with the main motive.

Regardless of the design chosen, the placing of two or more horizontal bands in the same basket is difficult. It is so rare to find the second band units woven exactly above the first and identical in every detail, that it must be concluded that the effect lacks aesthetic interest. The use of crosswise pattern bands is practically confined to fancy modern types. In these the second or other bands may duplicate the count of the first for the same reason given above: the number of sticks has been increased to its full requirement prior to the setting of the pattern.

A technical difficulty present in any design motive with irregular outline lies in the necessity for frequently breaking overlay strands. This feature will be dealt with more in detail in connection with Devices. If a weaver were to copy the foot design from a finished basket with the problem of setting the mark already solved, she would still consider the design hard because of its continual alternation of colors. Each successive change is started, ideally, with an overlay strand snapped off at completion of its previous use, possibly not more than three twining turns back. Consequently, a beaded effect along the slant edges of a flint or a wax'poo mark is sufficient to transfer those so-called easy designs into hard ones (pls. 21*a*, 26*b*).

Fig. 31. Hard designs, so-called because of the number of calculations necessary before starting the design.

No one dislikes hard designs particularly. Good weavers will state very frankly that they do not make certain marks because they are difficult to set. Nos. 5, 7, and 17 are among the most skilful of my informants. No. 7 has used the spread-finger design (fig. 32*g*, *h*, *i*) recently, but would only duplicate it on an order for that specific design; No. 17 admired flints-with-points (fig. 31*e*, *g*) but will not

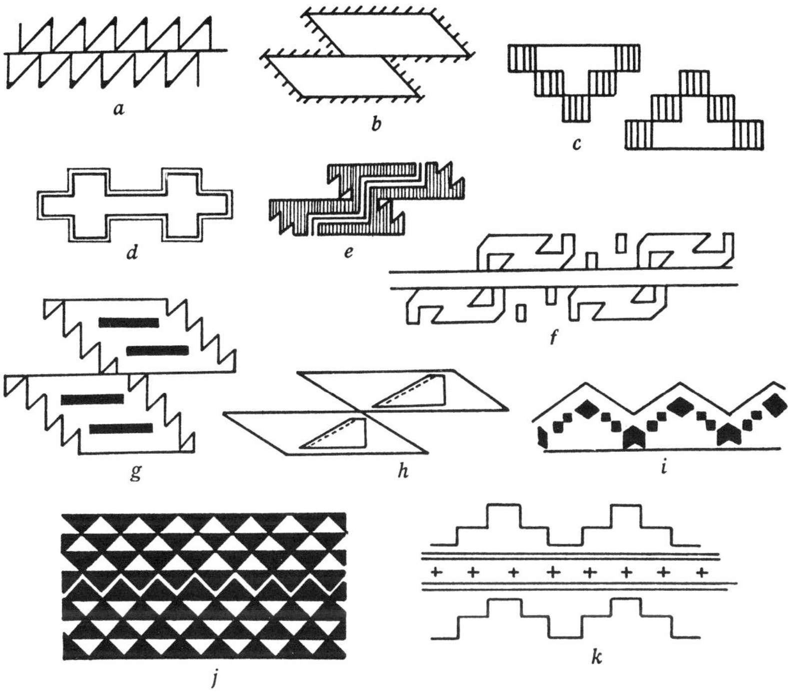

Fig. 32. Hard designs, so-called because of the counting and planning necessary at the start of the design.

make it for the chance customer. A very average weaver called my attention to the fact that guesswork and ripping took materials as well as time.

Designs called hard have been listed in table 14 together with informants so characterizing them. The column headings under which each informant is placed indicates my estimate of her ability. More than half of the forty-three women are represented and a sufficient number of reactions from those capable of excellent workmanship is recorded to make the design characterization convincing.

TABLE 14

"HARD" AND "EASY" DESIGNS

Design name	Illustration	Rating of informants' workmanship				
		Excellent	Good	Average	Poor	?
Cut wood	Figure 31*c*, *d*, *k*					
Hard:			10	8, 11		
Easy:		20, 24	6	42		13, 15
Flint, beaded	Figure 31*b*					
Hard:			17	8		
Flint-and-points	Figures 31*e*, *g*					
Hard:		14, 29	10, 17, 21	8, 10		
Foot*	Figures 32*a*, *b*, *c*, *d*,					
Hard:	*e*, *f*	14, 29	5, 18, 21	8, 11, 35	12, 19	3, 4
Easy:		28	5, 10, 22		12	
Spread-fingers	Figures 32*g*, *h*, *i*					
Hard:			1, 5, 7, 17, 25	8, 16, 27		3
Zigzag	Figures 29*f*, 31*a*					
Hard:			10, 17	11		
Easy:			6			

* The seeming contradiction in the cases of Nos. 5 and 12 is due to their evaluation of some foot mark arrangements as "hard," others "easy." This is in special reference to figure 32*a*, which is judged to be easier than in most of its forms. No. 28 makes this one mark over and over again; naturally, repetition has made it easy.

Design copying and plotting.—To copy an old basket of authentic shape and unquestioned traditional design is the easiest as well as the safest way to insure a good result. In former days whatever reproducing of very old baskets was done must have been largely from memory, as all a woman's possessions were destroyed at her death. Now it is not unusual to be told that your informant uses her mother's baskets, or that she cherishes them as an unbroken group (pl. 4*b*), or that she has finished some partly completed baskets to remind her of a deceased child. In line with this changed attitude a number of pattern marks were singled out as favorites of dead relatives, marks which are still made by informants because the designs give a basket a good, old look, or because the motive has sentimental associations. Very far from the recent avoidance of any mention of the dead, Yurok-Karok women now seem to take pleasure in recalling what and how things were done by them.

Practically all weavers copy from old baskets, some of which are kept solely for that purpose. No. 6 preserved baskets her aunt had used as models for her own weaving. They were left to the younger woman with the admonition to keep them, that they would save her much time. A weaver may even buy a basket, take off the count of the pattern, and resell the original when she has completed her own weaving. An expert will work faster from a model and it is frequently said that any woman can reproduce any design if the count for setting the mark is before her. With such aid there is no excuse for a poor joining at the completed circle.

Besides old soup baskets and caps past usefulness except as pattern guides, one Karok informant cleans and stores fragments of old baskets (pl. 4*c*). Most valuable are the entire bottoms which show the count for the pattern. Lacking the bottom, a design unit from the side is preserved. No informant had the least objection to the idea of keeping a whole basket for a model but, for some reason or other, this remnant device was disapproved of by nearly every woman to whom I explained it. Piecing together different phrases, I found the criticism amounted to this: when a good weaver makes a basket once, she can do it again from memory. That is the traditional workmanlike method. If No. 27 had been well taught and had talent for weaving she would require no artificial aids like basket fragments; she would just think of her basket and then make it. Therefore she could not be a real weaver.

An original device was described to me by a maker of Jumping dance baskets. She picks up the requisite number of sticks for a single unit of the pattern, holds them flat as if starting a dance basket, and works out the mark upon these loose sticks. If she is planning some new mark or initials for an order, this method allows the addition of an indefinite number of sticks. When she has progressed past the point of further difficulty she computes for the pattern in her basket and begins to work from her guide. The extra time involved is more than balanced, in her mind, by the certainty that there need be no ripping during the real weaving. It is partly the handling of loose sticks which discourages women from attempting Jumping dance baskets. Consequently the method struck several informants as curious rather than helpful.

There is no sketching of basket designs among Yurok-Karok weavers, according to my informants. The nearest approach to it is a diagram on paper. Diagrams are commonly used among white women to indicate the pattern stitches in crocheted filet lace. The method might easily have been suggested to Indian basket makers who crochet by the lace itself or by the pictures of work frequently shown in modern women's magazines. I have been in rooms completely papered with pages from these, although the occupants had never been inspired to translate the illustrated patterns in terms of drafting for their basketry.

Four Karok informants worked from diagrams; one Yurok was credited with doing so but denied being able to do more than copy baskets from a picture. The Karok women had different methods of making their patterns but each insured a mathematically correct division of the sticks for the all important first course of the design. No. 31 draws lines on a sheet of paper to check it into eighth-inch squares. Dots in certain of them indicate the pattern overlay. She may have to add sticks to her basket to make her design units all the same size but this necessity is clear before she begins work. She had taught the scheme to No. 27, her sister. No 27 taught her own daughter who does not weave, but who has become adept at reproducing on paper basket patterns from pictures or from memory.

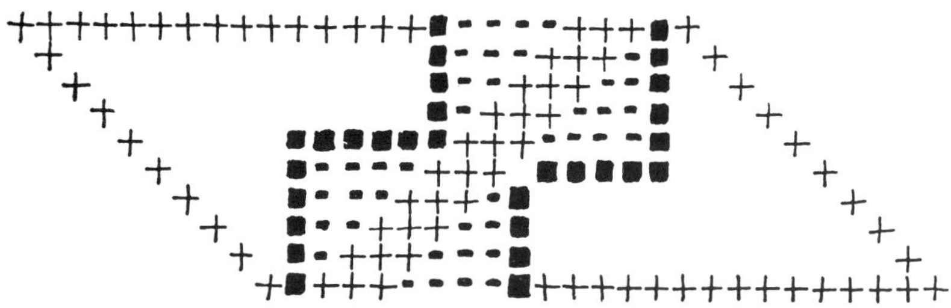

Fig. 33. No. 29's design draft. Made on plain paper but with indication of the number of sticks involved in the pattern, and the colors to be used.

Diagrams, of which No. 27 has a quantity also, and her basketry remnants already spoken of are looked upon with the same tolerant disapproval we might feel for a would-be mathematician who counts on his fingers. Aids may be excusable for an occasional pattern but reliance upon them is a confession. No. 29 is quick and observant. She plans a design on plain paper by a method original, so far as she knows, with herself. Her draft shows count and also the colors to be used. If she were to plan a snake mark in a flint (fig. 33), by way of illustration, she explained how she would put down X's for black, and dashes for the yellow quills to indicate the count for the first row. By diagramming a whole motive with due allowance for the addition of sticks she can bisect a unit and still feel certain of corners equal in size which they should be. She contrasted her draft with the cap in plate 28*a*; the latter shows an error in spacing.

SHORT-CUTS AND DEVICES

A short-cut, like crossing two sticks in twining instead of one, is known to all basket makers. All, too, have methods for freshening the cured grass to render it pliable. Some informants dip it in water then leave it spread on the ground all night; some soak the grass in cold or warm water just before using it. A method followed chiefly among Yurok weavers is that of burying the strands in a container full of damp sand. This method has the advantage of convenience because no harm can come to the grass as in oversoaking, but the strands are gritty to work with and unpleasant to hold in one's mouth.

If work could be done early in the morning, the materials would be at their best. Weavers, especially the cap makers, look forward to fog and rain. Sticks and weaving strands in fine baskets are so small that materials dry out quickly. When caps are made in the summer a weaver will close doors and windows in efforts to keep out the wind. During the afternoon the air is thoroughly dry and finer work is laid aside for less careful weaving, such as cooking and soup baskets, or even the sale fancy baskets. The beginning of any basket, including caps, is coarser than other portions of it. A weaver customarily makes up a number of centers on windy days or in the evenings. All baskets start alike but she sets limitations on the fineness of her subsequent work by her choice of the first sticks. As a usual thing even the best makers will select coarser sticks for the larger baskets; that is part of a well developed sense of scale. One Karok informant makes the beginning of a medium coarse basket, then cuts off the finer tip ends to use them in the start of a fine basket. Alternating the two she can use all her hazel sticks, scarce in her vicinity, and be ready to fill orders for different sizes of baskets.

When a pattern is developed by overlay, the fern or grass strand always faces the outer side of each root element. If the design occasions many color changes within a course, weavers characterize the pattern as one requiring much "breaking." To prevent the overlay from coming to the surface, a woman snaps the strand off against her left thumb nail and pushes the end through to the inside of the basket. Breaking the overlay means time and extra care. Where care is worth while in fine basketry it does not so impress the makers of household containers or fancy baskets medium-to-coarse in quality. Twisting the overlay in order to place it behind the root instead of snapping it off has always been a fairly common trick among both Yurok and

Karok weavers. This method reverses the pattern more or less exactly on the inside of the basket. It is not an unattractive effect for the larger types, and tedious breaking at the completion of a few twining stitches is obviated. No maker of a dress cap would resort to time saving by this method, nor would an old conservative weaver of modern fancy baskets; the craft ideal of such women is an inner surface as smooth as can be made; it shows plain root in contrast to the patterned outer surface. Some weavers do reverse the position of the overlay in weaving the more ordinary caps (pl. 30*a*, *b*). One single device of like character was given me by a Karok expert who uses porcupine quills in her small gift baskets. The quills are so short that a single additional turn of twining is welcomed. If black fern is to be worked in adjacent to the completed quill motive, the quill tip is extended for a stitch or so into the fern motive. The tip is a glossy black, only slightly different from maidenhair black.

Indian women use two old-time methods to mold their finished baskets to exact shape. No. 17 said she was a grown woman before she could make a basket that did not require to be filled with damp sand and patted into shape. That was commonly done to big storage baskets, which are even now kept tightly packed with old clothes to prevent sagging. With years of experience a weaver outgrows the need to give her basketry symmetry by finishing devices. Today's shapes, too, are less difficult to accomplish than the old ones. No. 28, who makes small modern trinket baskets, moistens them and fills them with beans to hold the shapes in position until the baskets dry out. A tiny cover is dampened, placed on the loaded basket, and held down with an iron ring which has been found the right weight for the purpose.

Cap makers use molds. Both Yurok and Karok informants showed me plain root caps made for this purpose. They are specially constructed on hazel sticks to insure rigidity. No. 20 keeps her work to the right size by frequently fitting it down over the mold; No. 41 dampens her mold before pressing the completed hat over it to dry. It is even possible to stretch a cap a little on one of them.

The ten-inch Indian plate should require no final shaping. The large hazel stick pans, thirty or more inches in diameter, are generally warped in the weaving. An old pan is placed bottom up on the ground and covered over with a wet quilt or rug. The new pan is pressed down over this and weighted with stones heavy enough to prevent any portion of the basket from springing back. By the time the rug is dry the new pan has been given its permanent shape.

No. 20 makes dozens of napkin rings for her holiday trade (pl. 51*d*). They are quick work and bring a fair price. Her method is to bind the eight sticks and insert additionals as for the start of a basket. About an inch from the center she turns all the sticks at right angles to begin close twining on the narrow cylinder. When the woven band is about two inches wide one napkin ring is finished. Leaving a space she makes a second and so on. Upon reaching the end of the sticks, she cuts between the bands.

Deliberately warping a basket to add to its appearance is evidence of expert control over technique. The very fault which betrays the unpracticed or inept weaver, too many inserted sticks to insure a smooth surface, is made capital of by No. 28 in weaving covers with high knobs (pl. 51*i*). Diameters of the knob tops range from three-eighths to three-fourths of an inch. The start is made in the usual manner with the first additions to the original eight sticks coming midway between the center and the turn. Where the knob appears constricted some sticks have been cut out (never done in ordinary weaving), others are carried inside for a core. New sticks are introduced at the base of the knob to allow for the cover proper. A wavy or fluted effect is given the surface by the insertion of more sticks than are required. Symmetry is maintained by the regular intervals between insertions. I did not hear of any other weaver who warped her basket surface and doubt the device being known. No. 28 works with her daughter only; all their products are sent out of the region.

Finishing Processes

The ends of the sticks, when the basket is finished, are usually cut off close to the last row of twining. According to some informants in both tribes the twining will not loosen and nothing is necessary to hold the ends of the two root elements which are presumably set fast in the drying. According to an old method a short length of hazel is folded over and held beside the last stick. One side of the folded length is treated as an extra stick, the other side doubles the size of the last regular stick. When twining has been done through the loop it is pulled down to secure the elements firmly. Nos. 1, 14, and 20 used this method of finishing; the last named occasionally transferred it to a loop of white string. All the women, to judge by numerous descriptions of it, know the root-loop finish but the majority of weavers sew over the basket edge with white string or thread. A technical inconsistency which is paralleled among primitive peoples working in other crafts is revealed by the casual way in which an essential detail is accomplished. Baskets of fine materials, with standards written in every feature of their making, will be ended with the most indifferent workmanship. To make their whipping stitches hold over the edge the Yurok-Karok weavers insert each successive stitch under a different course of twining. It is not uncommon to see stitches reaching down a half-inch, and spreading over a distance almost as wide. I found a single informant who thought the white threads unsightly, and she sewed with Indian string made from the fibers of the *iris macrosiphon* leaf because the American storekeeper told her her baskets would sell better if she used the native material.

Cleaning the basket.—From the very beginning of work there is concern for the completed basket. The base of each stick was stripped to half its diameter, not only to make its insertion less noticeable but also to render the end more easily scraped off when time came to clean the basket. The finishing process begins with a thorough drying. Frequently this is done in the sun or by propping up the work before an open fire. Now, with stoves, a woman puts her basket on the floor beneath.

Weavers of earlier days might partly singe the inside of the common food baskets by holding them over a blaze. That left only a portion of the ends to be scraped out with a sharp rock or shell. Informants at present use metal spoons, although No. 1 said she still kept to a mussel shell tool because it could not cut the root-twining elements. I found only one weaver who singed her basket, thus running the risk of a sooty product. She wove solely for her own use. A very careful weaver, No. 7, uses in addition to an old mussel shell, a small brush about an inch in diameter, made of the short discarded tips of hazel sticks (pl. 3*b*). After drying her basket she scrapes off with the shell all ends protruding on the inside and then brushes around with the stubby, stiffer end of her brush. When that is done she uses the side of the brush to rub off any bits of black fern edges from the outer surface, and finally smooths it gently with her fingers. If she has used porcupine quills in the pattern, each end must be clipped off close with a knife or pair of scissors. The fact that quills cannot be scraped like other materials is said to have prohibited the use of quills among the old people who lacked cutting tools fine enough for such work.

STANDARDS

STANDARDS FOR MATERIALS

A good basket begins with the choice of materials used in its construction. A food basket requires sticks, roots, and grass overlay. The work cap adds black or red-dyed fern to the three essentials; a dress cap or a fancy basket may call for as many as six kinds of fiber: sticks, tree-root strands for binding the start, willow-root twining elements for the center disc, overlay of black fern, grass, and quills. A woman at her basketry is fairly surrounded by materials.

Some generalization has already been made in the section on Materials regarding relative values of the roots and sticks. A weaver who runs short of supplies at the end of a year may be forced, for example, to substitute split willow root for pine root. Her lack is no reflection on her knowledge of craft standards. But certain things a good weaver will not do: she will not use fine and coarse sticks together, because a well shaped basket cannot be made from the combination. She watches the decreasing size of the sticks as work progresses, and replaces those thinner or poorer than the rest. If uniformity of sizes is not maintained, the surface of the basket will lack smoothness. When a stick snaps off, or needs extending, a weaver can make an almost invisible graft by cutting a deep cleft in the end of a new stick of similar size, then placing it to straddle the old stick an inch from its stub end. The twining elements hold the new and the old firmly together. As on every other occasion all ends are pushed to the inside of the basket. Again, a good basket maker will not use white grass blades of different sizes or renew two overlay strands at the same spot, because the surface will show unevenness, nor will she split a grass blade for a size to match that already in use. Primary sorting has been done poorly when either expedient is necessary.

Other refinements are so obvious to any informant, and so casually accomplished by the weaver at work, that an observer stumbles upon them by chance. For example: there is a glossy side and a dull side to white grass and dyed fern. The good basket maker inserts the base end of a new strand for an overlay pattern; she knows by the feel of the midrib that she has the dull side next to the root twining element. As with grass, there is a right side to porcupine quills which should be kept uppermost in overlaying. After moistening, quills are flattened by running, not scraping, the thumb nail over each one. A careless weaver knows these details but lets her grass twist; she seldom works with quills, which everyone recognizes are not only short but troublesome to handle.

STANDARDS FOR WORKMANSHIP

Criteria for Quality

In diagonal twining, double-stick work, as the Indians call it, there are the same two active elements as in plain twining. Each element passes over and under two sticks instead of one at a turn. On each successive row there is a progression of one stick to the right or left so that the crossing shifts from over sticks one and two to over sticks two and three, sticks three and four, and so on.[29] Twining over two sticks at once is variously rated by different weavers. Most of them say it is quicker than twining over a single stick at a time. The real point involved is whether or not a weaver with standards will make use of the short cut. According to No. 39 it never was considered nice work. Lazy or poor people with just enough baskets for actual use had only double-stick things, whereas the well-to-do, whose rooms were lined with fine baskets, made double-stick containers from waste sticks for acorns. In former times soup basket bottoms might be in double-stick technique. The man's soup dish was commonly begun in this manner, the woman's more often in single-stick work because she ate from the cooking basket which must be strong as well as water-tight. Here there was some difference of opinion with regard to double-stick work in a cooking basket. It does seem to have been customary to make several courses in the quicker technique, a device to straighten up a basket on the way to becoming wobbly.

The crossing of two sticks at once is never done in a cap except at the insertion of a new stick; the method is never used in developing any pattern other than twilling, which automatically develops from the combination of diagonal twining and an uneven number of basket warps. Today the motive behind double-stick work is frankly commercial, and not approved by some conservatives. Two weavers from the oldest age group, Nos. 1 and 17, four from group 2, Nos. 5, 25, 31, and 36, and one from group 3, No. 14, never use the speedier method. One of them questioned its being quicker. These seven

[29] Mason, Basketry, 234.

women keep to the old-time way of making the basket of uniform fineness throughout. Five weavers, Nos. 9, 10, 27, and 37 from group 2 and No. 15 from group 3 always use double-stick twining on the bottoms of their sale baskets; it is easier and as strong. The saleability is not impaired, according to No. 10, but she was quick to say that her mother, No. 7, and other fine workers would not lower the real quality of their baskets by descending to the easy method. Of the latter group only No. 37 has a reputation as an expert among her own people; among the seven who do not favor the method five are characterized as expert. No. 14, for instance, who overlays her entire basket except for the three-strand disc at the start, could not be expected to approve of double-stick work in plain root.

Sometimes a woman in her effort to make me see the ideal of technical perfection would describe a basket as being smooth as paper or painting. Fineness in a basket is less important than consistently even workmanship (pl. 46*a*, *b*, *c*). Different types have their own prerequisites. By comparison with a cap a food basket is coarse work; the sticks are larger, root strands and grass overlay relatively wider. It must resist strain of weight and handling. It has standards of its own to measure up to if it would escape criticism: uniform size of sticks, however coarse, untwisted root elements, and grass strands to make a smooth surface.

Less fineness is expected in caps of the red-white combination with black fern than of the black-white combination with porcupine quills. Plain root caps with grass and fern patterning will be called good in spite of their coarseness if they are well shaped, the marks are evenly spaced, and the overlay covers all of the root twining base. The same trio of qualities, shaping, spacing, and successful coverage might equally describe an admired quill cap with the exception of the adjective coarse. Table 15, of counts made on grass overlay, dyed-fern overlay, and plain root caps will illustrate this point. The count of the number of sticks and twining courses per inch was made immediately below the top three-strand twine (the Karok "arav"). This point is beyond the final insertion of sticks for size and shape, whatever the type of cap.

Evidence of superior workmanship as well as conformance to an old ideal is proved by the line of steps at the beginnings of successive rows of weaving. The coarser the work, the more clearly the progression from the end of the old course to the new one may be seen. In case of a color change at this point the step is doubly visible. A cap weaver always plans to make the step come at the center back, where it is hidden when the cap is worn, as an informant explained to me. A straight line of steps up a single stick is perfection. The line in plate 23*a* was given as a good example to contrast with the join in plate 44*b*. No addition of sticks, which it was admitted might shift the line slightly for a little distance, could be adequate excuse for the poor planning in the latter basket. No. 38 said it was reminiscent of her grandmother's work after blindness came upon her. Old women with dim eyesight customarily tie a root to the stick at the beginning of the new course in order to approximate a straight line of shifts from one row or one color to another.

TABLE 15

STANDARDS OF QUALITY AS BASED ON COUNT

Grass-overlay caps				Red-fern-overlay caps				Plain-root caps		
Specimen number	Plate	Sticks per inch	Rows per inch	Specimen number	Plate	Sticks per inch	Rows per inch	Specimen number	Sticks per inch	Rows per inch
1-20822		17	18							
1-4384	19*a*	16	25							
1-27877		16	20							
1-1692	24*b*	15	18							
1-1593	21*b*	15	16							
1-20834	26*a*	14	19							
1-1609	24*a*	14	17							
				1-26812	30*a*	13	19			
				1-27054	30*b*	13	18			
1-27175	23*b*	12	18							
1-20824	19*b*	12	17					1-27174	12	17
1-1610	25*b*	12	16							
								1-1496	12	15
				1-27055	31*b*	12	14			
1-1831		11	16							
1-1439	25*a*	11	13							
				1-374		10	17			
1-371	26*b*	9	13							
1-1804		9	13							
								1-1498	9	12

Tolerance

In spite of caustic criticism of different phases of basketry there is a surprising amount of tolerance shown. If a mistake was obvious, one that could not possibly be overlooked by an experienced weaver, the work was often attributed to an old woman. Age, as such, does not limit a weaver's activities; she goes for her own materials, makes her preliminary preparations, and weaves, often after she is half blind. Only one informant among my number wore glasses. It is not likely that any Indian women were wearing them at the time when the baskets were purchased for the University of California collection.

Therefore the work of a good many weavers must have become less representative of tribal standards with the years. Very simple designs like stripes, diagonal twining, running flint marks, or zigzags are chosen by old people. Miscounts within the same design, sometimes groups of four sticks, at others six sticks to a unit (pl. 15*a*) were pointed out as evidence of an old woman's failing eyesight; a scattered group of shapes, or a meaningless motive (pl. 25*a*), were often excused on the ground of a weaver's age. Concerning the last design, No. 16, my oldest informant, said her grandmother used to make marks like that when she had partly lost her sight and that the younger people of her household laughed at such effects. Any of the failures to attain high technical standards may be attributable to age. When a woman is obliged to tie a string or root on a foundation stick to indicate she has completed a round of twining, her knowledge of perfection is of little assistance. Several times my informants produced caps and other baskets made by some very old relative to show me the quality that could rightfully be expected of old people.

The same tolerant attitude was held for the unmistakable first work of a young girl. "Practicing," informants called it. In very few cases did an informant think this sort of poor work could have been done by an old woman. There were only four baskets among the four hundred fifty odd which, from their unconventional designs, might as reasonably have been made by an inexperienced young weaver as by a handicapped old one. The criteria in these few cases are apart from technical ability, which generally betrays to one basket maker the relative age of another.

RAPIDITY OF ACCOMPLISHMENT

No one of my Yurok-Karok informants would venture an estimate of the number of baskets she might be able to finish during a year. If she worked at her craft as a professional she said she made "lots"; if it were more in the nature of an avocation she "could not make very many." Only one of the forty-three informants, No. 7, gives unlimited time to basketry; the rest have household duties. No. 17, who has been selling baskets as a chief source of livelihood for forty years, worked at most three to four hours a day.

Getting at the number of days required for a single basket of a certain type is less difficult but not much more exact. There is the story of a Yurok girl who lived on the point at the confluence of the Klamath and Trinity rivers. Day after day she escaped the attentions of a persistent suitor by going very early in the morning to a spring; there she worked on her baskets. Each day at evening she came back with a finished cap. This is obviously a tale, but an old woman over a hundred years old, who lived near Wahsekw below Weitspus, is reputed to have duplicated the heroine's feat. From a more reliable source, No. 39's mother, a Karok above the Ti district, is said to have made a work cap in one day, although she is the only Karok known to have accomplished this feat.

TABLE 16

TIME ELEMENT IN BASKET MAKING

Basket type	Informant	Own estimate	Time required
All-stick			
Plates	20	Fast	One day for three about 10-inch size
Market, hand	24	Fast	One day for two, complete
Cradles	7	Not fast	One day for two, complete*
Close-twine			
Soup	9	Slow	One month for 8-inch basket; works all the time
	18	Fast	One week for the fast worker
	20	Fast	Three days, if on an order
	21	Not slow	One week, possibly; quick work with house to care for
Fancy	5	Slow	One day, possibly, for cup-size. She works too slowly for that
	8	Fast	Two days for one 2-inch gift size, order One month for four 2-inch baskets
	15	Very slow	One month for a basket
Cap	5	Slow	Two weeks quick work
	17	Fast	One week might be enough if able to work three or four hours a day. Two weeks for her; eyes tire.
	21	Not slow	Two weeks quick with housework
	28	Fast	Three or four days if one could sit down all day long. One week for average worker is quick work.
	39		Some can go no more than 2 to 4 courses in a day
Big storage	24	Fast	Thinks it would take one to two years to finish big sizes

* No. 7 traded her cradles to a white storekeeper. At the end of a year he had said that with three more cradles she would have made him a hundred. She picked all the willow; her sons peeled and stacked it; they all worked nights.

Reference to any of these achievements always provoked personal comparisons. No one now known is able to make the plainest sort of cap in one day. A fast worker was defined as the weaver who got up early in the morning when all her materials were damp and pliable. Early risers work most quickly and make the smoothest baskets.

There is, however, no stigma attached to being a slow worker, for while five women by their own confession take a long time to a basket, the number includes the best as well as average weavers. No. 8, an informant who is quick at turning out her products, said speed depended upon familiarity with the design and upon uninterrupted time almost as much as upon adeptness. A weaver cannot work steadily all day; the turning of a big basket against the knee forces the whole body to hold an unnaturally strained position. Incidentally, the woman with good teeth has an immense advantage over her less fortunate neighbors.

A custom which makes estimates largely speculative is that of having from two to twelve or more baskets at various stages of completion. For the professional weaver, this is good business since it offers the buyer a range from caps to hand baskets, a choice of designs, and fair assurance that the work will be delivered within the time promised. For the woman who works at her craft less steadily, several baskets started at one time is a device to save trouble in setting her designs (there may be duplicates), or it provides a diversity of work. Again, like our own women who do fine sewing, an Indian weaver may be years finishing some of her basket starts.

The factors mentioned leave any estimate open to correction; but, with appreciation of the varying hours in a weaver's "day" and her own opinion of her speed as a worker, table 16 shows a degree of consistency.

COOPERATION AND THE CONCEPT OF DESIGN OWNERSHIP

Cooperation among weavers implies a willingness to share designs. It involves the concept of ownership. Although everyone is positive that no single design belongs to any specific weaver and ridicules the idea of being able to keep a new motive uncopied, practice differs somewhat from theory. Anyone *may* work out any design, but it is a saving of hours of labor and worry to be allowed to copy a basket mark or to be given the count of the sticks in its elements.

Reactions to the possibilities involved in true cooperation are too varied to generalize other than in a broad way. First, there are weavers who prefer to work alone, and one gave as her reason that she has all her patterns in her mind. Younger weavers might be looking for something new and need help from each other. Basketry with her is a business; she does not make of it a social diversion. Second, two or three weavers may form an exclusive little group to exchange designs among themselves. No. 15 said of a pattern new to her that she could copy No. 8's basket if it were finished before her own. These women are cousins; Nos. 7, 10, and 14 are within a family circle; Nos. 24, 25, and 26 are distant relatives; Nos. 20, 21, and 33 are neighbors as are Nos. 26 and 27, also Nos. 24 and 27. In each of these groups one woman is the leader type, a weaver who can be relied upon to hold a pattern in her mind long enough to make it in a basket; the others count from her weaving. The leader would be as well, if not better off, independent of this cooperative spirit.

Among Yurok weavers around Weitspus there was a sociable old custom of taking one's materials to the creek. Some women always worked with the same friend; others went every day to join any group of four or five. Working in the cool shade where supplies could be kept damp with no trouble formed the ideal set of circumstances for free exchange of patterns.

Four weavers among my informants were referred to as "pattern makers." There is no implication of inventiveness in the term; it refers to the possession of a reliable memory. Three pattern makers are old women with experience in recognizing the basic form of any design, for which doubtless they know the usual counts. After the recognition of elemental forms it devolves upon pattern makers to see the relationship between units and to memorize one or two counts in any details new to them. One of the four informants used as illustration the design in plate 16*b*. She knew it for the wax'poo mark and, if her interest lay in the particular size and its proportion to the basket, her memorizing could limit itself to the number of sticks in the base of the small triangle. A conventional wax'poo mark is made up of lengths and widths in definite relation to each other. Apparently a weaver does not lose caste by admitting that she relies on the superior memory of some member in her family. No. 6 is one of three sisters, all professionals, but one weaves models for the other two to copy. No. 14 took several basket prints to her mother-in-law, No. 7, to have her look intently at the designs. The old lady analyzed the motive by counting out some one of its elements. All her life No. 41 has been the source turned to by her family of three professionals for old designs as well as innovations. She found among the prints a number of motives which have not lasted into her daughters' generation, some of which had been crowded out of her own memory.

The quest for a design tribally authentic and yet new to the weaver has never ceased. It forms, for some women, the greatest interest at dances or when visiting. No. 8, known as a very quick worker, chanced to be present at the conclusion of my interview with her neighbor. She admired a picture of a cap in the print collection and had partly completed a small basket with the cap design as the motive when I called on her several days later. She was not entirely satisfied with the proportions and said that a first trial of a new pattern would always be rather uncertain. She thought this particular mark would look better in a larger basket; she would duplicate it at once to fix the counts in her memory. If the attempt turns out successfully, the weaver makes the design again and again until it finally takes its place in the repertory of the immediate locality. An up-river informant gave as her theory of variations in old marks the fact that a weaver's first duplication of a design made from memory could rarely be checked against the original. If the design deviated slightly, subsequent attempts based on reproductions of reproductions would ultimately result in basket marks with little relation to their prototypes. Exactness, she thought, could never be relied upon in working from memory.

A negative view of the matter of cooperation stresses a false ownership of designs which can last only so long as the basket is kept from the sight of acquisitive eyes. It seemed incredible to some women that weavers should want to hide their work; basket marks are common property and all a weaver should have to do is to ask the owner to lend her basket from which to copy. Evidently that request does not always receive the same answer. Nos. 25 and 34, experts representative of two generations of weavers, took it as a matter of course that weavers hid their patterns. No. 24, also Karok, complained that No. 20 asked to see others' baskets but never showed her own. The trouble here is that No. 24 is outside the neighborhood group. Yurok weavers are equally culpable. No. 16, my oldest informant, has a basket of her mother's make (the largest in her basket group, plate 2*b*). No. 7 greatly admires the old pattern but is not allowed to see it or the reproductions of its motives. The excuse always given is that the owner's work is not comparable to that of No. 7, but the old lady frankly acknowledged the real reason behind her pseudomodesty to me, a stranger. In these last cases there is no question of unfriendliness or selfishness, primarily. No. 13, who told me of drying her baskets in a box near the fire to prevent the patterns being seen by visitors, would lend a whole boatful of baskets to any friend "making a dance," or give from her own store to some woman who could not make a sturdy food container. It seems very like hugging a secret which loses any value it may have once it is known.

PROPERTY MARKS

Kroeber refers to property marks as "occasionally introduced in the weaving, certain small areas being covered with overlaying."[30] To begin with, a distinction had to be set up in the informant's mind between a design looked upon as a private possession and a basket made by or belonging to a specific weaver, as might be signified by a pattern detail. Some women were skeptical that any weaver would put into her basket a personal symbol; others were amused at the idea. The majority had never made or seen a property mark. In all, thirteen reactions are covered under these generalizations. My informants were certain no two weavers could make the same pattern identically alike, and the notion that a woman would not know her own baskets if she could handle them was ridiculous. At dances there are so many baskets that they are stacked in piles and yet a weaver can pick out her own.

But although there were Yurok and Karok women willing to speak thus broadly for their tribes, some old weavers remembered marks unrelated to the designs in a basket. Nos. 27, 34, and 35, the last two living in isolated communities, knew of them. No. 35 had outlined a few figures in black fern to identify her own baskets more quickly; No. 27 recalled the instance of an old woman who put the same pattern on each soup basket which she made to take to the dances. This old woman had told my informant it was a common custom in her own time.

By check of the actual baskets at the museum, four of the food type were found to include red-dyed or black fern design elements in their makeup. It would be illogical to consider them deliberate attempts to vary the decoration. Two of these baskets are shown in plates 16*a* and 18*a*. The other examples have an irregular series of twining turns of black fern at intervals near the top of the basket, or short lines of fern which look like identification marks. The variance of opinion coupled with the range in ages of those informants who deny the custom make it improbable that property marks were universally used or locally well developed.

---

30 Kroeber, Basket Designs, 116.

MEN'S ATTITUDE TOWARD THE CRAFT

A basket maker takes for granted that the men of her household know more or less about her craft. Men, they say, are used to seeing baskets around; they know the names of designs, the worth of a good basket, and something of the difficulties involved in the making of one. While it may be true that in the old days men did not help in the gathering of materials there were exceptions; I was reminded there would always be men who think it beneath them to offer aid in women's work and that some men are like that even now. Today, when basketry means income, most women take for granted not only their men's knowledge but their active help. With increasing distances to go for supplies their collection is becoming less and less strictly the job of women weavers. Men of group 1's generation brought in grass and roots for their wives and taught their sons how to choose good stock. The boys of an extremely shiftless Karok informant had been taught through practice and criticism to recognize qualities and prepare materials. A Yurok weaver had had to buy supplies only three times in her lifetime. Husband and sons brought in stuff from all directions, all "made," which meant sticks peeled, roots cooked or scraped. Her ability to turn out the hundred cradles that she wove during one year was made possible partly by her sons' help. Another old Yurok weaver who has not made baskets for many years still has annual supplies brought in by her husband. She gives them to her friends. Perhaps the most unusual case is that of a white man over ninety, according to his statement, who has an Indian wife. He explained to me in detail how he had learned the values of the several kinds of necessary materials from watching the progress of the work. Now his wife is old and he must do the gathering. Annually, he takes a pack horse back into the hills twenty miles or so. To the customary complaint of modern shortage he added his own: cutting down Christmas trees and pulling them through the giant fern is ruining the patches.

Occasionally the men of the family stayed the full time of an interview with their wives, two hours, a half-day, even a whole day. There was never the slightest self-consciousness on the basket maker's part at their presence, or any attempt to be jocular or patronizing on their own part. The women passed prints to all in the group, and a weaver often referred a subject to her menfolk for additional details. One husband who protested he knew very little about basketry proceeded to set aside all the examples of new-style patterns as we came to them among the pictures. The most interested listener and participant during a long interview with his aunt was a Yurok boy of sixteen. The women of his family depend upon him to go for those supplies from distant localities. The aunt discussed with him the pattern names, good and poor work, mistakes in design placing. He looked at every picture and frequently made comments about the start of a basket, the new-style strap handles, the shaping of an Indian all-stick plate, or the probable age of the weaver of a poor basket. It was all matter of fact; he had no interest in impressing me with his knowledge.

Men, probably with an eye to a sale, will evaluate their wives' work for a potential buyer. Behind such statements as "my wife makes dance baskets," or "she is the best cap maker on the river," there is a real pride. Something additional is involved here: such reputations are largely maintained among the Indians themselves. The cap maker, for instance, lives at Ko'ǫtep on the lower Klamath. She had sold one of her products in the Panamenik district, Karok territory. There is much more to that as a feat and as an indication of skill than in any sale of fancy baskets to white people.

FOREIGN WORK AND WORKMANSHIP

YUROK KNOWLEDGE OF KAROK AND HUPA

Trade, visits occasioned by ceremonial gatherings, and the interchange of wives made the Yurok, Karok, and Hupa acquainted with each other. Knowledge is patchy as far as basketry is concerned but with regard to gaps there is complete indifference.

The Yurok women know more about the Hupa than about the Karok. No. 12, who is unusually inquisitive, thought the Karok might make good baskets but she did not know. One or two other informants had heard of No. 20's work but they had relatives within the up-river territory which partly explained their information about Karok weavers. Yurok knowledge of the Hupa is more satisfactory. The Yurok traded chiefly with the Indians along the Trinity, taking to them redwood dugouts, sea food, and dentalia in exchange for inland foods and skins.[31] Yurok women say specific things of Hupa basketry and of its makers: that the only ones in the valley who do really good weaving are Yurok women married to Hupa men; that Hupa women

[31] Kroeber, Handbook, 132.

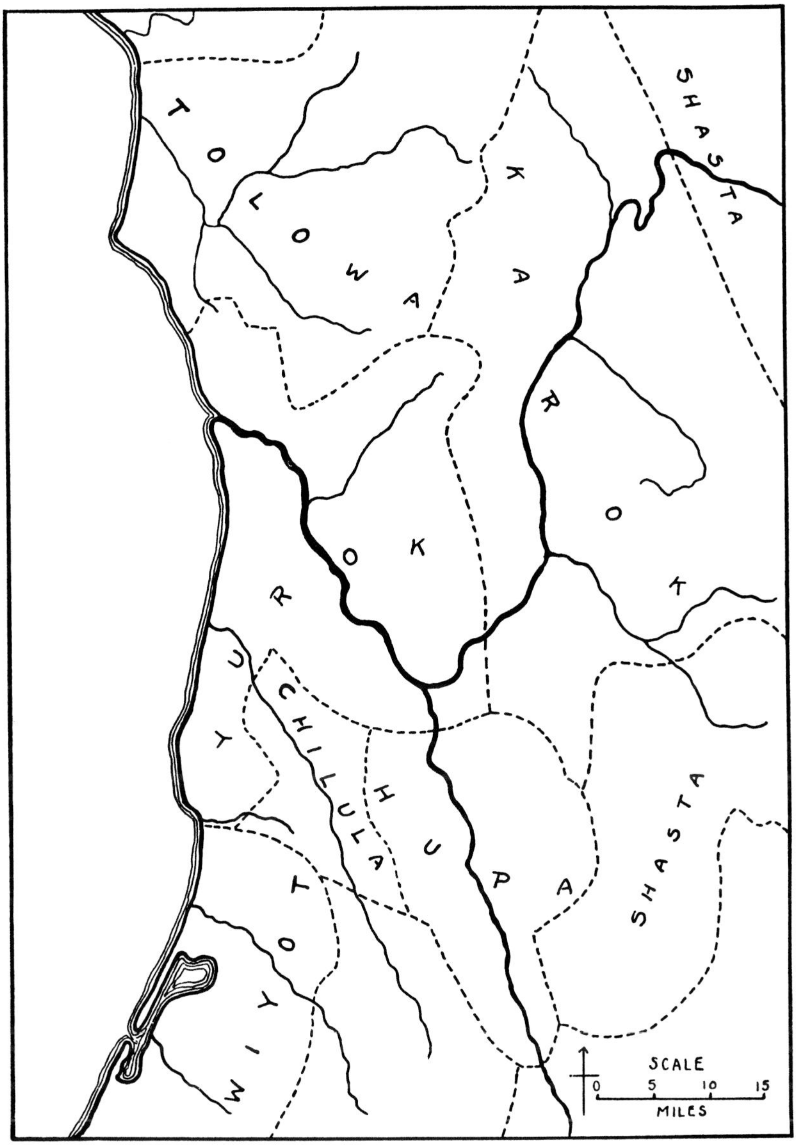

Fig. 34. Map to show the location of tribes adjacent to Yurok and Karok peoples.

lack pride in their work. Obviously such statements require corroboration from the Hupa angle. Probably the one basketry detail most often mentioned is the difference between the Yurok plaque-like sifter, which is shaken up and down, and the Hupa conical pan, which is tapped to shake through the fine meal. There is amusement at the form and wonder that any women can accomplish results with it; Yurok women confess their own inability.

The Hupa, according to Yurok informants, often betray their advanced notions in some unusual feature. As far away as Rekwoi, No. 1 asked me to confirm her suspicions that four globular baskets with new-style handles, covers, and knobs were Hupa products (pl. 48*a*). There is nothing about the baskets which could not have been achieved by any expert weaver, but to a Yurok the Hupa are the innovators. In these cases the intuition was correct, but to place any reliance on chance accuracies would be dangerous. There is so little upon which to base an identification of Yurok and Hupa workmanship, that those baskets with incomplete provenience data cannot be told apart positively.

KAROK KNOWLEDGE OF YUROK AND HUPA

Karok and Hupa peoples of the old days were generally on friendly terms but their products were too characteristically inland to stimulate contacts through barter.[32] From the craft aspect almost nothing definite was known of Hupa basketry by present-day Karok weavers. They recognized a general elaboration of pattern among the dance basket designs which, to them, was unmistakably Hupa, or something else, in feeling. In eight of the ten instances the baskets are actually Yurok, but it is the attitude which is significant. At present, the Karok enumerate the modern European details of ornamentation, ribbons, tinsel, and novelty effects in braids, which as substitutes for fur strips, feathers, and the other traditional embellishments have crept into Hupa dance regalia. The Karok say there is a similar trend in Hupa basketry and regret the cheapening. They, too, like the Rekwoi informant, suspected the Hupa of the new-style features, the handles and covers on baskets. (The baskets in question were purchased thirty years ago.) This implied criticism is from the conservative Karok who, it must be remembered, have never been in close contact with white settlers or thrown with members of other tribal groups

[32] Kroeber, Handbook, 132.

on a reservation, as have the Hupa. In fact, Karok informants know little of old Hupa customs although they make frequent trips into the valley to the government school.

If the Hupa are the progressives in Yurok minds, the Yurok are seen in that light by the Karok. Down-river traveling must have been common at all times, and intermarriages frequent. About a fifth of my informants had a parent or a husband from the other tribe. Among the Karok there is matter-of-fact recognition that Yurok weavers have a natural advantage in their quantities of available basket materials. A Yurok informant, married to a Karok, thought that abundant supplies explained the generally better quality of down-river basketry. Especially at Weitspus, she said, everything is handy and the workmanship is correspondingly uniform. A much older Yurok in Karok territory, No. 19, gave the palm for variety of patterns to the people down-river where, she said, everybody knows how to make good baskets. Nos. 24 and 33 made less complimentary remarks: Weitspus people invent marks; Karok weavers use the reputable old ones. Nos. 29, 32, and 41 accused the Yurok women of copying the up-river marks seen at dances. Sometimes the designs were changed a little, or there was an inaccurately rendered detail which betrayed a reliance on memory, but at base the designs were Karok. No. 32 admitted the Karok might be expected to do the same when they went to the down-river dances, yet thought there was less inclination among their people to look outside the tribal pattern catalogue. That statement would be open to argument, were opportunities afforded. However, with little question from the Karok standpoint, the adventurous ones, be the implication complimentary or not, are the down-river and Hupa people.

Table 17 setting forth the provenience ascribed to different baskets by Yurok and Karok weavers may be of interest. The details which led to allocation are not infallible, but they evidenced to some informants, at least, the probable origin of the specimens.

Within the much larger group attributed by Karok women on stylistic grounds to Yurok or Hupa weavers, the dance baskets (pls. 55, 56) may be considered illustrative of local developments in a highly specialized branch of the craft; the globular fancy baskets (pl. 48*a*) are results of modern tourist influence; and customs such as mud-dyeing sticks and storing tobacco in caps are as well-known foreign features as the conical Hupa sifter. These subtractions reduce the actual number, distinguished solely by their designs as foreign

TABLE 17

INFORMANTS' ATTEMPTED IDENTIFICATION OF BASKETS AND DESIGNS

Informant	Illustration	Ascribed to Y	Ascribed to K	Ascribed to H	Reasons	Provenience* Y	Provenience* K	Provenience* H
Yurok								
6	Plate 31*a*		?	?	Not seen on the river			x
10	Figure 31*d*	x			Lower river; not typical; cross-stitch pattern	x		
4	Plate 9*b*		x					x
8	Plate 9*b*			x	Seen at Hupa			x
6	Plate 17*b*		x		Not down-river mark		x	
Karok								
32, 41	Figure 20*n*				Not our mark	x		
28, 29	Plate 6*b*	x			Down-river mark	x		
41	Plate 6*b*	x			Down-river mark	x		
28, 29	Figure 31*d*	x			Seen at Weitspus	x		
41	Figure 31*d*	x			Down-river mark	x		
28, 29	Plate 22*b*	x			Karok do not make it	x		
41	Plate 22*b*	x			Never seen before	x		
41	Plate 25*a*	x			Never seen before	x		
41	Plate 25*b*	x			Never seen before	x		
35	Plate 34*a*	x			Men up-river use caps	x		
41	....	x			Mud dyes, down-river	x		
41	....	x			Laced-on cover; not up-river style	x		
29, 41	Plate 56*c*			x	Not up-river style			x
41	Plate 56*d*	x			Long, stiff, placing of feathers	x		
29, 30	Plate 55*d*			x	Not Karok style	x		
29, 30	Plate 55*c*			x	Not Karok style	?		
29, 30	Plate 56*b*			x	Not Karok style	?		
29, 30	Plate 55*a*			x	Not Karok style	x		
29, 30	Plate 56*a*			x	Not Karok style	?		
29, 30	....			x	Not Karok style	?		
29, 30	Plate 55*e*			x	Not Karok style			x
29, 30	Plate 55*b*			x	Not Karok style	x		
41	Plate 48*a*			x	Handles, loops, etc.			x
41	....			x	Handles, loops, etc.			x
41	....			x	Handles, loops, etc.			x
41	....			x	Handles, loops, etc.			x

* As shown in museum records. Y, K, H stand for Yurok, Karok, Hupa.

to Karok territory, to six baskets. The tabulation, then, instead of suggesting regionally characteristic groups of motives recognized by Karok weavers as Yurok or Hupa motives, indicates that basketry designs, equally in use among the three tribes, form an extremely large percentage of the total number. Actually, the design in plate 17*b* is the single "Karok" mark, and rarely found, at that. Fragments of its history told in another section make it probable that it was once known among the Yurok also. To be sure, Karok women, like Nos. 28, 29, 30, 32, and 41 and her family, exclaim at "our" marks, or say that they can always tell their marks, but the implication of something tribally typical more often means that they recognize a favored design developed in white grass on a ground of the more plentiful alder-dyed fern. It is the combination of form, material, color, and established pattern which is recognized. Show Karok weavers the same pattern in black fern on the white grass ground of a cap and the basket might be a Yurok basket; show it on a globular form with handle, cover, and strap or knob lift, and both Karok and Yurok weavers will say it looks like Hupa work.

YUROK-KAROK KNOWLEDGE OF OUTSIDE TRIBES

If an informant shows indecision in locating the probable origin of familiar shapes and patterns within Yurok-Karok-Hupa territory, her doubt vanishes at once when she is shown baskets made by "outside peoples," as other tribes are called. The print collection included about a hundred fifteen baskets representative of the Tolowa, Wintun, the Wailaki group (Lassik, Sinkyone), Wiyot, and Chilula. Of these, twenty-eight baskets provoked comments from one to four informants; the Wintun specimen will be dealt with separately. Reactions were varied. At most, whether a Yurok or Karok woman was being interviewed, there was a tolerantly superior attitude toward the others' work. What seems to be their standard does not approach Yurok-Karok quality. Possibly, my informants offered, others' materials are different, or very old women made the baskets pictured, in which case they hardly deserved criticism. One Yurok and one Karok informant made sincere efforts to evaluate the outsiders' work; they pointed to this or that detail as an achievement. To the rest of the women the technique was incomprehensible from the standpoint of adults' weaving; it was a waste of time to look at it. Out of regard for the interviewer, polite attention was often forced, but on occasions there was indifference, and even impatience. Some women handed back the whole hundred prints after glancing through a half-dozen. Purposely, a volume containing reproductions of many beautiful baskets was left about conspicuously so that a family of expert weavers might look it through. These women are avid for new ideas but to my knowledge the book was not opened; the baskets are not their type in design or technique. Lack of curiosity is no more true of the Yurok than of the Karok; both peoples reveal the vaguest information concerning other tribes through hearsay, have known almost no Indians other than those on the Klamath and Trinity rivers, and have seen very few foreign baskets. In answer to a question about the smallest object a weaver had ever made I was frequently told of two tiny baskets no larger than seeds. A salesman has shown the baskets in several localities, but who or where the makers are is unknown to the Yurok-Karok, and uninteresting. I do not recall ever hearing a reference to the coiled work of neighboring tribes.

After the first amazement at the consistently inferior technique, Yurok informants reacted to the obvious similarities between other peoples' designs and their own. No. 17 had never seen any baskets not made on the Klamath. She marveled at the tottering food containers and pointed carrying baskets of the Wailaki group. In spite of disinclination to find relationships in such poor craftsmanship, she acknowledged the sturgeon back mark and flint variants, ladder mark, isosceles right triangles, and sharp points—all basic elements in the river patterns. No. 10 did the same, quickly assuring me that she did not know whether the Lassik copied the Yurok basketry or not, but at least the Yurok are independent of Lassik inspiration. At the same time she found several baskets to admire within the group: the Lassik basket in plate 58*b* is not only a hard mark to set, but the accurate planning at the bottom must also have included visualizing the requirements for the topmost pattern courses. This is the difficult double horizontal band effect of the Yurok-Karok weavers multiplied several times. The pattern is by no means perfect but the effort was approved. The Wyot basket in plate 57*a*, an elemental stripe pattern of alternating overlay and root courses, was called pretty by a lower river weaver. New features which appealed to her are the oversized, decorated strengthening root on the outside and the crossed-stick finish at the top.

No. 16, my oldest informant, had never seen any Indians from outside the region but she knew of the Redwood or Bald Hills (Chilula) people. It is to this locality that Weitspus women go for their white grass. Both Nos. 16 and 7 described the Chilula as a moving people with no established homes, as wanderers after edible seeds and game. They are said by the Yurok to glut themselves after a fortunate kill, and then go hungry until the next. No. 7 used the tribal name as an adjective; she characterized her lazy, dirty, or improvident neighbors in the village as tsulula'. No informant had ever known of Chilula basketry and it so happens that the only coiled specimen in the northwestern California collection is said to have been obtained from Bald Hills. The technique in itself stamped the aberration an outsider even had its ovoid form remained unnoticed.

Waterman says "the Yurok were much better acquainted, and were much more intimate in every way, with the Karok, and the

Hupa . . . . than they were with the Tolowa, who lived twenty miles up the coast."[33] Applying this to basketry, No. 17 exclaimed at the Tolowa "so far away" using an identical form of the familiar Yurok ladder design. Nos. 7 and 10 knew a little of the Shasta and of the Tolowa; these tribes border a region within which basketry is homogeneous. Beyond the present towns of Happy Camp (in the Asisufunuk district) and Crescent City, they said basketry was different. The Shasta use white grass, maidenhair fern and porcupine quills, but they twine on Indian string instead of on hazel sticks and their baskets are flexible. In addition, the Yurok women said, the Shasta are reported to incorporate beads in their weaving. At Rekwoi, where summer employment attracts Indians from all the surrounding tribes, No. 1 disapproved of the soft, unsteady-looking Shasta basket she had obtained in exchange for one of her own firm, shapely root baskets. She had never seen other peoples' work to recognize it; she supposed a Lassik specimen she gave me was an American product.

At Weitspus allusions were made by several informants to an Arizona woman of a forgotten tribal affiliation. She had come north years ago with her Yurok husband. Her coiled baskets were described to me as totally different from the twined variety of the region, as made over heavy, soft rings of grass. She learned from No. 14's mother to make the Yurok type of basket and then she moved away. What little was still remembered of her was in terms of her neighbors' wonder that she should allow her children to play with her rare foreign baskets. The designs in them had been admired for their bold forms and bright colors but neither had been copied. At the end of my trip No. 5 from the Ko'otep district on the lower river gave me an addition to the foreigner's story: she had gone back to visit her tribe in Arizona and had taught her people how to make twined baskets according to Yurok-Karok methods. No. 5 heard her tell on her return to the Klamath district of her difficulties as an instructor.

Through an error in labeling, the basket pictured in plate 58*a* was left among the Yurok-Karok-Hupa prints and was accepted by six Yurok informants as one of their own baskets. It is a Wintun basket patterned with a variant of the foot design. It impressed four of the six women as a hard mark and one of them as an unfamiliar design arrangement. The zigzag effect in the case of a wide pattern zone is commonly expressed by the space between alternately inverted motives; when found as a continuous pattern band, the zigzag width seems

[33] T.T. Waterman, Yurok Geography, UC–PAAE, 16:184, 1920.

narrow in proportion to the pattern-zone width. My informant thought this a new feature. Two Karok weavers, however, recognized the flexible Wintun basket. Possibly family connections in the Shasta territory, where Wintun baskets are fairly well known, explains acquaintance with the foreign product. No. 41 knew from its type that it was outsiders' weaving.

The Karok are in a position to know the Shasta. Kroeber mentions the Karok following the Salmon river since the American settlement and their living among the Shasta Konomihu at the forks of the river.[34] No. 25 remembered seeing, years ago, the long caps which came down low over the ears; No. 27 knew of the hats woven over Indian twine, not sticks, which could be bought in the Asisufunuk district. The Karok name for them, ka apxan, means a hat from "above" or "way up the river." In earlier days No. 24 had retrieved quills from these hats to re-use in her own caps. No. 31's husband is a Shasta and she knew of the flexible caps from his mother's weaving. My informants all remarked at the ability of a weaver to twine over pliable warps. No. 23 used to see the tule mats from the lakes north of Karok territory. There was, at most, curiosity in isolated details but no specific interest in any phase of Shasta basketry, and no one could tell of a single process or device in use among the Shasta.

Designs fared better. Nos. 22 and 23 recognized the design in plate 37*b* as one from Konomihu (Shasta) territory. If it had been a pattern typical of the Klamath region, they said, its motives would have been smaller and alternately inverted from a line centering the pattern zone. No. 37 called the familiar wax'poo design in plate 36*b* the wild geese mark. "Flying geese" is the name given undivided rows of parallelograms by the Achomawi; the Yurok-Karok customarily called the forms flint marks.[35] As noted in the table of terms for the Karok uswufumas design, "wild geese" was also applied to the interpenetrating triangles in the specimen in plate 35*b*. No Yurok informant used that name for any design.

Miscellaneous bits of information were incidental: one woman had seen a coiled basket of unknown provenience in the possession of a tourist; No. 41 had been told that the swastika was a mark belonging to Indians "across the ocean";[36] No. 40 knew that Indians near the present town of Crescent City buried their hazel sticks to make them

---

[34] Kroeber, Handbook, 100. [35] Kroeber, Basket Designs, 160.

[36] Compare the Yurok concept of geography in T. T. Waterman, Yurok Geography, UC–PAAE, 16:189–192.

black. Remembering that a separation of twenty-five miles was on one occasion invoked logically to explain a difference in Yurok and Karok cap shapes and the different methods of starting a basket, I was interested to find an informant beyond Ti district who was aware of a Tolowa detail in technique. As will be seen by the instances cited, any attempt to piece together a composite account of the border tribes' basketry from information gathered along the Klamath river would yield meager results. Childlike, Yurok-Karok weavers say they could make the others' shapes and designs if they wanted to; possibly they did once make the designs and lost them through less frequent use of them. At the same time my informants pointed to the others' self-evident technical inferiority by comparison with that in their own baskets; to copy anything from the outsiders, even had it once been their own, is now out of the question.

No one knew of any foreign marks coming into the region at present but those weavers below on the river thought the chances for evidence along this line were better farther up in Karok territory. Even there the instances are few. No. 41's family living at Inam own a number of baskets whose isolated design motives and spaced arrangements suggest similarities with baskets of the Atsugewi (Hat Creek Shasta) pictured by Mason in plates 177, 178.[37] The professional weavers in this family are credited with starting the innovations for the upper river basket makers.

THE COMMERCIAL ASPECT OF YUROK–KAROK BASKETRY

The oldest group of informants remember a time when baskets were made for use only. It is true that caps, wood packing baskets, hoppers, and Jumping dance baskets have always been made by experts and sold to Indian women who made them poorly, if at all. But in the main, a Yurok or Karok woman worked at her household containers in leisure time, occasionally finishing an extra piece for sale or gift. No one, they declared, got a living from the craft even were she an expert cap maker. Then the settlers and miners came to the region; dishes and metal utensils were incorporated into the family's equipment; fewer baskets were used and more were sold. No. 21 remembers that her mother sold footed-bowl types (pl. 54*a*)

[37] Mason, Basketry, pls. 177, 178.

to the Chinese cook at a mine. Much later, tourists became buyers to be depended upon and for the continuance of their custom, Indian women on the Klamath have perpetrated aesthetic atrocities. They are still willing to. Left to themselves weavers revert to old shapes and old patterns as the line of least resistance. Very often in admiring a basket picture an informant told me that that was the sort of basket or design a weaver might make for herself. But with every woman making baskets for sale, the obvious precaution is to produce results that will attract buyers.

Perhaps the least expected phase of the Yurok-Karok attitude toward basketry is the enthusiasm which the women display toward their work. To see a weaver go through the mechanical motions of twining, inserting sticks and overlay almost automatically, is one aspect; to hear a matter-of-fact looking woman of nearly sixty tell that she forgets to eat when she is weaving, and another admit that she has never tired of basket-making after forty years of selling for a livelihood, is the other aspect. Several informants were unable to offer much assistance on details, but not one was indifferent to the subject. A single weaver, Karok, reminded me that the price of a basket included nothing but the actual weaving, that it was hard to keep at weaving all day long, and that it was tiresome to go through the months of preliminary preparation of materials. Yet she herself could hardly stop her work in her eagerness to complete a pattern motive. The economic pressure is very real in most cases. A few men do day labor on the roads, intermittently; and during the fall months fighting the almost incessant forest fires can be counted on for income. I knew of one husband who was regularly employed; of several others who worked unprofitable little patches of ground. For basketry, then, to continue to be the fascinating occupation it apparently is despite its necessity, the craft must represent something more than a means of adding to the scanty resources.

As stated in the Introduction, the tastes of white buyers, interpreted in terms of basketry, are fundamentally responsible for its maintenance. Native ceremonials make few demands; the new soup basket for the medicine man officiating at a Brush dance or at new year's festivities is simple work; the large close-twine seed basket now used solely for collecting Brush dance medicine is generally very old, and Jumping dance baskets may be used over and over again for years. Only caps are sold to any extent among Indian women; white people are less attracted to the cap shape with its partly hidden designs than to the other types. Specifically, forms, structural details—such as handles, covers, and knobs—patterns, colors, and technical standards are in appreciable measure influenced by tourist trade. Of them all, forms are most indicative of fashion's changeable demands.

INFLUENCE OF WHITE PATRONAGE

Trade Influence on Structural Form

Except for collectors and curio seekers, white buyers have limited their interest very largely to the bowl and tray types of Yurok-Karok basketry; these include tobacco storage baskets, food and water containers, sifters, and mealing trays. Out of the bowl has developed the fancy basket with its sticks more or less sharply indrawn toward the top, as described in the section on Traditional Forms. The term "fancy" is not limited to this type; a regulation soup or cooking basket if made with some embellishment out of keeping with the Indians' concept of the container is a sale basket. Of these there are a variety of sizes made for the white woman's sewing tools. The shapes, as the plates show, are fairly close to the parent bowls. Informants say the basket with an indrawn top, done after the manner of the cooking basket, is preferred by white customers to a basket with straight or slightly flaring sides characteristic of some soup cups. Baskets from two to three inches in diameter, to which weavers give their attention for the holiday trade, are miniatures of the larger fancy baskets, identical in materials and patterns. Practically all Yurok-Karok weavers make miniatures, if not in close-twined technique, then in all-stick work to duplicate the market basket types. From the trays have come decorative plaques to hang on walls and table mats for hot dishes. The latter are frequently oval; they represent the one basketry object commonly made in that form. Oval baskets are rare even among modern products. Mats and plaques do not pretend to be native in shape or use. Before the whites came there were no "flat" basketry objects with the exception of the sifter, itself slightly dished; all sizes of pans and trays were concave although No. 13 was certain that the pan for drying fish was supposed to be flat.

So far, the objects made for white trade have a visible relation to Indian forms but, as mentioned in speaking of footed-bowl types (pl. 54*a*), some of the informants in each of the three age groups actively participated in an era of eccentricities (pl. 51). There are few remnants of the period in which basketry spoon holders, handled vase forms, and fruit dishes with pedestal bases were made regularly. Every craft is exposed to demands as incongruous and even now it would be possible to procure any of the above forms, but only on specific order. The fashion for them has gone out completely; only an occasional request goes into the region for a close-twine patterned basket analogous to a fisherman's catch basket. Nine of my informants had made cups and saucers. As many had woven basketry covers and stoppers for liquor and perfume bottles. No one does these things today and no weaver thinks the chance of a sale immediate enough to have such objects on hand. Of there being ultimate sale for them among tourists there seemed little doubt, but a weaver would have to wait indefinitely. No. 33 had noticed an increasing demand within the last two years for wood baskets, small and large, for Indian all-stick plates, and for the more common root baskets. White people seemed to be getting away from the fine grass overlay types, to be inquiring for the sturdier baskets. Other weavers, too, were noting the tendency.

Trade Influence on Structural Detail

Next after form, the most conspicuous additions to the native basketry tradition are handles and set-on covers with lifting knobs, or with straps (pl. 48*a*). These details are less in vogue at present among white women than formerly. The natural sequel to decreased demand functions on the Klamath river: fewer such details are being made. Something of the controversy over the relative "age" of handles and covers was given in the section on Basket Types. There is not much doubt that it is the concept of a cover that is troublesome. The oldest baskets had flat plaque lids tied on with elk thongs, or conical-shaped covers with knob-like protruberances, or inverted baskets of the seed-gathering type. Today, a "cover" means a plaque with a straight half-inch rim fitting down over a collar (pls. 49*a, b,* 50*a, b,* 51*a, b*). No 40 had started the making of covers in her district following the unsuccessful efforts of her neighbors, who were professional weavers. The material achievement was less in her mind than her triumph over the experts; they had copied foreign objects; she had adapted an old idea to a new use, as she explained. A "knob" signifies a ball-like handle to most Indian women and is the result of white influence. So, also is the strap of grass plaited over a length of thong, a type found on some fancy basket covers. No one of my informants dissented on that score. Any form of knob is in better repute than a lifting strap. A knob is regarded as a natural outgrowth of the traditional form. Thus, No. 29 made a distinction between her mother and herself, who put the variant type of knob on their covers, and No. 20, who makes, among other unaccepted innovations, the newer strap handles on hers. The Hupa, they told me, make fitted covers without the means to raise them.

Plaited carrying handles (pl. 48*a*), too, were unknown until baskets were offered for sale.; now they are admired quite generally. The facts concerning structural details, because of difference of opinions, were made the object of special inquiry among a group of the most conservative up-river weavers, Nos. 33, 34, 35, 36, and 37.

The usual method of finishing a Yurok-Karok basket is to clip off the sticks close to the last course of twining (pl. 41*b*). Openwork spoon baskets, serving also for odds and ends, have coiled edges of grass and black fern over a foundation of sticks bent to lie flush with the top of the last course. The coiled finish (pl. 44*a, b*) has been transferred to fancy baskets, especially by the Karok weavers. Yurok weavers see it in the light of compliance to foreign taste. No. 10 doubted whether any woman would make a coiled finish on her own basket; No. 5 had filled orders specifying such a top finish. From the standpoint of a professional cap maker the idea of a spoon-basket top being considered superior to the clipped cap finish is ridiculous. No. 42, Karok, thought that the difference in top finish constituted a tribal difference: down-river people leave their baskets unfinished; up-river people use the coiled finish. Only caps and food baskets should end abruptly, this informant thought; a fancy basket top should be an attractive feature with an edge such as the Karok make on them. She had refinished the tops of some down-river baskets by ripping out a portion, inserting new sticks, crossing them, and ending the weaving with a grass coil. In exchange the storekeeper gave her new cloth. The following check will show that finish is an unreliable criterion for determining provenience:

	Yurok	Karok	Hupa
Fancy baskets in the print collection	17	11	10
Clipped sticks, no top finish	15	10	9
Crossed sticks, coiled top finish	2	1	1

To be just to No. 42, the coiled top finish is more often found according to her generalization in today's baskets; and Karok weavers of today do prefer that finish on their sale baskets. The customary abrupt ending of the weaving must have impressed some buyers as inadequate. No. 14 made baskets for a storekeeper, who planned with her a narrow border of alternate black and white twining stitches topped with a line of solid black (pl. 47*b*). The finish was extra work and the dealer paid more for it, at the same time giving the Indian woman a new slant on the refinements to which basketry lends itself.

Trade Influence on Pattern

Some patterns have a measurably better sale value than others. It may be understood when a weaver says she likes certain marks very much and makes them again and again, that her baskets produce more than aesthetic enjoyment. I never heard a woman regret that she must deny herself the making of a favorite mark because it would not sell, and conversely, an informant never complained of being weary of flint and wax'poo marks in spite of her repetitions of them. Several women recalled difficulties in disposing of baskets with crochet patterns or designs from obvious non-basketry sources in them. Even the swastika motive had delayed the sale of some baskets. No. 23 adapted a mark from a pictured Navaho blanket. The storekeeper refused the basket until she proved its Indian source. But, as a rule, the women are wary; there is too much at stake in terms of weeks of time and effort to gamble with unproved designs. White customers have never shown any preference for new designs; a letter chosen randomly from a newspaper, *X*, or *Z*, or *H* is an unwise venture (pl. 25*b*). Occasionally an order will come for a motive of initials, of Merry Christmas, or the Christians' cross—none of which, it is protested, can be made to look like an authentic basket mark. At picnic grounds it was once profitable to display baskets with the name of the site or Fourth of July woven in them. Nos. 11 and 26 had done this, but only to vary their work, to try something different; neither informant considered the results other than amusing.

A tabulation of basketry designs cited by informants as most in demand shows a laudable consistency. All of them are genuine old Indian marks expressive of native good taste; they are simple and "showy," which means they are divided into a few, fairly large color areas. Generally, in Yurok country, designs are developed in black on white; a red fern basket does not sell so well there. In Karok districts, where both white grass and black fern are comparatively scarce, the ground area is usually red with white patterning. This color balance is considered more striking than the reverse. The nicest baskets in both tribes have bright spots of yellow-dyed porcupine quills, more favored at present than has been noted for some years past. No one except No. 7 has, to date, ever received orders involving package dyes; until that happens there is little danger of their acceptance. One family leans toward their use but the output so far is noticeably un-Indian in color. Besides, dyes are expensive.

TABLE 18

DESIGNS WITH SALE VALUE

	"Easy" designs*			"Hard" designs*			
Informants	Flint	Wax'poo	Snakenose	Spread finger	Flint-and-points	Cut wood	Foot
(*Yurok*)							
1	x						
5	x	x				x	
6	x	x	x				
7		x		x			
8	x	x	x				
9	x				x		
10	x		x				
11	x		x				
12	x	x					
13		x					
14		x					
15		x					
16		x					
17		x		x	x		x
18	x	x					
(*Karok*)							
20			x				
21		x					
22			x				
25		x			x		
26	x						
27		x					
28	x	x					x
29	x						
30	x	x			x	x	
31		x					
32	x	x		x	x	x	
33	x	x					
34	x	x					
36				x			
37	x						
38	x		x	x			
39	x						
41			x				
42	x		x				
Totals:	20	20	9	5	5	3	2

* See illustrations of easy and hard designs, figures 29-32.

Designs characterized as easy to make are in large majority in table 18. Toward the hard marks weavers hold different attitudes: either the designs are passed by because a white buyer who knows nothing of relative values demurs at a price commensurate with the extra time involved; or, a hard pattern is woven because the buyer does know values and is willing to pay primarily for the additional effort. This last is especially true of storekeepers whose experience aids them to balance the time required by one design against that for another. There is, too, from a different standpoint, the mental attitude of the craftswomen: one says no more is to be gained by making a hard mark and that a good basket sells regardless of its design; another says that weaving a pattern she likes renders time and potential difficulties matters of indifference to her. It must not be assumed that the so-called easy designs are always simple. Although flint is the name given, there are no solid flint marks in today's baskets; each form has a secondary design within it to be reckoned with. Again, marks easy or hard, if repeated often enough through demand for them, become less trouble to set and weave. This fact was noted for the foot mark, which is difficult to most weavers, but is easy to No. 28 who is called upon to make it often.

Attitudes toward duplication of designs are fairly uniform. Most Yurok-Karok women care little about the number of times they repeat a design that sells well. The most expert put the same mark on a cap and on various sizes of fancy baskets. Two professionals answered naïvely that they would as soon make several designs alike as not since the baskets went to different places when sold. No. 15 makes duplicates as a precautionary measure: two customers may want theirs alike. She has four main designs which she makes in rotation. Other women are more exacting. One will not make the same pattern twice in succession; another varies the repetition slightly to give it interest; a third chooses a simple element like the isosceles right triangle for her most frequently made design because the triangle allows a number of stylicized changes in arrangement. That duplication has always been more or less common is indicated by the recognition of some old designs as favorites of certain weavers. Numbers of times an informant was reminded of some woman, usually dead, who had made the design shown in the print. There was always the chance when the basket had been purchased in that locality that the intuition was sound. To us, one good basket looks very like another, but the personality of a weaver may be as visible in her product as an architect's or writer's is in his.

Trade Influence on Color

Yurok-Karok weavers know commercial dyes; they know grass and fern will take various colors, but the demands of white buyers are inflexible: there must be no colors but black, white, red, and yellow in the closely woven basketry of the region. A storekeeper sent a professional weaver at Pekwututl six bunches of grass dyed with package dyes in imitation of porcupine quills. She was to make the grass into caps to be traded for supplies. She had no apparent reluctance to using the dyed material; if white people did not know or care, she need not concern herself. The yellow which appears in caps of her own planning is dyed quills; she substitutes no grass for them.

Fully a third of the informants expressed themselves on the subject of commercial dyes. They have a specific use in the handled baskets of willow or hazel sticks woven like our own market types. From Rekwoi to the Asisufunuk district there was agreement of opinion that dyes were not appropriate for the "old" types. They are too bright to color fern the customary red, but more than that, a basket does not sell when commercial dyes are used. Storekeepers and buyers from the outside strongly advise against them. Among the Indians they rate lower in estimation than woven shades for electric lights and initialed baskets. But for all-stick clothes and market types purple, green, red, and blue are conventional. No yellow is used; it does not look "right," and it does not "show off." So established is the use of the other colors for this type of basket that some weavers were at a loss to say why they did not use yellow; they had not appreciated the fact of its omission until their attention was called to it.

Trade Influence on Technical Standards

There are few references to technical standards in connection with the economic aspect of the craft. As has been stated, the best work of which a weaver is capable goes into her orders; if there is a "good enough" attitude, it is reserved for her household necessities. No. 14, speaking of the care essential to preparation of materials, said her mother had made money at basketry because she knew quality beginning with the raw stuffs. She herself saves the best sticks and roots for orders; she uses the sortings for her own containers.

What is looked upon by conservatives as a questionable procedure, diagonal twining or double-stick work, is actually an asset to sale baskets. The method, as stated in the section on Standards for Workmanship, has no caste among those who do it and no excuse except for being a short cut. The white purchaser, perhaps, picks up one basket to find a pattern in the bottom similar to the center one in a cap; the next basket will be patterned, he thinks, by diagonal twining. The easy technical method may be the more attractive in appearance to him and helps sell the basket. Although Indian women are still more or less apologetic about stooping to the quick way, only the most conservative are unyielding. No. 7 filled an order for a number of baskets of double-stick work throughout. This, to her, was a matter of her customer's taste and not to be questioned. It is the same ignorance of the traditional which has done away with the two encircling roots on the outside of cooking baskets. After one is accustomed to their decorative effect, a large modern sale basket with plain unbroken surface has an unfinished appearance even to a white buyer. Just as in the matter of black fern in cooking baskets, an Indian law requiring the strengthening roots can be set aside by the more practical considerations of trouble saved and buyers' complete satisfaction without them.

Roughly speaking, the shape of the basket and the design in it are less influential to effect a sale than are size and workmanship. Weavers tell of former prices paid for their weaving in days when a quarter seemed reasonable and fifty cents high for a plain cap. Everybody wanted to sell and no one knew how much her work was worth. Usually it was food that was given in exchange and even now that course is followed by some merchants; others pay in cash, an alternate policy which amounts to the same thing in a one-store community. Today gift-size baskets are measured either by encircling them with thumbs and first fingers or by lapping the fingers for the smaller sizes. Some weavers scale their sizes to prices: No. 20 sells a root and grass basket about thirteen inches across the top, a measurement which she gauges by putting her arms around it, hands lapped, for ten dollars: No. 6 makes a larger basket, which she measures in the same way, for twenty dollars. No. 14 has three standard sizes and her orders come for baskets of a specified price: her two-dollar-and-a-half size is as wide across the top as the distance from the knuckle to the first finger tip; the three-dollar-and-a-half size is as wide as from the knuckle to the second finger tip; and the six-dollar-and-a-half size, a covered basket, measures from the second finger tip to the wrist. All are woven with very fine sticks, grass, and black fern (pl. 46*b*, *c*).

A weaver is naturally proud of some of her sales. If she is a cap maker it is assumed that she will get four to five dollars for a dress cap disposed of among her own people. A fine quill cap is worth six dollars and the buyer as well as the seller advertises the price. White customers are asked more with no apology for the action.

TABLE 19

TODAY'S PRICES FOR YUROK-KAROK BASKETS

Informant	Plate	Spoon	Wood	Doll cradle	Soup	Cook	Gift	Fancy	Cap
5									$6
6					$1	$20	$1		
						$22			
7									$6
9					$3	$35			
12		$0.75							
14							$2.50	$6.50	
							$3.50		
17				$0.75	$1		$3.00		
18							$1.00		
							$2.00		
19	$0.50		$2.50						
20	$0.50				$1			$10	$10
								$15	
23								$ 8	
27						$10			$3
									$7
28								$15.00	
34								$ 3.50	$4
								$ 5.00	
36							$1	$ 2.50	
37									$10
41									$6
									$10

It may be of interest to glance at present prices for Yurok-Karok baskets (table 19). The list includes only such recent sales as were given me by my informants. In general, sizes and quality are unknown. Comparison of the worth of the different baskets in the table is impossible; however, No. 9's work is so mediocre-to-poor in quality that the buyer of one of her baskets for the sum mentioned was either indiscriminating or charitable. No basket of the cooking type is worth thirty-five dollars and the women would be the first to say so.

ATTITUDE TOWARD THE VIRTUOSO

One of the best, if not the best, Karok weavers in the territory today has never made freak baskets nor copied foreign shapes. No. 28 cannot be considered typical. She and her family have had more contact with white people than is usual, and for a long time her tastes have been molded, perhaps unconsciously, by the likes and dislikes of a patroness who contracts for the family's entire output. As a partial result she and her daughter have never sought to invent marks, because only the old ones are requested. Her one attempt to vary the usual repertory of designs by copying a modified old mark was clearly lacking in favor. Both informants repudiate the tourist fancies as un-Indian and in poor taste. But, inconsistently, a basket with the legend Fourth of July woven in it was given center place in their photographed group. A frequent question when looking at an obvious European design was "Why do they want to do it?" And yet, No. 28 admitted, so strong is the feeling that their craft must be profitable as well as pleasurable, and much as she might dislike to, that she would accept even a commission to make table mats. If her patroness asked for them she would execute the order as if it were a detail like color arrangement. Basketry is a business with the Yurok-Karok women, molded by their traditions and conventions, to be sure, but yielding in all but technique to the demands of trade.

Novelty Shapes

Whatever may be the attitude toward the result, the weaver, who can control her technique to effect an unusual or even freakish shape, is accorded admiration and a reputation. It takes ability and effort, for Yurok-Karok weavers characterize all invention or ingenious adaptation as hard. Thus, it is hard to make a new mark, or to copy initials as sketched by a customer; hard to make a basket smaller than two inches in diameter; hard to develop in basketry a cup and saucer or other dish; hard to cover bottles; hard to make oval shapes. When No. 39 remarked that only a good weaver would try these things, I checked over the list of informants and found some corroboration for her statement.

Not all the capable weavers, as may be seen from table 20, tried their hands at fads and not all the average weavers were discouraged by anticipated difficulties. Of the total forty-three informants, I estimated twenty-three to be good or excellent craftswomen and fourteen to be average or less in ability. For six informants, I saw no work upon which to base an estimate. In this connection, thirteen of the twenty-three good weavers have experimented with technique to produce foreign shapes as against five, or less than a third of the average and poor weavers.

TABLE 20

CORRELATION BETWEEN ABILITY AND ATTEMPTED NOVELTIES

	Freak shapes	Cups and saucers	Bottle covers	Initials, legends
Good work:	18, 20, 31, 34, 41	6, 17, 18, 20, 30, 37	5, 6, 7, 17, 20, 41	5, 38, 40
Average work:		8, 26	11, 26, 39	11, 26, 43
No examples seen:		33		13

Realistic Designs

Animals and men are not considered fit subjects for basketry patterns. The majority of my informants have never seen any attempts at realism; a few remember certain weavers who, in years gone by, had been known for their skilful representations; not one Yurok or Karok weaver aims to do anything of the sort at present; there is no

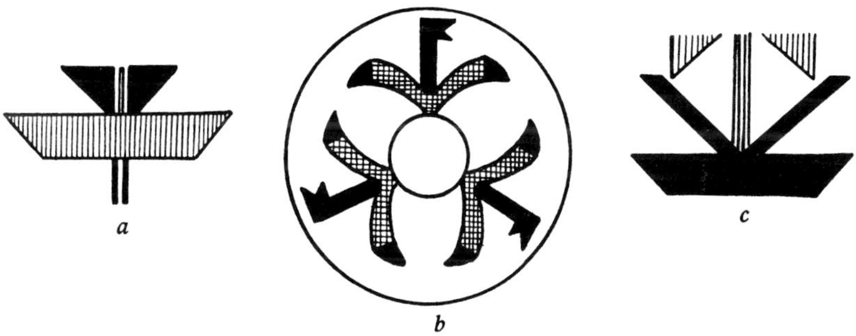

a b c

Fig. 35. Realistic designs. *a, b,* sketched from baskets in a private collection. *c,* No. 20's original design (partly finished).

demand for realism. The cases referred to were looked upon as evidences of high technical proficiency, but as nothing of the kind was known by informants on the lower river, it is clear representation could not have been regarded, within memory, as an important accomplishment. In Weitspus there was once a woman, long since dead, who encircled her basket with men holding hands. She is given credit for originating the design. At its completion she was afflicted with a painful eye trouble. My informant did not believe the design indissolubly connected with punishment, but she did think realism might be tempting fate. On the upper river a woman of the same age as my Pekwututl informant was emphatic on the subject of realism: it is against Indian law to work whole or parts of animal forms into basketry motives. Other nature forms are in a different category, not particularly appropriate perhaps, but not dangerous. Three Karok weavers, all experts, were admiringly spoken of; they were able to make life-like pictures: No. 18 once put flowers and birds in her fancy baskets and novelties; No. 20 still weaves potted plant motives based on quadrilateral elements, although different from any other basket mark (fig. 35*c*); and No. 34 made very small butterflies which were, according to her, an original motive.

Virtuoso effects are viewed differently. If they are far enough removed from the conventional designs so that there is no clear suspicion of a familiar foundation element which might have undergone change, they receive a good deal of admiration. The designs are "new," of no rank, but their makers have overcome not only all the known difficulties which are faced by any weaver, but have overcome, also, unknown difficulties incidental to developing a tangible something out of a concept. From other than the curio seeker's standpoint, novelty shapes and fantastic representations are a deplorable misuse of talent; from the Indian woman's they are proof of the conquest of technical obstacles.

Dreams

Basket weavers of other tribes acknowledge inspiration through dreams;[38] the dream element is totally lacking on the Klamath river. One informant hazarded the opinion that a woman might say she had dreamed a design just to be different, but no old weaver would tell anyone such a tale. Other informants had been so eager to begin work on new baskets that they dreamed of starting them, or they went to sleep trying to calculate mentally the motive counts in an untried mark. But no informant took dreams seriously, and no one had ever seen or known of a new mark that appeared in the locality as the result of a dream.

---

[38] F. Boas, *et al.*, Coiled Basketry, 302.

CONCLUSIONS

Basketry as practiced by a Yurok-Karok weaver is thoroughly molded by a compact body of established traditions. Moreover, it exacts nothing of her which she considers unreasonable or stultifying. Tribal standardization begins with her learning the craft from a preceding generation of weavers identically as they were taught by their mothers' or grandmothers' generation. Standardization continues by prescribing materials: all the needed supplies grow within the region; dependence upon those outside the circumscribed area, which might conceivably make for changes, is unnecessary. There is no locality which does not have one or the other of the alternates for foundation sticks, twining elements, and decorative overlay. There are choices, to be sure, and the Yurok weavers are in a more advantageous position to obtain those rated as superior than the Karok. To the observer the red-dyed-fern baskets of the Karok are not less beautiful, perhaps, than the white-grass-black-fern baskets of the Yurok. To the natives of the region the larger quantity of red used indicates less plentiful growths of the more desirable supplies. With the exception of the Karok use of myrtle for foundation sticks and mullein for yellow dye, the two tribes gather, prepare, and weave with exactly the same materials. The identity goes beyond this: weavers use materials according to the same conventions. Alder-dyed fern, for example, is no part of the "nicest" dress cap in which white grass and black fern overlay cover the major areas. Fern has its own place: it is the basic color area of a cap to which smaller black and white areas give emphasis. This is not an inflexible rule. If a weaver wanted to render a small design element in red fern in her very nice cap, no Indian law is trangressed, or no bad luck follows, but she would thereby depreciate the value of weeks of work, and display what is to beholders an incongruous selection of colors and materials. Naturally, she follows custom in self-defense. So, too, the avoidance of red fern and yellow-dyed quills in the same basket is not a matter of individual taste: the combination would be, according to majority opinion, an overriding of established conventions.

For the twining process there is no thought of substitution; most weavers never heard of a basket completely made by coiling, the method occasionally used to finish off the tops of fancy baskets. To a Yurok or Karok woman basket making is accomplished by a single variety of technique; to change the technique means to stop weaving. Those rare examples of coiling which have drifted in and out of the region are so fundamentally different in materials and workmanship that they are looked upon as curiosities, nothing more.

Forms and proportions have come down practically unchanged. Older weavers are able to point to differences, mostly in sizes of baskets, but never is there any doubt as to the intended type. If it is bowl-shaped it is a food basket, or if it has a grass overlay surface, it is a cap or modern fancy basket. The latter is woven more or less according to the proportions of the bowls. With these exceptions identification is rendered positive by unmistakable forms for specific types. In all these details the basket weaver follows old habits, the line of least resistance. To consciously vary the shape of soup or cooking baskets would be a foolish waste of effort. They are utensils. Whatever individuality is to be expressed will be afforded opportunity in the choice of the design. The work cap shape fits the head snugly; it is unreasonable to suppose any basket maker would try to improve that prerequisite. The dress cap shape is purely conventional: it touches the head only at the rim and is flat-topped. Here any deviation would be an overthrow of tradition. No one knows how long the present shape has been in vogue. Some informants remember a slight difference in contour. It is extremely improbable that an object worn only for display during festivities of a ceremonial character would yield to marked variation. The cap measurements which are rigorously adhered to by today's cap makers are demonstrated just as meticulously by the oldest woman in the Klamath region. There are no other measurements; whatever modifications are seen to have taken place in a cap are at once put down to ineptness, and not to a desire to foster stylistic change.

The sections on Design review in detail the concepts of "old" and "new" designs, the latter term synonymous with tribally unrecognized motives. A weaver is interested in a new mark, it is admired and copied, but it is a passing thing and always labeled as such. Up to the present, at least, no woman will make a prophecy that in time an invented motive or one taken over from white sources will ever become incorporated into the Yurok-Karok system. Informants say some person will always be left to recognize the design's original, or half-caste character. With this attitude toward invention and the resistance of the older conservatives to changes, whatever alteration of patterns goes on is slight or is tolerantly disapproved of. The weaver who shows aptitude for modification, even if her result has been carried thereby out of tribal recognition, is given grudging commendation. There were, other weavers say, plenty of smaller changes she might have made in old patterns to vary them for the sake of renewed interest. Any flair for the original which is due to meet similar response would have to come from a woman who was technically proficient and of established reputation. Nos. 20 and 39, when the latter was an active weaver, and No. 41's family seem to have maintained not only their positions as experts thoroughly conversant with tradition, but also were able to evolve at times something new for their districts. No. 43 is now known as an innovator. She is only twenty-one years old—not yet in the expert class—but she is daring and frankly dissatisfied with the old designs and forms. If she represents a tendency to be shown a few years from now by the fifteen-year olds at Ko'otep on the lower river, there will indeed be radical changes in Yurok-Karok basketry. Their real effectiveness, however, may be doubted. Between the Ko'otep and Ti districts there is no basket maker under thirty-five years of age except No. 14. The daughter of an expert with wide reputation, she is at present closely associated with her relatives, Nos. 7 and 10, both reactionaries. No. 14 herself is quite content to be as bound by traditional conventions as the older women. Granted, also, that some women between the two districts may take up the craft later, they will be taught the old things and years will pass before they are in control of technique to an extent where freedom from old designs is possible. Perhaps by that time these women, too, will have seen how much easier it is to copy the traditional models than to go through the arduous calculations essential to setting an untried design motive. It would seem, then, that as long as there is Yurok-Karok basketry in the Klamath region it will be made according to traditional convention, which has established choices of materials, selection and arrangement of elements, and the placement of these as design motives.

In this respect the northwestern Californians are presumably not unique. Formalized composites of prescribed units are common to other crafts. Both Lowie and Kroeber concluded in their separate studies of parfleches that the significant feature in a design was the disposition of the combined geometric elements with relation to each other rather than the elements themselves.[39] Spier found in analyzing

[39] R. H. Lowie, Crow Indian Art, AMNH–AP, 21:279, 1922. A. L. Kroeber, Ethnology of the Gros Ventre, AMNH–AP, 1:171, 1908.

Plains Indian parfleches that one shape, the lozenge, never occurred except as the center of a motive, but that another, the single triangle, never assumed the central position.[40] In a different field, pottery, Boas quotes Dr. Ruth Bunzel's description of Zuñi water jars.[41] They are divided into decorative zones each with its appropriate design chosen from a strictly limited range. The proper design, in turn, is always to be disposed within a field according to a definitely established scheme. This last tendency is in consonance with the restrictions imposed upon the weaver of Yurok-Karok dress caps. The mildest criticism of a basket mark varying a little from its usual expression is tolerance for some weaver who apparently wanted to make that particular change; the most severe criticism repudiates the result as an individual's vagary, of no rank among tribal designs. What remains to the weaver is opportunity to rearrange colors in a motive, providing they are the correct ones to start with, and to vary to some extent the arrangement of certain elements. As has been noted in the section on Legitimate Modifications, the boundary separating the approved from the challenged in this last possibility is so elusive that an Indian woman's concept of it is an enigma.

Originality, as a result, is lacking to a large degree and ingenious play with technique is not worth the trouble. To find twenty women giving the flint mark as their favorite design element and as many others admiring the combination of quadrilaterals and right isosceles triangles known as the wax'poo mark, indicates the narrow groove in which Yurok-Karok basket makers seem content to travel. Few liberties are taken with designs and these are of the simplest. Tastes are for plain patterns; complexity and exuberance of detail leave weavers indifferent, whereas there is enthusiasm for a solid rectangle terminated with triangular forms—the combination in good proportion to the size of its field (pl. 9*a*). It is thus with respect to the native designs; when the weavers admire and copy something of ours in their baskets, the results are open to question from the standpoint of good taste.

Standards are conventionalized. The fact that more baskets than ever before are being sold does not lower but raises the quality of workmanship. So-called slipshod methods are evidenced in few sale baskets. The white buyer, from his many opportunities to handle

---

[40] L. Spier, An Analysis of Plains Indian Parfleche Decoration, UW–PA, 1:100, 109, 1927.

[41] F. Boas, Primitive Art, 166–168, 1927.

textures, appreciates even spacing and smoothly held overlay materials. A roughly made basket is as obvious to him as to the best Indian weaver. Substitution of materials may enable a woman to finish a basket quickly; short cuts may save her time, but they are unimportant disadvantages in a basket not made for cooking in or eating from—that is, the use to which we put our purchases need not take into consideration a structure upon which specific demands are wont to be made. Technically the standards are high. They may be initiated by pride in ability, but they are maintained at uniform level by the added incentive of an established reputation among other weavers and by the hope of better prices for one's products.

Conventions transmitted from one generation to the next have simplified the work of the Yurok-Karok basket maker. In the main they have set up few irksome prohibitions. A weaver is not required to be original or even ingenious. Her design choices, if she has no definite desire to go outside, are readily available within a range of traditionally authorized variations of standard motives. The size of her basket is a matter of instruction; where to begin her pattern is governed by formula; the width of the design zone is predetermined by basket proportions; the colors to use are strictly defined. Technical problems not repeatedly met are few and those regarded as unusually difficult are confined to the basket types in which a few weavers have always specialized. Far from being deadened by a craft in which so much is reduced to conformity, the women of the two tribes have developed an appreciation of quality, design-to-space relationships, and effective color dispositions which are discriminating and genuine.

APPENDIX

INFORMANTS' CHARACTERIZATIONS

The characterization of each informant which follows is in two parts. The first paragraph is an assembling of statements which each woman made concerning her own work incidental to other matters under discussion. To this first part has been added my impression of her ability. The second paragraph is partly composite. Wherever several informants' numbers are grouped, the separate evaluations as given are summarized in a sentence. In the remaining cases, an individual weaver's opinion of another was equally illuminating as to her own attitudes or skills, and no modification has been made beyond

TABLE 21

INFORMANTS' WORKMANSHIP AND ACCOMPLISHMENTS

Author's rating	Informant	All-stick types				Close-twine types			
		Market	Plates	Cradle	Wood	Storage	Jumping dance	Hopper	Cap
Good	1								
Average	2								
?*	3			x					
?	4						x		
Good*	5								x
Good*	6								x
Good*	7			x	x	x		x	x
Average	8								
Average	9								x
Good	10								No
Average	11								
Poor	12								
?	13								No
Excellent	14						x		
?	15								
Average	16								
Good	17	x	x						
Good	18						x		
Poor	19		x		x				No
Excellent	20	x	x	x					x
Good	21			x					
Good	22						x		
?	23								No
Excellent	24	x			x				No
Good	25	x	x		x	x	x		No
Average	26	x	x		x	x			x
Average	27								x
Excellent	28								x
Excellent	29								
Good*	30	x		x					x
Good	31								No
Good	32		x						x
?	33								x
Excellent	34					x			x
Average	35								x
Average	36								
Excellent	37							x	x
Good	38								
Average	39								
Good	40	x							
Good*	41				x		x		x
Average	42								
Average	43								

* No examples of weaving seen.

minor changes in wording. For convenience, table 21 gives my own ratings of informants' workmanship in terms of poor, average, good, excellent. The more unusual types of baskets each informant has made are also listed. It is assumed that every weaver makes or has made the plain root types and the fancy close-twine sale baskets. No effort was made to gather the information in the table, but it is correct for the types each woman weaves at present. The past record of accomplishments is incomplete. Big storage baskets are no longer made except for a rare order; the two lower age groups of informants cannot be expected to have had experience with them.

The Expert Weaver

To the question of who is the expert weaver in the locality there was always an immediate reply. Even if the answer necessitated declaring that the woman being interviewed was herself the best weaver, the information was given without affectation. Usually some other woman shared the honor with her or was equally adept in another line of basketry. If an informant felt that her statement needed corroboration she might say that everyone agreed she made the finest caps, or that anyone would tell me she did the best work. Of course there is envy. When one informant tells you that for her three-dollar basket another woman can ask five dollars, there is an implication of superior workmanship to which there cannot be indifference; but neither is there anything to be done about it. Many times informants have said that their best materials and work went into their sale baskets, that if they lowered their standards it was in those baskets made for household use. Consequently there seems to be no feeling of injustice about prices paid or that effort, as such, demands compensation beyond the estimated value of the result.

There is a laudable reluctance to condemn another's weaving among the Yurok-Karok women. The best workers are easily discovered; reference to poor weavers is usually lacking. The characterization of a woman's baskets as "pretty good" implies, as it does with us, mediocrity. If it were suggested that one's time would be wasted in interviewing some basket maker the prophecy would be worth heeding. Interrelationships are at the bottom of much of the tolerance; a relative's work may be described as average when her results are poor.

The map (fig. 36) shows in a graphic way the distances an expert's reputation will travel. Each woman who was referred to outside her immediate locality—local references are not indicated—was known by name and for the basket type in which she specialized, or for what she was able to charge for her work. In addition, the variety of details that travel covers a wide range. This is illustrated by the sentences concerning No. 20, the best known and the most independent weaver on the Klamath.

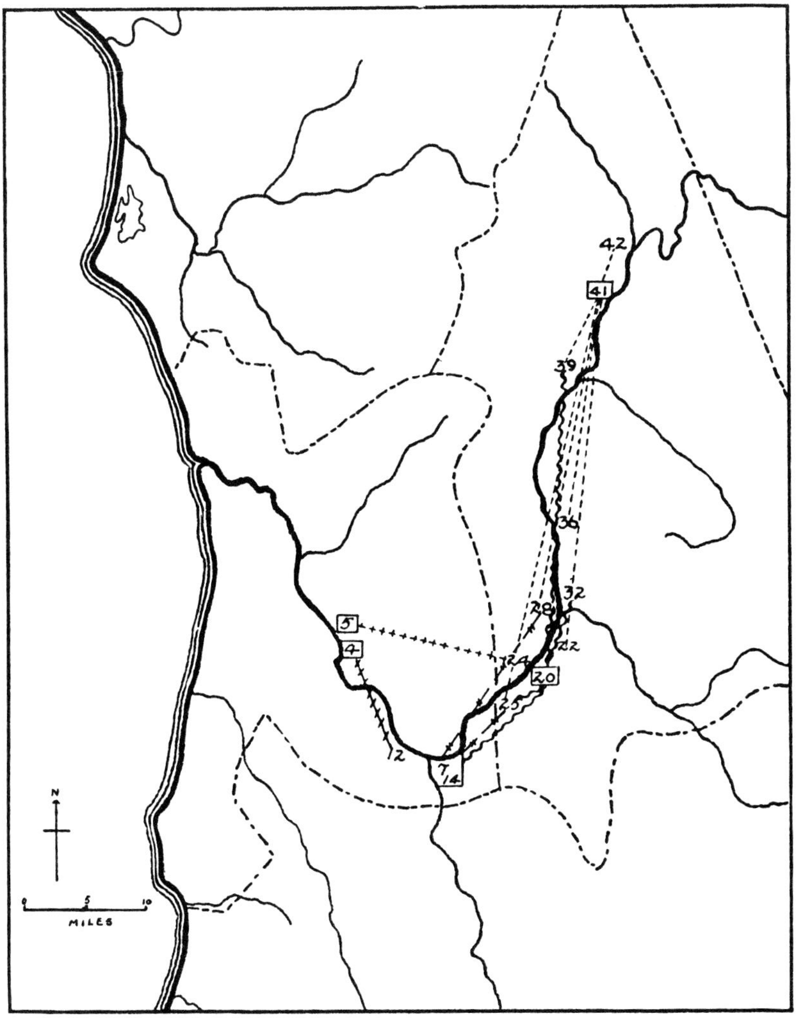

Fig. 36. Map to show the distances reputations of experts have traveled. All travel follows the river, considerably increasing the number of miles in reality.

No. 1, a Yurok at Wetlkwau; about sixty-five years old; one of three sisters all known as basket makers with high standards. No. 7, a professional at Pekwututl, is the best known of the three. No. 1 makes fancy baskets of the cooking type in different sizes, also grass overlay baskets of modern style; she admired a globular, handled basket and began at once to copy the photograph—this eagerness is in direct contrast to her sister's ultra-conservative attitude toward new things. No. 1 regrets there are so few old weavers left in the Rekwoi district and that the young women do not care for weaving.

No. 2, a Yurok at Ho'pau; about seventy years old. Since becoming prosperous and interested in a religious cult she does not make baskets; she gave some corroboratory information regarding old designs but in a manner to suggest rather superficial knowledge.

No. 5 said No. 2 was never a good basket maker even when she did weave.

No. 3, a Yurok at Ayotl; about fifty years old; a cousin of No. 17. My interview with her was very short. She seemed to know designs and their conventional requirements more categorically than any other Yurok on the lower river; she made fine distinctions as to proportions which other informants missed. She was beginning to weave all-stick open-twine Indian pans and cradles and criticized her own efforts; she knows how they should look but has failed so far to make as good open-twine as close-twine baskets.

No. 4, a Yurok at Sregon; about forty-five years old; a weaver with old traditions. She has taught her seven-year-old daughter as she herself was taught. I saw none of her work although she has a reputation as a dance basket maker. Her invented mark is shown in figure 18*g*.

No. 5 said No. 4 makes all kinds of baskets; she also crochets. She uses old basket marks in her weaving. No. 6 said No. 4 makes fine porcupine quill caps. No. 12 had heard the husband boast of his wife's Jumping dance baskets.

No. 5, a Yurok in the Ko'otep district; about forty years old; one of the most intelligent informants. She is the expert cap maker on the lower river with all the old traditions and conventions in mind. Whatever she said of basketry was based on her experience from young girlhood in a community where everyone weaves. She herself enjoys weaving and everything connected with it.

No. 24, Karok, displayed her cap bought from No. 5 "who lives on the lower river where they do the finest work."

No. 6, a Yurok in the Ko'otep district; about fifty-six years old; slow and very conservative. There was no one in the informant group who spent as long a time looking at the basket prints; she looked methodically at each one commenting on workmanship, proportions, and designs; no point in technique escaped her notice. Her statements corroborated and unified many incidental remarks; she was the only informant to try to see value in baskets made by outside peoples.

No. 7, a Yurok at Pekwututl; about seventy years old; a professional basket maker for many years; sister of No. 1 at Wetlkwau. She has made all kinds of baskets (pls. 5*a*, 53*b*), selling them to Indians and white tourists. Among her own tribe she had a reputation for the finest caps and the best cradles, two extremes seldom attempted by a weaver. She has no false pride about her work: it is good and everyone knows it. No. 7 has kept her standards high in spite of raising a family on the proceeds of her sales; her work is now past its prime for quality, but her store of knowledge is large and authentic.

Nos. 1, 11, 12, 13, and 15 said that No. 7 made the most baskets in the vicinity and made them best; that she had never done anything else but weave baskets; that she got good prices for her work; that she turned out her weaving quickly; that she made caps that fit well.

Nos. 28 and 29 knew of No. 7's caps from a long time ago.

No. 8, a Yurok at Weitspus; about thirty-six years old; a cousin of No. 15. Effect and the quick saleability of a basket count; this aspect is one of the newer attitudes toward the craft. No. 8 uses easy marks that are woven quickly; she characterized those patterns in the basket prints involving frequent changes as too slowly made to interest her. She would not try a design which promised uncertain results; her reason was that it takes a long time to make a basket even if there are no design difficulties to overcome and mistakes to rip out. The simplest flint marks, rarely varied, are her favorites. Her invented design appears in figure 18*b*.

Nos. 9, 12, and 15 said, admiringly, that No. 8 is a fast worker. No. 10 described No. 8 as willing to make anything that would sell, including small fancy baskets for tourist trade, which she makes better than her neighbors.

No. 9, a Yurok at Weitspus; about forty-six years old. She works under unspeakably dirty conditions; she sells to white people from her own house; she does not trade at the store. She camps, in the summer, with her husband on the grounds of a millionaire sportsman. She has been spoiled by patrons who pay her four times the value of any of her baskets. The dozen she had ready for the annual visit were mediocre in workmanship and dirty. She looked through the prints with an acquisitive eye, commenting only on those designs which she had sold well. She said that people called her a good weaver and acknowledged with pride her ability to make caps; she prefers to do open-twine weaving in shapes similar to the modern waste baskets, and large food basket types. Her main contribution was an original mark seen in figure 18*h*.

Nos. 10 and 12 said No. 9 is industrious, and interested; she cannot make a good basket; she is careless.

No. 10, a Yurok at Pekwututl; about forty-six years old; a daughter of No. 7, a cousin through her Karok father of No. 25. She has grown up in an atmosphere of professional basket-making; she collects supplies for her mother and sister-in-law, No. 14, and takes great pride in her quantities of prepared materials (pl. 3*a*). She is conservative in all her work and she knows standards; she weaves less steadily than her mother but makes all the ordinary types of close-weave basketry except caps.

Nos. 12, 13, and 15 said that No. 10 is one of the best makers in the locality; that she gets good prices for her work; that she uses old marks.

No. 11, a Yurok at Ertlerger; about forty-seven years old; the mother of a large family. She likes to make baskets but knows weaving demands more uninterrupted time than she can give to it. Her sale products are of the acorn basket variety. During the craze for novelties she made the usual types of covered bottles, cups and saucers, etc. Her main value as an informant lay in the fact that she knows fine workmanship and devices, alfhough she herself cannot achieve results up to her own standards.

No. 12 said No. 11 is a fast worker but cannot make enough baskets to make weaving worth while; it is hard to weave, she thinks.

No. 12, a Yurok at Ertlerger; about fifty-six years old. She does not make many baskets to sell; her house and husband need all her time. Possibly the frank confession that she has always been a poor weaver is more nearly the correct explanation. Her efforts are limited to open-twine spoon baskets of mediocre quality, and to table mats begun in close-twine like caps. The edges of her mats are finished with interlaced scallops copied from our cheap modern stick work. Her preferences are for the open-twine which she considers easy; her designs are simplified to the type commonly made by very old or very young weavers; if her basket gets out of shape from the addition of too many or too few sticks, she loses her interest in it. Her husband helps her gather materials but she admitted he could not boast about her basketry. Possibly the best commentary on her ability as a weaver is the fact that she was never mentioned by any informant as being a basket maker. Here is a woman who weaves simply to be weaving with other women, in contrast to unsuccessful workers who have taken up crocheting or dropped crafts altogether. She knows designs as her rating on the old-new design argument proved; she was very valuable in her gossipy way. Her information led several times into additional lines of inquiry.

No. 13, a Yurok at Ertlerger; about seventy years old; an aunt of No. 17; related to No. 25; the only woman in the vicinity who does not attempt to make baskets. No. 13 likes dishes because cleaner; she grinds her acorns in a patent mill; but she sifts her flour from a basketry tray bought from a good weaver. She used to make fancy and small baskets for tourist trade. Caps were always beyond her: they have to be a good shape. She called herself a poor weaver; she took up crocheting, which she did faster and with more satisfaction to herself. In criticizing a basket print she pointed to a stick so small it could hardly be seen, to show me a fault she herself used to commit. She knew as she was working that her basket was not developing as it should, but kept on with the weaving; she called this lack of control over her work not having a gift for weaving. Perhaps her very inability to achieve according to her standards made her quick to evaluate those of other weavers. She knew old conventions and she recognized violations of traditions.

No. 14, a Yurok at Pekwututl; about twenty-seven years old; the daughter of an expert maker who is still referred to by down-river weavers. No. 14 makes as fine a basket as any weaver does today. She has made all sizes of fancy close-twine baskets (pl. 46*b*, *c*); she used to make Jumping dance baskets by the newer method of weaving cylinders and then slitting them the long way. She likes plain, old-fashioned designs which she reproduces faithfully; she uses the flint mark most often because it suggests so many variations.

Nos. 9 and 15 said No. 14 made the best baskets of anyone in the locality and got the best prices for her work. No. 10 said No. 14 is the only one of the younger generation who wants to make fine baskets; other girls think the craft old-fashioned. No. 14 makes a fine basket, too fine; she likes to do it that way. Everything in her work must be small. No. 10 and her mother save the ends of sticks, the smallest porcupine quills, and the finest grass strands for No. 14. No. 25 said No. 20 makes finer baskets than No. 14's best quality.

No. 29, a Karok in the Katimin district; about thirty-five years old; daughter of No. 28. Except for the difference in age, what is said about the mother applies equally well to the daughter. They make the same type of covered basket and send their work out on the same contract. No. 29 is thoroughly familiar with all the details of making, and furthermore, took intense interest in getting them properly presented to me. When she acted as interpreter, she brought out comparisons of methods used by different weavers, taking great pride in every old-time way that pointed to the conservatism of the Karok. Many points seemingly too obvious for direct mention were obtained through her efforts to make basketry, as practised by the Karok, appear completely molded by convention. She is one of the most tribe-conscious of the informants.

No. 10 said No. 29 makes baskets as well as does her mother. No. 28 thought her daughter makes as nice baskets as her own.

No. 30, a Karok in the Ti district; about twenty-nine years old; a niece of No. 36. She lives some distance south of the Klamath but comes back to her old home to gather supplies. Sticks only are available in Scott valley, and Karok women who have moved there are accustomed to making annual trips back to familiar localities for ferns and grass. No. 30 and the others would like to come in the early spring for better qualities of willow but the fare is an item, so the summer trip when more kinds of materials are at their best must suffice. She makes baskets to eke out the county money allowed her family. She weaves small storage baskets and the popular modern fancy basket types, novelties, table mats, cradles, market and clothes baskets. Comparatively few women cover a range from caps and miniature fancy baskets to the all-stick types.

No. 29 thought No. 30 as good as any other Karok weaver but said that she is handicapped through lack of basketry supplies.

No. 31, a Karok in the Katimin district; about fifty years old; a sister of No. 27. She makes no baskets to sell and few for herself. She comes from a family of weavers and knows old patterns and the conventional methods but has no actual interest in the craft. She once made open-twine fancy baskets and food types. She admits being unable to get the shape of a good cap. She is proud of her ability to plot designs on squared paper. She does not fear the complications in any mark because she can diagram it before beginning work.

No. 35 said No. 31 made footed bowl types when they were in fashion; that she does nice work; that she draws marks to guide her in pattern setting.

No. 32, a Karok in the Katimin district; about forty-eight years old; a very hard working woman with a family of small children. She crowds in her basket making to help earn the living and because she enjoys it. She weaves all kinds from caps to the large all-stick drying trays. Her sale baskets are usually of the food types, strongly made. She still makes and uses baskets as part of her household equipment (pl. 5*b*); she is conservative and content to follow the old procedures to the letter.

No. 28 said No. 32 is a good weaver; that she uses simple, old marks.

No. 33, a Karok in the Panamenik district; about sixty-five years old. She has made baskets for many years, though less regularly for sale in the recent ones. She can weave close-twine and open-twine types. At present there is better sale for all-stick trays, so she is specializing in them. She is very proud of her friendship with No. 20, an acknowledged leader in her district; she quoted her opinions often to corroborate her own.

No. 21 said No. 33 makes a pretty good basket—this means she does average work.

No. 34, a Karok in the Ayis district; about seventy years old; an expert weaver of established reputation among her own people although she has not made baskets for six or more years. Examples of her work are even and smooth (pls. 32*b*, 45*a*, *b*). She used to make all kinds of basketry except miniature baskets. Her big storage baskets were bought by collectors. She also made novel shapes for the trade. According to her own statement she was always able to charge good prices for her work.

No. 28 said No. 34 used to make the very nicest baskets. No. 35 remembered that she made butterflies in her baskets and that she got high prices—up to five dollars—for the small sizes with hard designs in them. No other weavers made the type of designs she was able to make unless they copied from hers.

No. 35, a Karok in the Ayis district; about sixty years old; sister of No. 37. She lives in an isolated spot across the Klamath from her nearest neighbors. She has been making baskets for many years but of late years has woven only the easier food types. She sticks to old shapes and designs although she knew of innovations in both. She admired the makers of novelties. She has always worked alone; she knows all the old marks by heart. Her greatest pride is her ability to make porcupine quill caps but she has not had an order for one for many years.

No. 28 knew No. 35 as an old-time conservative; that she used to make good baskets.

No. 36, a Karok in the Ti district; about fifty years old; mother of No. 43; aunt of No. 30; a weaver of old-time forms and patterns, at the same time a great admirer of her daughter's developing reputation as an innovator. No. 36 is known as a good worker and her comments on points involving traditions were given with authority. During her interview with me, her whole family came around her. Occasionally she stopped her conversation to drill one or the other of the younger girls on design names or technical details; doubtless the method used in teaching basketry essentials.

No. 30 said her aunt and No. 37 are the best makers in the district.

No. 37, a Karok in the Ti district; about fifty-five years old; sister of No. 35. She is the expert cap maker of the vicinity. Her products are sold regularly from Katimin to the Inam district. One of her caps was displayed by an informant in Ertlerger as the work of the finest maker up-river. No. 37 is the only informant who is still making basket hoppers for her own needs and to sell to Indian women. She said of herself that she could make anything. A reputation for ability to weave caps and hoppers would prove that statement.

No. 13 had bought a cap from No. 37, paying ten dollars for it. No. 28 said No. 37 makes hats small at the top in the older style; that she can weave all types of baskets. No. 35 said of her sister that she made all the hard things like cups and saucers, and that she could make letters in baskets. No. 42 knew of the high prices No. 37 could ask for her caps.

No. 38, a Karok in the district above Ti; about thirty-seven years old; daughter of No. 39. She is one of the cleanest workers in the region. Her house is immaculate and her basketry materials in perfect order. She is proud of her weaving, and of the fact that she uses only the old-fashioned designs. She has made novelty baskets on order, but they are not her choice.

No. 42 knew of No. 38, and that she had once made a basket with ABC in it.

No. 39, a Karok in the district above Ti; about seventy years old; mother of No. 38; sister of No. 42; a fine type of old-time weaver. She has made baskets for many years and can tell much about passing traditions. She said she used to make nice fancy baskets as well as the novel shapes; she made porcupine quill hats, for which she got a high price. Now her work is getting coarser and she weaves mostly for her own use. She stopped trying to make caps when they failed to measure up to her standards. She has much interest in the craft, knew what other weavers were doing, and cleared up several obscure points on design changes.

Nos. 10 and 13 referred to No. 39 as an old weaver with a high reputation for fine work in former years. No. 40, the interpreter, remembered her own mother ordering hats from No. 39.

No. 40, a Karok in the district above Ti; about fifty-five years old; a slow talker, accurate in all her statements. She has not made baskets for a number of years due to other demands upon her time. She has never lost interest completely, but recognizes that she is out of practice. Her two partly finished baskets of fine craftsmanship showed her an able weaver. She means to take up the weaving again but will start on coarse sticks before she attempts to continue with fine work. She made all-stick types but was most proud of her improvement upon an unsuccessful fancy basket cover which had its start in the vicinity.

No. 41 and her family, Karok at Inam; No. 41 about seventy years old. This family is known the upper length of the Klamath river for their ownership of old Indian ceremonial objects, their ''making'' of the largest new year's festivities in the region, and their basketry (pl. 2*a*). They are all professionals. No. 41 has been and still is of great influence; the two daughters and the niece are recognized experts. They are full of the traditions of the craft, but do not hesitate to turn from them to meet any demand for innovations. One daughter, especially, is credited with superior ability to invent new objects and designs. Since an interpreter was necessary, no one of the women can be singled out as most helpful. Generally, the mother voiced the opinions for the family after a discussion among themselves. She is much admired for her memory: she remembers the new pattern, comes home, weaves it in a basket, and the others copy it.

No. 22 had bought a cap made by one of the daughters; she liked it for the variation of an old mark which had been woven in it. Nos. 25, 28, and 42 referred to the caps made by the family; that they make a right size and well fitting caps; that ten dollars is the price for one of their quill caps. No. 36 spoke especially of the talented daughter, saying that she could make anything in basketry. No. 39 knew that the family was hired to make the Jumping dance baskets for the Hupa dances and that the daughters are the innovators for the locality. No. 40 mentioned the cover idea the family had taken over from the whites' dishes and the fact that she had been able to improve upon the idea.

No. 42, a Karok of the Asisufunuk district; about seventy years old; sister of No. 39. She has been a good basket maker and still tries to maintain her standard. Her white husband offered the information that her ability was not equal to her ideals; he said she was always ripping out her work to correct mistakes. Her original mark is shown in figure 18*d*. She was one of the two people who owned a basket similar to an unusual specimen in the University collection. Her basket is shown in plate 17*a;* its design story is told in the section on Designs with Histories. Her mother was a down-river woman. No. 42 was in a position to contrast the traditions of the two tribal areas in addition to remembering some of the oldest ways of doing things in basketry.

No. 43, a Karok in the Ti district; about twenty-one years old; the daughter of No. 36; a unique combination of the modern girl who wants change and novelty and the Indian craftswoman who has grown up among tribal conventions. The mixture where it concerns her results is unsatisfactory; she is out of harmony with both aspects. Her materials were wound with rags in the most approved Indian manner; she sat in an airless room so that her basket sticks should not dry out; but she wove baskets with Merry Christmas legends in them, using commercially-dyed fern. Her ideal is to win admiration for innovations such as initials, woven names, and unusual shapes. Her basket with its original design elements is described in the section on Invented Designs (fig. 18*i*). For standard work she draws upon her mother's memory of old marks; she herself knows few names of tribal motives. Her basket-making sets her apart from girls of her own age who, in that region, rarely go beyond the simple techniques. She is very proud of her ability, and her mother is much prouder.

No. 30 knew that No. 43 used package dyes for fern. No. 34 had noticed package dyes were being used for fern and thought the tendency was being fostered by No. 43. No. 36 said that her daughter used package dyes together with the native plant dyes.

EXPLANATION OF PLATES AND FIGURES AND MUSEUM NUMBERS OF SPECIMENS ILLUSTRATED

Specimens possessing the prefix 4– are in the University of California Museum of Anthropology; those preceded by 2– are in the Washington State Museum; those with the prefix G– are from photographs made in the field by Pliny E. Goddard; CA as a prefix indicates that the specimens belonged to the former collection of the California Academy of Sciences; those without numbers are baskets in private collections.

Plates

Plate 1. Informants. *a*, No. 6, Yurok. *b*, No. 19, Karok.

Plate 2. Informants. *a*, No. 41, Karok. *b*, No. 16, Yurok.

Plate 3. *a*, No. 7, Yurok. *b*, hazel twig brush and mussel shells for cleaning finished baskets.

Plate 4. *a*, first weaving of Yurok-Karok girls; x .6. *b*, No. 18's baskets. *c*, No. 27's pattern fragments.

Plate 5. *a*, Yurok; 2–40; girl's acorn soup basket. *b*, Karok; 2–41; boy's basket. *c*, Karok; 2–51; man's plate for fish. *d*, Yurok; 2–43; man's soup basket. *e*, Yurok; 2–44; dipper for serving from cooking basket. All x .47.

Plate 6. Yurok soup baskets. *a*, 1–1475. *b*, 1–1698. *c*, 1–1472. All x .44.

Plate 7. Soup baskets. *a*, Yurok or Hupa; 1–1206. *b*, Hupa; G–454. *c*, Hupa; G–442. All approximately x .44.

Plate 8. Soup baskets. *a*, Hupa; 1–1493. *b*, Yurok; 1–1437. *c*, Hupa; 1–11639. All x .44.

Plate 9. Hupa soup baskets. *a*, 1–1517. *b*, 1–1495. *c*, 1–11644. All x .44.

Plate 10. Hupa soup baskets. *a*, G–448. *b*, 1–1863. *c*, G–458. All x .44.

Plate 11. Food baskets. *a*, Hupa cooking basket; G–426. *b*, Northwestern California soup basket; 1–28140. *c*, Yurok; 1–1578. All x .44.

Plate 12. Yurok cooking baskets. *a*, 1–1202; x .44. *b*, 1–1201; x .5.

Plate 13. Cooking baskets. *a*, Hupa; G–455; approximately x .44. *b*, Yurok; 1–1880; x .44.

Plate 14. Cooking baskets. *a*, Yurok; 1–1579. *b*, Hupa; 1–1494. Both x .44.

Plate 15. Cooking baskets. *a*, Yurok; 1–1483; x .44. *b*, Karok; 1–1583; x .36.

Plate 16. Cooking baskets. *a*, Yurok; 1–1473. *b*, Karok; 1–1764. Both x .44.

Plate 17. Karok cooking baskets. *a*, private collection; x .48. *b*, 1–1762; x .4.

Plate 18. Cooking baskets. *a*, Yurok; 1–1481. *b*, G–438. Both x .44.

Plate 19. Caps. *a*, Yurok; 1–4384. *b*, Hupa; 1–20824. Both x .5.

Plate 20. Yurok caps. *a*, CA–10. *b*, CA–91. Both approximately x .5.

Plate 21. Caps. *a*, Hupa; 1–27875. *b*, Yurok; 1–1593. Both x .5.

Plate 22. Yurok caps. *a*, CA–87. *b*, 1–1577. Both x .5.

Plate 23. Caps. *a*, Yurok; CA–92. *b*, Northwestern California; 1–27175. Both x .5.

Plate 24. Yurok caps. *a*, 1–1609. *b*, 1–1692. Both x .5.

Plate 25. Yurok caps. *a*, 1–1439. *b*, 1–1610. Both x .5.

Plate 26. Caps. *a*, Northwestern California; 1-20834. *b*, Hupa; 1-371. Both x .5.

Plate 27. Hupa caps. *a*, G-6. *b*, G-5. Both approximately x .5.

Plate 28. Hupa caps. *a*, G-94. *b*, 1-20819. Both x .5.

Plate 29. Caps. *a*, Northwestern California; 1-27876. *b*, Yurok; 1-1425. Both x .5.

Plate 30. Caps. *a*, Karok; 1-26812. *b*, Yurok; 1-27054. Both x .5.

Plate 31. Caps. *a*, Hupa; G-2. *b*, Yurok; 1-27055. Both x .5.

Plate 32. Caps. *a*, Hupa; G-93. *b*, Karok; private collection. Both x .5.

Plate 33. Northwestern California caps. *a*, 1-27878. *b*, 1-27164. Both x .5.

Plate 34. Yurok trinket baskets. *a*, 1-1661. *b*, 1-330. Both x .5.

Plate 35. Yurok trinket baskets. *a*, 1-1507. *b*, 1-1571. Both x .5.

Plate 36. Yurok trinket baskets. *a*, 1-1659. *b*, 1-1424. Both x .5.

Plate 37. Yurok trinket baskets. *a*, 1-1674. *b*, 1-2275. Both x .55.

Plate 38. Trinket baskets. *a*, Yurok; 1-1605. *b*, Karok; 1-1598. Both x .5.

Plate 39. Yurok storage basket. 1-1089. x .16.

Plate 40. Fancy baskets. *a*, Hupa; G-445. *b*, Yurok; CA-444. Both approximately x .5.

Plate 41. Karok fancy baskets. *a*, 1-1595; x .42. *b*, 1-1807; x .52.

Plate 42. Fancy baskets. *a*, 1-1806. *b*, 1-27056. Both x .53.

Plate 43. Karok fancy baskets. *a*, 1-1801. *b*, 1-26814. Both x .55.

Plate 44. Karok fancy baskets. *a*, 2-48. *b*, 1-26815. Both x .53.

Plate 45. Karok fancy baskets. Private collection. Both x .53.

Plate 46. Yurok modern gift baskets. Private collection. All x .5.

Plate 47. Northwestern California fancy baskets. *a*, 1-27886, *b*, 1-27887. Both x .3.

Plate 48. Covered fancy baskets. *a*, Hupa; G-239. *b*, Yurok; 1-1888. Both approximately x .6.

Plate 49. Covered fancy baskets. *a*, Karok; 1-26813ab. *b*, Yurok; 1-27871ab. Both x .53.

Plate 50. Modern fancy basket cover. *a*, *b*, Northwestern California; 1-27888b. x .64.

Plate 51. Modern sale objects in basketry technique. *a–d*, Northwestern California; *a*, 1-27894ab; *b*, 1-27166; *c*, 1-27872ab; *d*, 1-27170. All x .5. *e–k*, private collection. All x .12.

Plate 52. Mealing tray. *a*, *b*, Yurok; 1-1435. x .2.

Plate 53. Open-twine baskets. *a*, Northwestern California; 1-11868; x .2. *b*, Yurok; private collection; x .33.

Plate 54. Miscellaneous types. *a*, Yurok; 1-27057. *b*, Hupa; 1-2487. Both approximately x .3.

Plate 55. Jumping dance baskets. *a*, Yurok; 1-1997. *b*, Yurok; 1-1998. *c*, Yurok; 1-2273. *d*, Yurok; 1-2222. *e*, Hupa; 1-988. All x .18.

Plate 56. Jumping dance baskets. *a*, Yurok; 1-2270. *b*, Yurok; 1-2271. *c*, Hupa; 1-20825. *d*, Yurok; 1-1461. All x .18.

Plate 57. Baskets from neighboring tribes. *a*, Wiyot; 1-9404. *b*, Wiyot; 1-11626. Both x .35.

Plate 58. Baskets from neighboring tribes. *a*, Wintun; 1-2500; x .53. *b*, Lassik; 1-2541; x .32.

Figures in Text

KEY TO FIGURES OF DESIGNS SHOWN ALSO IN THE PHOTOGRAPHICALLY REPRODUCED PLATES

Fig. 4. *a*, pl. 31*b*. *b*, pl. 35*b*. *c*, pl. 43*b*. *e*, pl. 34*a*. *h*, pl. 5*c*. *i*, this series, 1: 21, 1. *p*, pl. 5*e*. *r*, this series, 1: 24, 2. *s*, this series, 1: 22, 1.

Fig. 5. *c*, pl. 16*b*.

Fig. 7. *a*, pl. 26*b*. *b*, pl. 26*a*. *c*, pl. 27*b*.

Fig. 8. *a*, pl. 14*a*. *b*, pl. 10*a*. *c*, pl. 10*c*. *d*, pl. 11*a*. *e*, pl. 8*a*.

Fig. 9. *b*, pl. 7*c*.

Fig. 10. *a*, pl. 34*b*. *b*, pl. 36*b*.

Fig. 11. *a*, pl. 6*c*. *b*, pl. 29*a*.

Fig. 13. *a*, pl. 33*a*. *b*, pl. 38*a*. *c*, pl. 27*b*. *f*, pl. 10*c*. *g*, pl. 9*a*. *h*, pl. 20*b*. *i*, pl. 11*a*. *j*, pl. 48*b*. *l*, pl. 10*b*.

Fig. 14. *a*, pl. 29*a*. b, pl. 8*a*. *c*, pl. 6*c*.

Fig. 16. *a*, pl. 8*c*. *b*, pl. 35*b*. *c*, pl. 49*a*. *d*, pl. 37*a*.

Fig. 18. *g*, pl. 46*c*.

Fig. 19. *a*, pl. 25*b*. *b*, pl. 28*b*. *c*, pl. 25*a*.

Fig. 20. *a*, pl. 22*a*. *b*, pl. 8*b*. *c*, pl. 21*b*. *d*, pl. 22*b*. *e*, pl. 24*b*. *f*, pl. 43*a*. *k*, pl. 6*b*. *m*, pl. 9*b*. *p*, pl. 38*b*.

Fig. 21. *b*, pl. 37*a*. *c*, pl. 6*c*. *d*, pl. 28*a*. *f*, pl. 54*a*. *g*, figs. 6, 12. *h*, pl. 13*b*. *j*, pl. 17*a*.

Fig. 22. *a*, pl. 19*b*. *b*, pl. 21*b*. *d*, pl. 51*j*.

Fig. 23. *a*, pl. 32*a*. *b*, pl. 32*b*. *c*, pl. 46*c*. *d*, pl. 51*e*. *e*, pl. 51*k*.

Fig. 24. *a*, pl. 32*a*. *b*, pl. 7*c*.

Fig. 29. *c*, pl. 45*a*. *e*, pl. 10*c*. *g*, pl. 10*a*. *h*, pl. 24*a*. *i*, pl. 9*a*. *j*, pl. 28*b*. *k*, pl. 23*a*. *l*, pl. 20*b*. *m*, pl. 19*b*.

Fig. 30. Pl. 11*a*.

Fig. 31. *b*, pl. 26*b*. *c*, figs. 6, 12. *e*, pl. 28*a*. *f*, pl. 9*b*. *h*, pl. 23*a*. *i*, pl. 8*b*. *j*, pl. 42*a*. *k*, pl. 15*a*.

Fig. 32. *a*, pl. 15*b*. *b*, pl. 11*c*. *c*, pl. 37*b*. *d*, pl. 11*a*. *e*, pl. 13*b*. *g*, pl. 32*a*. *h*, pl. 17*a*. *j*, pl. 41*b*. *k*, pl. 40*b*.

PLATES 1 TO 58

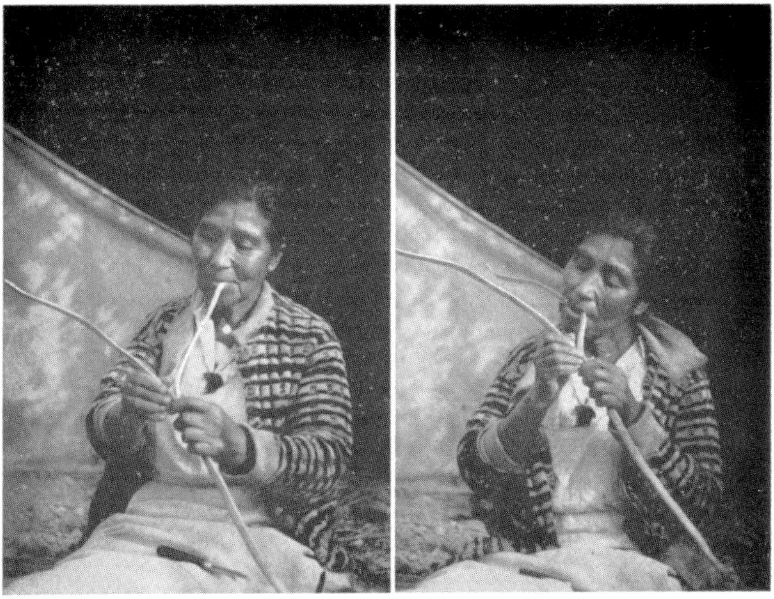

a

b

a. No. 6, Yurok, splitting "cooked" spruce roots for twining elements.

b. No. 19, Karok, peeling willow shoots for her stick baskets.

a

b

a. Cooking and serving baskets used by No. 41 at the Karok new year's making.
b. The oldest informant, No. 16, Yurok, and baskets of her making.

a

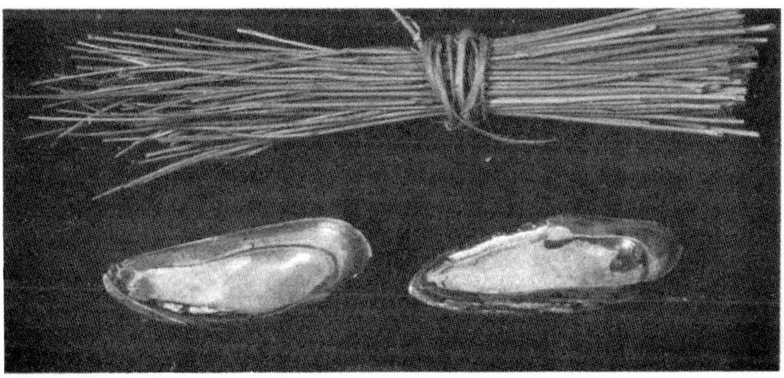

b

a. No. 7, Yurok, with a year's supplies prepared for storing.
b. Only tools used by Yurok-Karok weavers to scrape and clean a finished basket.

a

b

c

a. First weaving attempts of two six-year olds, Yurok.

b, c. Old baskets (No. 18's) and fragments (No. 27's) preserved to copy from.

a

b

c

d

e

An old-time "set" for acorn soup: girl's and boy's baskets, man's basket with plate, dipper.

a

b

c

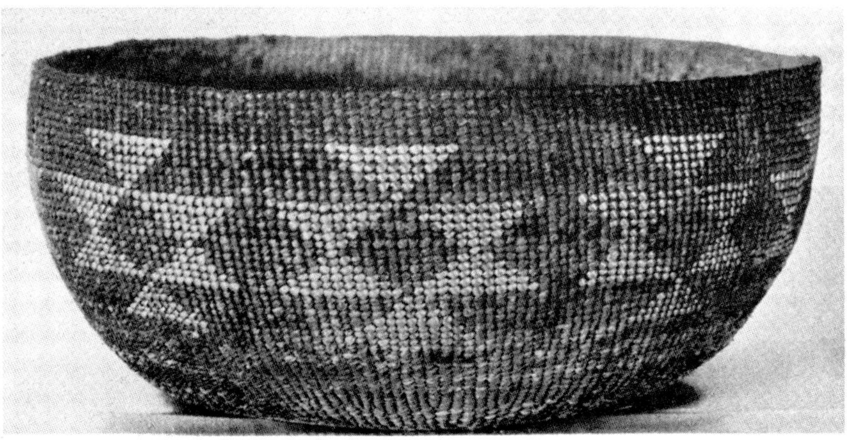

a. Soup basket with an old mark varied by the straight lines in the ground.
b. Soup basket with a much discussed design; not ''old'' by two-thirds' majority.
c. Soup basket with unconventional arrangement of familiar design element.

a

b

c

a. Good shape; criticized for lacking plain root courses at the top edge.
b. Design criticized as out of scale with size of the basket.
c. Design criticized for ornateness; use of black fern in food baskets "wrong."

a

b

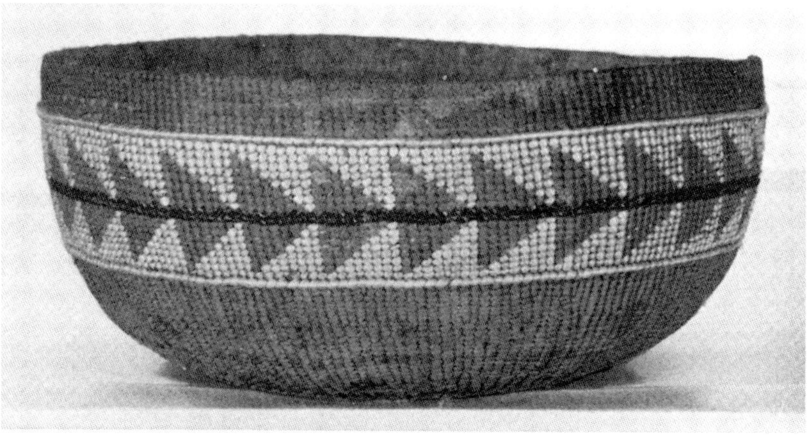

c

a. The wide shallow soup basket of former times.
b. A design lacking taste; out of scale with basket size and too broken up.
c. An admired design; use of black fern disapproved of.

a

b

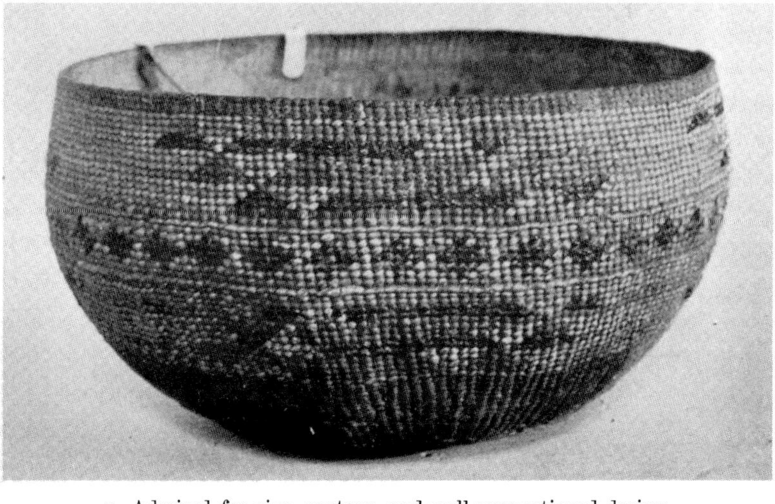

c

a. Admired for size, contour, and well proportioned design.
b. "Hard" design and confused effect; called a Modoc mark by up-river informants.
c. Use of black fern in food baskets criticized.

a

b

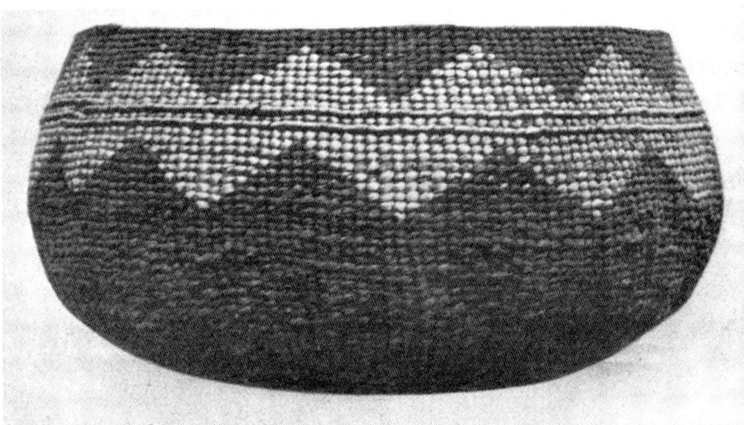

c

a. Asserted to be as old a mark as one could find; shape and work criticized.
b. The newer high, narrow shape for soup baskets.
c. "Easy" design for use in a girl's soup basket; workmanship criticized.

a

b

c

a. The tribally recognized foot design, "hard" and greatly admired.
b. The foot mark ground developed as pattern; loses standing and name in the change.
c. The foot mark carried by variation beyond tribal recognition.

a

b

a. A cooking basket admired for shape, design, and workmanship.
b. The correct finish for the top: several rows of plain root twining.

a

b

a. A well shaped basket; design requires more careful calculation than was made.
b. Contour criticized; design a hard one to space evenly.

a

b

a. Criticized for rough workmanship and angles which fail to come to a point.
b. An old mark varied by giving it a quarter turn.

a

b

a. Attributed to an old woman with hands too weak to pull the weaving tight.
b. A well shaped basket; criticized for low placement of the design.

a

b

a. Black fern thought by some informants to be an ownership mark.
b. Good shape and well placed design; various explanations for the rectangle.

a

b

a. Evidence of poor planning: addition of sticks made within a pattern motive.
b. The mountainside mark; a difficult design requiring exact calculations.

a

b

a. Suggestive of ownership mark. *b*. Spoken of as "all just right."

a

b

a. Very fine cap; placing of design criticized; conventional borders lacking.
b. Contour right for a cap; design in right scale for size.

a

b

a. Criticized for placement of dividing motive off center.

b. Criticized for choice of center design, for placing of main mark, for widths.

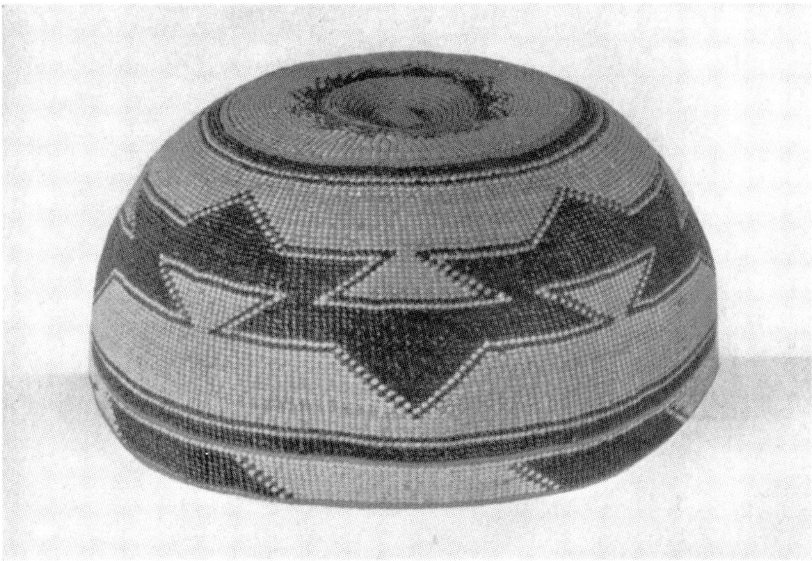

a

b

a. An "easy" mark made difficult by bordering line.

b. A disputed design; claimed both as an invention and as a legitimate variation.

a

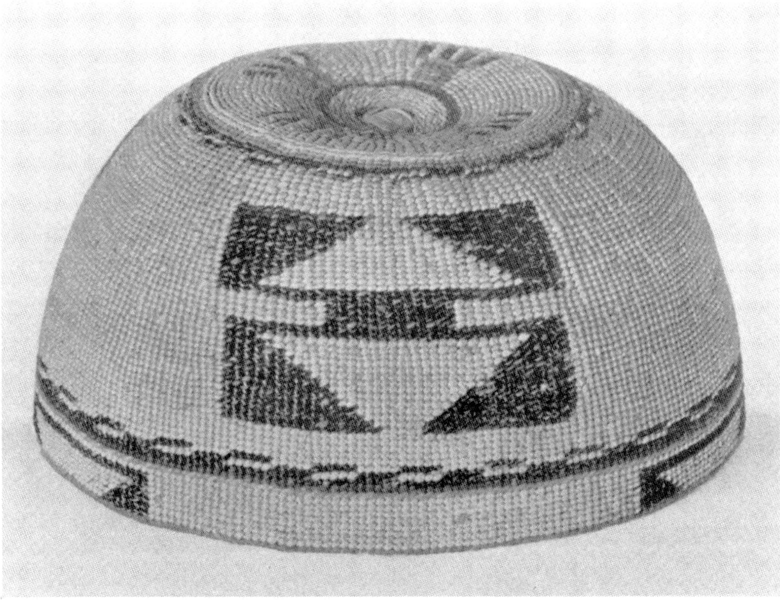

b

a. Unanimously criticized for poor choice of designs to combine in the same basket.
b. Generally repudiated as a traditional design; recognized by a few weavers.

a

b

a. Admired for well proportioned flint marks and perfect joining of the pattern.

b. Criticized for lacking some small motive in the lower border, "half finished."

a

b

a. A cap for a young girl; simplicity of pattern admired by all.
b. Unequal sizes of flint marks criticized; inner motives not conventional.

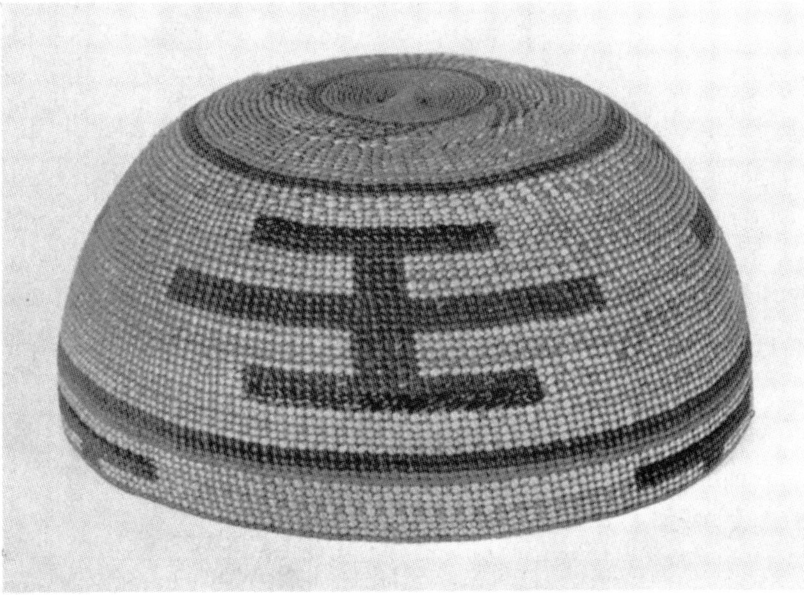

a

b

a. Unanimously declared to be an invented design.

b. Criticized as a design copied from a newspaper.

a

b

a. General admiration for contour, design, and workmanship.
b. Too high to be correct shape; beaded border "hard" to make.

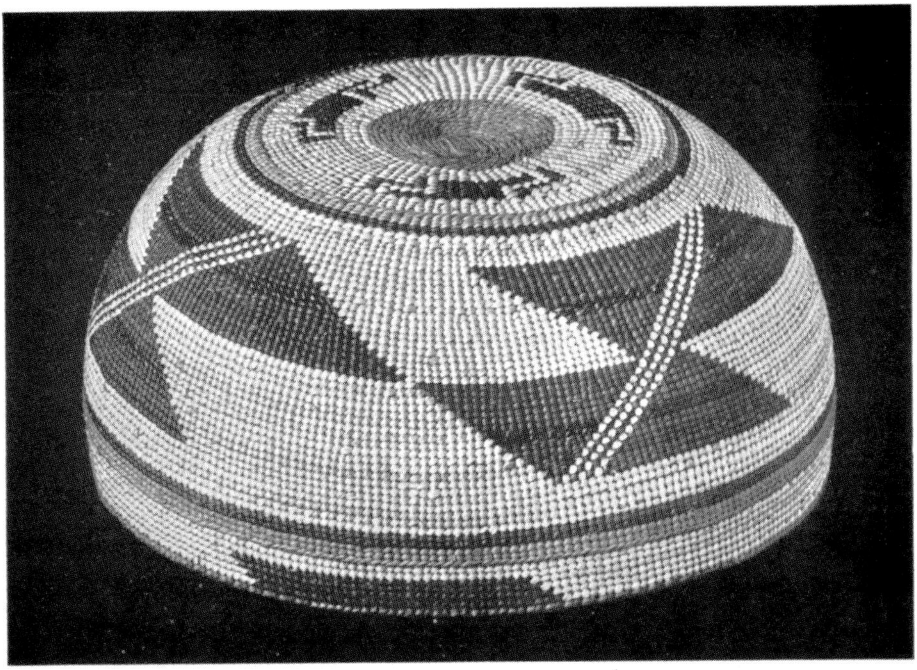

a

b

a. Excellent in every way except for unrelated small top design.

b. Unanimously criticized for contour; also, choice, size, and spacing of motives.

a

b

a. Admired for its design; criticized for its contour.
b. Very poor shape for a cap; X design unanimously disapproved of.

a

b

a. Typical arrangement for small design motives; should center zone exactly.

b. Scattered effect criticized; needs a stabilizing line through center.

a

b

a. An admired type of inner motive for flint marks.
b. A "hard" pattern with many points requiring much breaking of overlay.

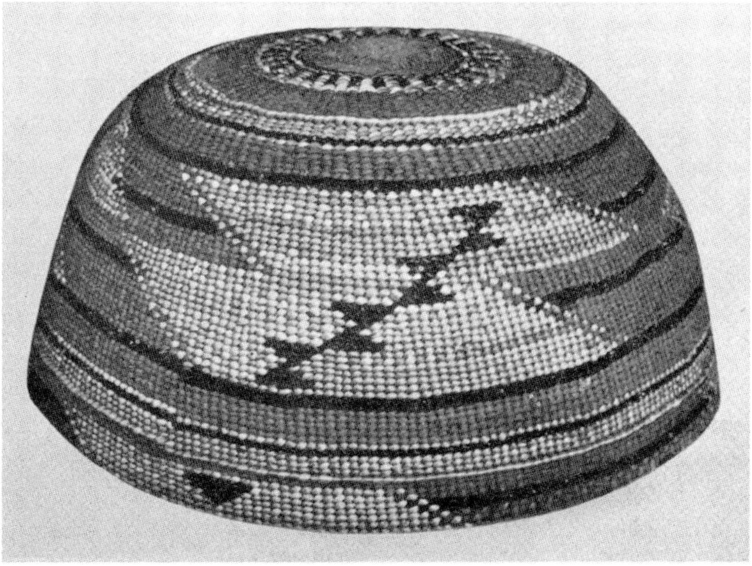

a

b

a. Disputed arrangement of old elements; criticized for off-center placing.
b. Too many little marks in flints; tribal good taste avoids crowded effects.

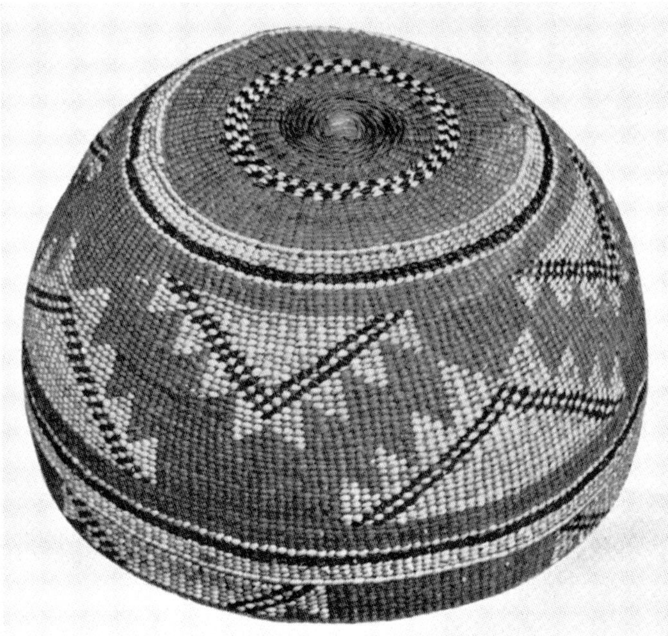

a

b

a. A hard design to make; considered a striking mark.
b. Variation of the design in *a;* very fine workmanship; made by No. 34.

a

b

a. The plain, undecorated flint mark remembered by older informants.

b. Rare to find among cap examples: a filler indicative of poor planning.

a

b

a. The small-mouthed trinket basket of former times.
b. An elaborate "running" mark taken over from the large storage baskets.

a

b

a. Trinket basket in "double stick" weaving; used for less important containers.
b. An old shape, high, small-mouthed; design admired for simplicity.

a

b

a. Trinket basket of former times; called "good" in spite of coarseness.
b. A "double" mark; twice as difficult in design placing as the one in plate 34*b*.

a

b

a. Criticized as unstable in form; story of design known to all Karok informants.
b. Hard, striking design, well spaced; considered a variation of the foot mark.

a

b

a. The snake mark conventionally a secondary design; should not be used alone.
b. Criticized as a transference from painting; not a real basket mark.

Yurok storage basket; thirty-four inches tall.
Y's indicate number and position of added sticks; inverted Y's indicate number and position of eliminated sticks.

a

b

a. Criticized for the unequal lengths and widths of its pattern motives.

b. A filler, always translated as inadequate planning before starting pattern.

a

b

a. Variation of the spread-finger design on a fancy basket zoned like a cap.
b. Typical design for a big storage basket; considered hard to make.

a

b

a. All-over designs hard to do; criticized as too spotty for effectiveness.
b. Too many different design elements used together to be in good taste.

a

b

a. Arrangement of triangles makes this a "new" mark; borders taken from caps.

b. Considered a very striking mark; universally admired.

a

b

a. Modern fancy basket made by No. 36; spread-finger design considered difficult.

b. Modern fancy basket; criticized for inexcusably poor "stepping" of the rows.

a

b

a. Modern fancy basket made by No. 34; snake mark used alone not traditional.
b. Modern fancy basket made by No. 34; fine shape and workmanship.

a

b

c

a. Gift basket made by No. 10.

b, c. Gift baskets made by No. 14; very fine work; design in *c* disapproved of.

a

b

a. Modern fancy basket based on old water basket shape; difficult design.

b. Modern fancy basket based on old cooking basket shape.

a

b

a. Modern fancy basket; handle, cover, and strap lift for white buyers.
b. The old covered trinket or tobacco basket with tied-on disc cover.

a

b

a, b. Modern fancy baskets; covers directly due to white influence.

a

b

a, b. Surface and reverse side of a modern cover; weaving technique and design old; knob, plaited edge, flange due to white demand.

a *b* *c* *d*

a–d. Group of objects made in response to demands of white buyers.
e–k. Baskets with features and design variations showing European influence.

a

b

a. Surface side of unfinished mealing tray.
b. Reverse side of *a* showing willow braces to prevent pulling in during weaving.

a

b

a. Old time carrying basket for fish; one or more close twine bands for strength.

b. Modern fancy basket after the manner of *a*.

a

b

a. The subject of many arguments as to origin; probably copied from lamp or dish.

b. Brush dance basket in which seeds are gathered; or, cover to storage basket.

a

b

c

d

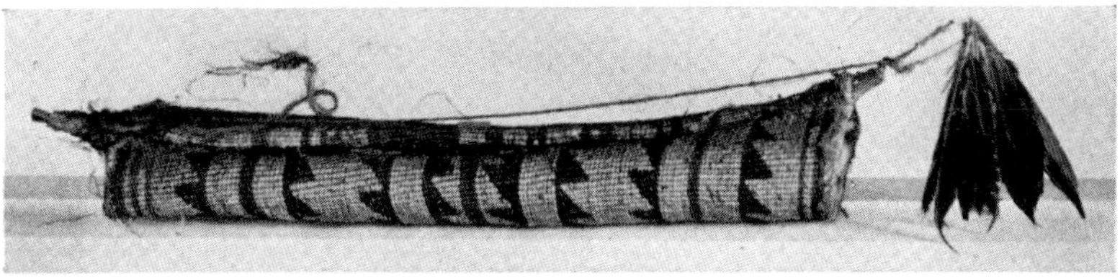

e

a. Too short for traditional Jumping dance basket.
b. Approved in size and pattern by old Karok informants.
c. Judged best shape and workmanship by Yurok informants.
d. Not well made.
e. Nearest correct of all, according to Karok expert, No. 22.

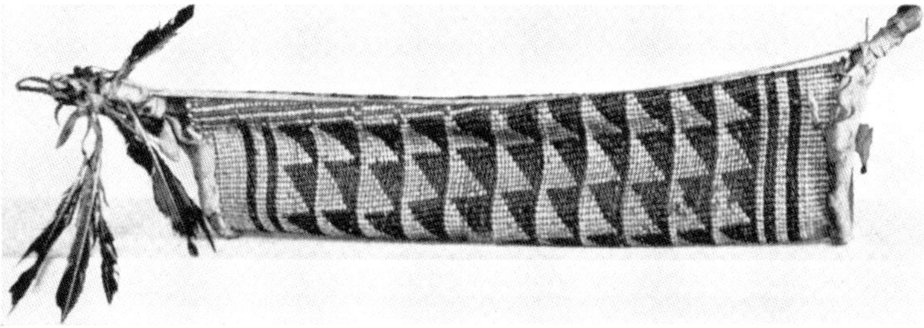

a

b

c

d

a. Too many little marks for Jumping dance basket.
b. Too long, according to No. 4, a maker of dance baskets.
c. Criticized by ten informants as showing modern trend toward ornateness.
d. Design approved; workmanship criticized.

a

b

a. Wiyot basket admired for its unusual pattern and ornamented outside roots.
b. Wiyot basket with modified wax'poo mark recognized as "ours."

a

b

a. The Wintun foot mark; admired as hard to do; criticized as crowded looking.
b. Appreciation shown for difficulties in setting this Lassik pattern.

ABBREVIATIONS USED

A	Anthropos.
l'A	L'Anthropologie.
AA	American Anthropologist.
AAA-M	American Anthropological Association, Memoirs.
ArA	Archiv für Anthropologie.
AES-P	American Ethnological Society, Publications.
AGW-M	Anthropologische Gesellschaft in Wien, Mitteilungen.
AJPA	American Journal of Physical Anthropology.
AMNH	American Museum of Natural History—
-AP	Anthropological Papers.
-B	Bulletin.
-M	Memoirs.
-MA	Memoirs, Anthropological Series.
-MJ	Memoirs, Jesup Expedition.
BAE	Bureau of American Ethnology—
-B	Bulletins.
-R	(Annual) Reports.
CNAE	Contributions to North American Ethnology.
CU-CA	Columbia University, Contributions to Anthropology.
FL	Folk–Lore.
FMNH	Field Museum of Natural History—
-M	Memoirs.
-PAS	Publications, Anthropological Series.
IAE	Internationales Archiv für Ethnographie.
ICA	International Congress of Americanists (Comptes Rendus, Proceedings).
IJAL	International Journal of American Linguistics.
JAFL	Journal of American Folk-Lore.
JRAI	Journal of the Royal Anthropological Institute.
MAIHF	Museum of the American Indian, Heye Foundation—
-C	Contributions.
-IN	Indian Notes.
-INM	Indian Notes and Monographs.
PM	Peabody Museum (of Harvard University)—
-M	Memoirs.
-P	Papers.
-R	Reports.
PMM-B	Public Museum (of the City) of Milwaukee, Bulletin.
SAP-J	Société des Américanistes de Paris, Journal.
SI	Smithsonian Institution—
-AR	Annual Reports.
-CK	Contributions to Knowledge.
-MC	Miscellaneous Collections.
UC-PAAE	University of California, Publications in American Archaeology and Ethnology.
UPM-AP	University of Pennsylvania (University) Museum, Anthropological Publications.
USNM	United States National Museum—
-R	Reports.
-P	Proceedings.
UW-PA	University of Washington, Publications in Anthropology.
ZE	Zeitschrift für Ethnologie.

ABOUT THE AUTHORS

LILA MORRIS O'NEALE (1886–1948) was one of the leading textile scholars of her generation. She earned her anthropology doctorate in 1930 with this volume and went on to a productive career as Professor of Decorative Art at the University of California, Berkeley. In addition to her work with California Indian basketry, she was known for her research with the textiles of Guatemala and ancient Peru.

MARGOT BLUM SCHEVILL is an anthropologist who focuses on ethnic textiles worldwide. She is a guest curator for The Fine Arts Museums of San Francisco, M. H. de Young Museum, where she is working on the Jeff Appleby Andean textile collection. Her most recent publication is *Maya Textiles of Guatemala* (University of Texas Press).